Beginning Visual Web Developer 2005 Express

From Novice to Professional

Paul Sarknas with Rick Delorme

Apress®

Beginning Visual Web Developer 2005 Express: From Novice to Professional

Copyright © 2006 by Paul Sarknas and Rick Delorme

ISBN (pbk): 1-59059-482-7

Printed and bound in the United States of America 9 8 7 6 5 4 3 2 1

Lead Editor: Ewan Buckingham
Technical Reviewer: Mark Horner
Editorial Board: Steve Anglin, Dan Appleman, Ewan Buckingham, Gary Cornell, Tony Davis,
    Jason Gilmore, Jonathan Hassell, Chris Mills, Dominic Shakeshaft, Jim Sumser
Project Manager: Sofia Marchant
Copy Edit Manager: Nicole LeClerc
Copy Editor: Freelance Editorial Services
Assistant Production Director: Kari Brooks-Copony
Production Editor: Katie Stence
Compositor: Pat Christenson
Proofreader: Elizabeth Berry
Indexer: John Collin
Artist: April Milne
Cover Designer: Kurt Krames
Manufacturing Director: Tom Debolski

Distributed to the book trade worldwide by Springer-Verlag New York, Inc., 233 Spring Street, 6th Floor, New York, NY 10013. Phone 1-800-SPRINGER, fax 201-348-4505, e-mail orders-ny@springer-sbm.com, or visit http://www.springeronline.com.

For information on translations, please contact Apress directly at 2560 Ninth Street, Suite 219, Berkeley, CA 94710. Phone 510-549-5930, fax 510-549-5939, e-mail info@apress.com, or visit http://www.apress.com.

The source code for this book is available to readers at http://www.apress.com in the Source Code section.

I would like to dedicate this work to my family in appreciation
for all their help and support over the years.
Paul Sarknas

I would like to dedicate this work to my two beautiful children, Jaxen and Kendyl,
and to my amazing wife, Jenn, without whom none of this would have been possible
because she is my anchor.
Richard Delorme

Contents at a Glance

Contents

About the Authors

 **PAUL SARKNAS** currently serves as the president of his own consulting company, Sarknasoft Solutions LLC, which provides enterprise solutions to a wide array of companies that utilize the .NET platform. Sarknas specializes in C#, ASP.NET, and SQL Server. He works intimately with all aspects of software, including planning, gathering, designing, architecting, developing, testing, and deploying.

Sarknas has worked with Microsoft technologies for over eight years and has used .NET since its conception. Along with authoring and technical reviewing for Apress, Sarknas has also co-authored for WROX Press.

Sarknas may be contacted via his consulting company's website, http://www.sarknasoft.com, and he welcomes questions and feedback of any kind.

RICHARD DELORME is a technical consultant. He lives in Ottawa, Ontario, Canada. He has an MCSD for Microsoft .NET. He is working on enterprise applications for the postal industry.

About the Technical Reviewer

 **MARK HORNER** is principal enterprise architect and .NET application consultant with Torville Software. He is a 25-year veteran of the industry and has worked with a host of blue-chip organizations, including Citibank, NRMA Insurance, ANZ Banking Group, Unilever, Hewlett-Packard, British Aerospace, and CPA Australia. You can contact him at markhorner@hotmail.com.

CHAPTER 1

■ ■ ■

Introducing Visual Web Developer

Welcome to Microsoft's Visual Web Developer (VWD)! This book most likely attracted you because you are new to programming and want to know how to build a web application. You have come to the right place. This book will guide you through the necessary steps and teach you all the relevant information you need to build solid web applications with VWD using ASP.NET 2.0. As the book progresses, you will gain a deeper understanding of the technologies involved. Throughout this book, we thoroughly examine all aspects of building websites with ASP.NET 2.0, from building your first simple web page to building your first dynamic web application and leveraging the starter kits. By the end of this book, you will be off to the races. We begin with the following topics:

- What ASP.NET is and how it works

- How to install VWD

- How the Internet works

- The principles of object-oriented programming

- How to build and run your first web application

What Is ASP.NET?

In 2001, Microsoft released Microsoft .NET, which represents a paradigm shift in the way web applications are built. For the purposes of this book, you only need to know that .NET is a platform that provides the framework for ASP.NET, which provides a simple development model for building highly interactive web applications. Although you can build static websites using ASP.NET, its real power comes from its ability to manage user interactions from the web page all the way back to a data store without the need to know client-side scripting. With ASP.NET, a lot of the heavy lifting occurs on the server, thus reducing the amount of client-side scripting a programmer needs to know. However, ASP.NET still supports all client-side scripting, so those of you who are more familiar with it can definitely leverage it where appropriate. When users interact with an ASP.NET web page, they send a processing request to the server, where it is executed and returned back to them. One of the beautiful things about ASP.NET is that you do not need to know much more than what you've just read to get it up and running. However, if your curiosity is aroused and you would like to read more about the .NET Framework, take a look at some of these well-known resources: `http://www.asptoday.com` and, of course, `http://msdn.microsoft.com`, an extensive library of resources from the Microsoft Developer Network (MSDN). We will get back to building applications with ASP.NET 2.0 shortly, but for now, let's talk briefly about VWD.

Visual Web Developer

You may be wondering where Visual Web Developer comes into play. All the way back to the old versions of Visual Basic, ASP, and the like, it was always possible to build applications using something like Notepad. You would simply type up your code files in any text editor, save them to disk, and then compile them on the command line. The command line is a non-Windows-based utility. If you had any errors, you would open the file, fix them, and then go back to the command line and try again. This was a tedious and time-consuming way to build any application. If you are like me, you like results and you like them fast. This is where the power of VWD comes into play. It provides a nice graphical user interface (GUI) that provides an Integrated Development Environment (IDE) to wrap up all the details we just discussed. An IDE integrates all kinds of different development tools into one environment. Here this environment is the Visual Web Developer. There is no need to go to the command line for anything. In addition simply to camouflaging the compiling of your applications and running them in your favorite browser, the IDE also provides a wide array of productivity enhancements, such as IntelliSense, on-the-fly code validation, an assortment of wizards that write code, and elements to create and manage databases. You may be asking, If all this functionality is provided by VWD, why would anyone ever use Visual Studio? Let's quickly answer that question now.

Visual Web Developer vs. Visual Studio

For all intents and purposes, there is no significant difference between Visual Studio .NET and Visual Web Developer. Visual Studio is the full entourage of Microsoft's Visual Programming suite, including VB .NET, C#, Windows Forms, and, of course, ASP.NET. Visual Studio is heavy. A lot of its features geared toward enterprise development are irrelevant for our purposes here. Microsoft released a suite of smaller development tools known as the Express versions. There is an Express development tool representing each aspect of Visual Studio. So VWD is just about everything you need from Visual Studio to build web applications, without all the extra baggage. And, of course, VWD has a lower price tag, much lower. Although there are some subtle differences, we will not bore you with them here; we will see that they are relatively unimportant. Next let's get going and install VWD so we can start building some cool web applications.

Installing Visual Web Developer 2005

Installing applications is easier than ever, and VWD is not an exception. In this section, we will quickly work through installing the development environment so you can get to the really fun stuff. For the purposes of this book, you need to have Visual Web Developer 2005 and SQL Server Express 2005 (discussed in Chapter 3). To set it up, double-click the installation file (.msi). When the installation starts, you will receive a series of dialogs. The installation begins with a welcome screen as shown in Figure 1-1.

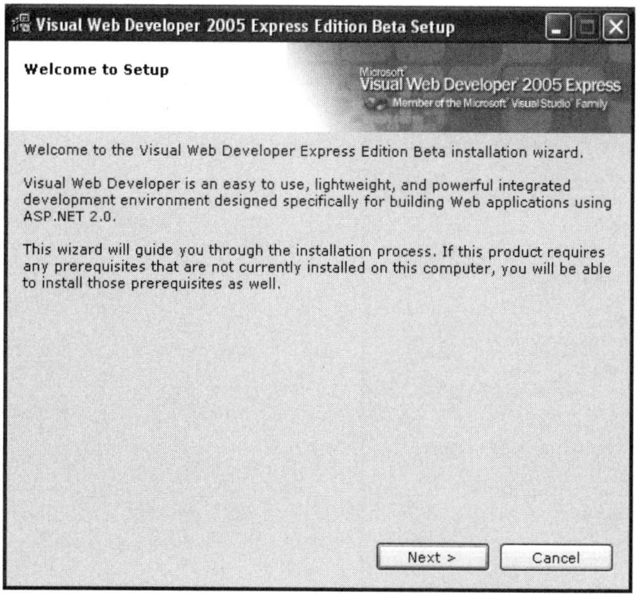

Figure 1-1. *Visual Web Developer setup welcome page*

Click the Next button. You see the standard Microsoft End User License Agreement (EULA) form (Figure 1-2). Read through the licensing agreement, and if you agree, click the Accept button.

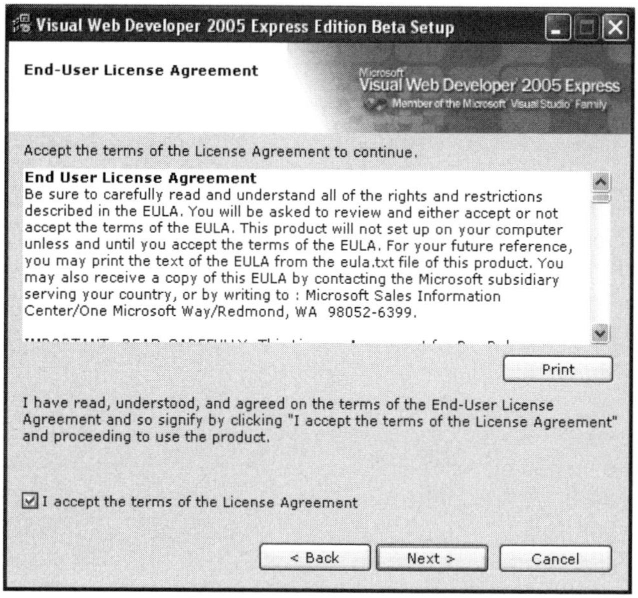

Figure 1-2. *Accepting the End User License Agreement*

If you accept the EULA, you will be presented with your installation options (Figure 1-3).

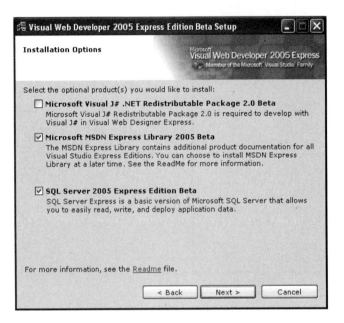

Figure 1-3. *Visual Web Developer installation options*

With the Visual Studio Express products, your installation options are limited. You need SQL Server Express Edition and also the MSDN Express Library. To speed up the installation, leave J# unchecked. It is implied that you want Visual Web Developer. Ensure that the two check boxes are selected as in Figure 1-3. Click Next to proceed to the next step of the installation.

As shown in Figure 1-4, you may now select the location where you want the installation to copy all of the necessary files and lists. A summary of the options you have selected to install along with the necessary disk space requirements appears. At a minimum, your list should match my list in Figure 1-4 because all these components are required in the rest of the book. If you are satisfied with the selected installation location, click Install.

Once you click Install, you see the installation progress screen (Figure 1-5). This screen lets you know how the installation is moving along, with green check marks indicating which parts have completed and the red arrow showing what portion of the installation is in progress.

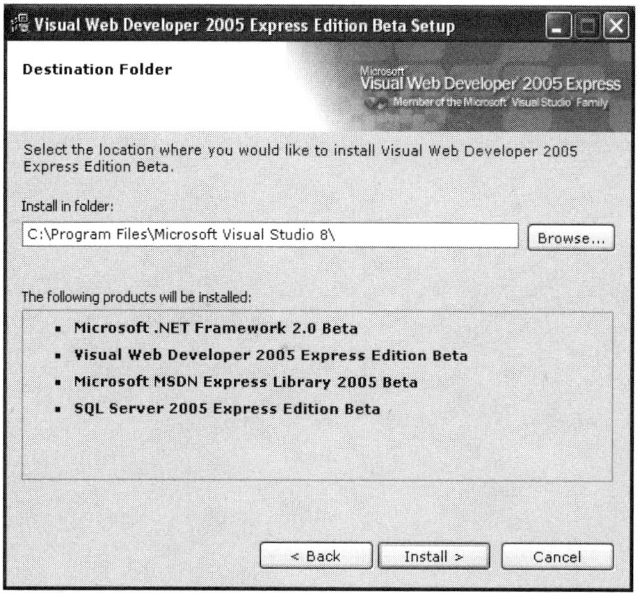

Figure 1-4. *Installation location and selected products summary*

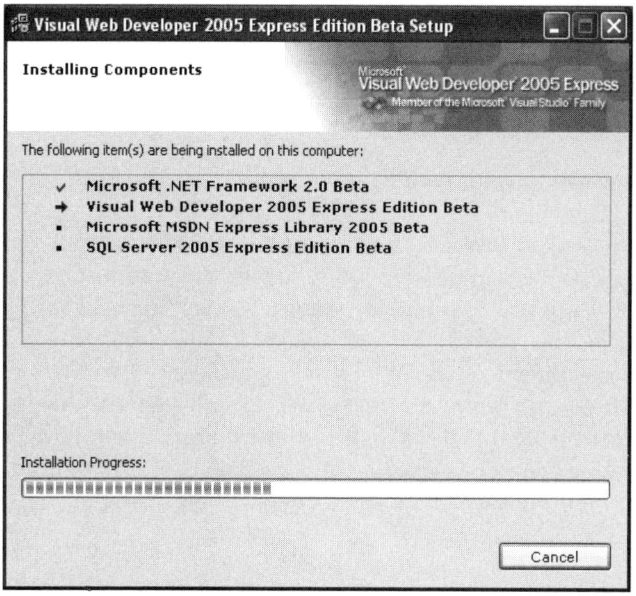

Figure 1-5. *Installation progress*

Once the installation is complete, you see the final page of the installation wizard (Figure 1-6), which informs you of the status of the installation and whether or not there were any errors. A link to a Windows update is provided so you can check for any updates to the software and your computer environment in general. You are also required to activate your software. If you do not, it will cease to function after 30 days. Click the Exit button and verify that VWD is installed.

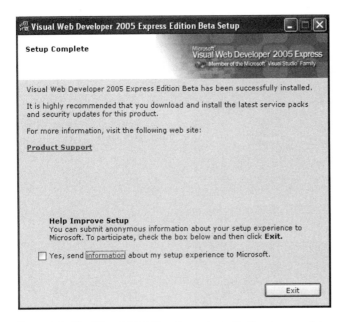

Figure 1-6. *The Visual Web Developer installation is complete.*

Go to your Start menu and open Programs. You should see a new item for Visual Web Developer 2005 Express Edition. Click on this item to open VWD. You are now looking at the Visual Web Developer Integrated Development Environment (Figure 1-7). In Chapter 2, we explore this environment in great detail.

You now have a fully enabled development environment to help you build cool web applications. Why wait any longer? Let's dive in. In this next section, you will build your first web application. We introduce important concepts briefly as we work through this sample; however, if you are unclear about something or it is not explained fully here, don't worry. It will all be covered as you work through the more advanced examples throughout the book.

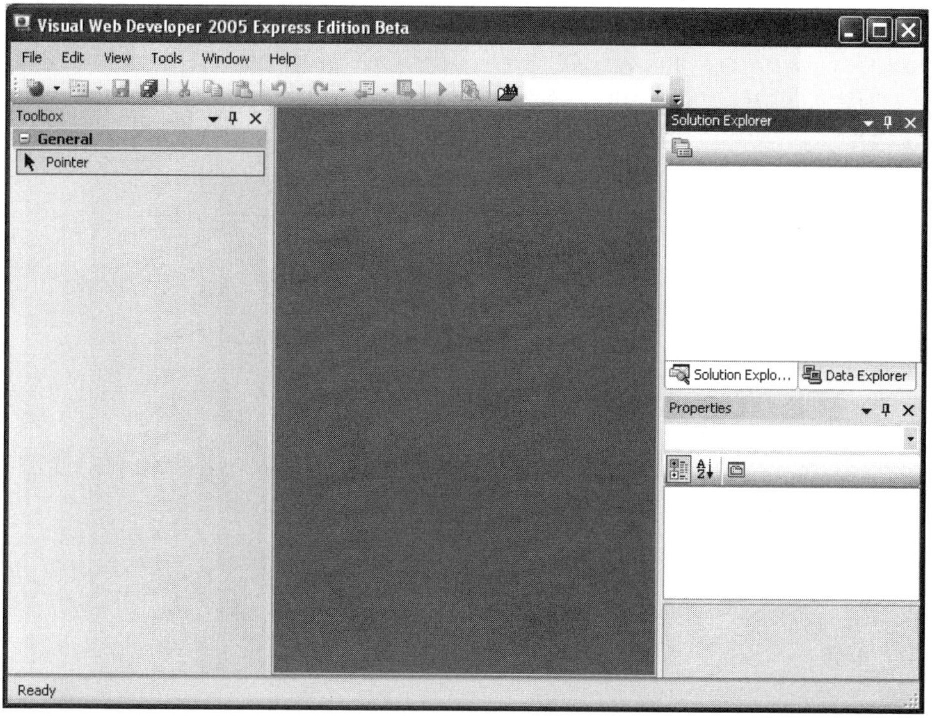

Figure 1-7. *Introducing the Visual Web Developer Integrated Development Environment*

Principles of Object-Oriented Programming

To work effectively in ASP.NET, you need a basic understanding of object-oriented programming (OOP). In this section, you will learn the principles of OOP and how the .NET Framework is organized. The .NET Framework is object oriented. Whether you are working in VB .NET or C# .NET, you are dealing with an object-oriented language. The basic terminology and their applications as well as key terms are described in the following sections. (For a more elaborate explanation of OOP, refer to the Apress book *Beginning Object-Oriented ASP.NET 2.0 with VB .NET*).

The purpose of OOP is to encapsulate the functionality and data of a particular entity within a specific class that is reusable. By encapsulating the functionality and data, consumers (client application or users) of the class need not worry about the inner workings. They can simply use the class and know that it knows how to do its job. Let's use the analogy of a car to further explore this principle.

A car is made of many components. As drivers, we do not necessarily know exactly how each of these components does its job. For example, the braking system and the transmission are two of the many components. We do know that if we press the brake, the car will stop, and if we accelerate with the gas pedal, the transmission will handle the changing of gears. Imagine the braking system is represented as a class. The class exposes an interface, the brake pedal. We can invoke the brake method by applying our foot to the brake pedal. This is the contract provided by the brake system class interface of a car. We have just used a lot of terminology. Let's take a brief look at each term in turn and see how each term looks in code.

Class

The *class* is the basic building block of OOP. Everything in an OOP language is represented as a class. The class defines an object. The class encapsulates functionality that is specific to the entity it is representing. A class can inherit from another class if the two are the same type of entity. For example, a Car class can inherit from a Vehicle class; so can a Truck class. If you look at our previous car analogy, you can write the code for the Truck class as follows.

```
Public Class Truck

Private fuelLevel as Integer

Public Property FuelLevel as Integer
Get
Return _fuelLevel
End Get
Set(byval value as Integer)
_fuelLevel = value
End Set
End Property

Public Sub New()
_fuelLevel = CheckFluidLevel()
End Sub

Public Sub DepressBrake()
End Sub

Private Function CheckFluidLevel() as Integer
End Function

End Class
```

A class is created by starting with the class keyword (*keywords* are words that VB .NET reserves for its own use; they cannot be used in variable names or in other constructs). The public class is followed by the name of our class, in this case Truck. Your class has two methods, one called New, which is the class constructor, and one called DepressBrake. New is another keyword, which tells Visual Basic that this particular method is a constructor. A *constructor* is a special method that is called by the .NET runtime when a class is instantiated. A class is instantiated with the following code:

```
Dim myBrakingSystem as BrakingSystem = New BrakingSystem()
```

When the class is instantiated, the first method to be called on the class's interface is the New method. The New method, as you can see in the sample, is called a default constructor because the method does not have any parameters. We would use this method if we needed to perform any logic to initialize our class. For instance, you may want to check brake fluid levels before permitting the successful instantiation of the BrakingSystem and initialize class data to represent the fluid level. You can do this by calling the CheckFluidLevel method and initializing the class member variable _fluidLevel to the value returned.

In this sample class, you also see the use of the public and private keywords. These words, called *modifiers*, are used to determine the scope of a method or property. It is always good design to limit the scope of methods to only what is necessary. For example, the CheckFluidLevel method is private because only this class needs to know how to do that; it does not need to be made publicly available. Let's take a look at the modifiers available in Table 1-1.

Table 1-1. *Modifiers*

Name	Description
Public	The public modifier makes the method/property available to anyone who instantiates the class.
Private	The private modifier makes the method/property unavailable to anyone. The method/property is only available from within the class.
Protected	Any methods/properties declared as protected will be only accessible from within the class it is created from and any classes that inherit from it.

A project can accumulate quite a large number of classes, so we may want to organize them more effectively. The .NET Framework consists of thousands of classes. It would be cumbersome trying to locate them if they were not organized. This organization comes from the use of *namespaces*, a way to specify a logical grouping for similar classes. For example, classes pertaining to vehicles such as cars, trucks, motorcycles, and so on, may be placed into a Vehicles namespace. All classes that deal with the mechanics of the vehicle may be placed into a Mechanics namespace. This organizes the code so when you access it via IntelliSense (as you'll see later), it is easier to drill down and find the classes you are looking for. If named well, it also makes it easier to determine where a class might be if you are looking for a specific type of functionality. For example, if you want to delete a file on your computer with VB .NET and you are not sure which class would do it, you might drill into System, then into IO, and then you would see the File class, which presumably would contain the Delete method for a file. Specify a namespace by wrapping the class in a namespace declaration as follows:

```
NameSpace Vehicles
Public Class Car
End Class
End NameSpace
```

The class is the basic building block for OOP. Table 1-2 summarizes some of the essential key concepts and terminology.

Table 1-2. *OOP Key Terms*

Term	Definition
Interface	The publicly exposed elements of a class. A class can be created as an interface for other classes to implement. At the root, you access an instantiated class by calling the exposed members of its interface.
Class	The basic element of OOP. Everything in an object-oriented world is based on a class. A class is a logical entity, such as a `Person`, an `Employee`, or a `Book`. You work with classes by creating an instance of them and invoking the methods or properties provided by its interface.
Method	One element of a class's interface. A method is called by a consumer of the class to invoke some behavior.
Property	One element of a class's interface. A property is the element that holds a class's data. A property is accessed in order to get data about the class's current state (e.g., the background color of a web page).
Encapsulation	The concept of hiding the implementation of a class from the users of the class. Any consumers of a class should never know about any implementation details of a class, only the interface it provides.

Your First Web Application

Next you'll see how easy it is to build your first web application. If you are new to Visual Web Developer and .NET, simply follow the instructions here, and you will be impressed with how easy it is to build a website. The concepts you see here will be elaborated in greater detail later in the book. Let's build a simple website that allows people to sign up for a mailed newsletter.

First, if you have not already done so, start up Visual Web Developer. It should be located in Start ➤ All Programs.

Follow these steps to create a website:

1. Select File ➤ New Website. You will see the New Website dialog (Figure 1-8).

2. In the Templates window, select ASP.NET Website.

3. In the Location drop-down box, select File System, and in the Language drop-down box, select Visual Basic.

4. In the Location box, replace WebSite1 with **EmailWebSite**.

5. Click the OK button to create the website.

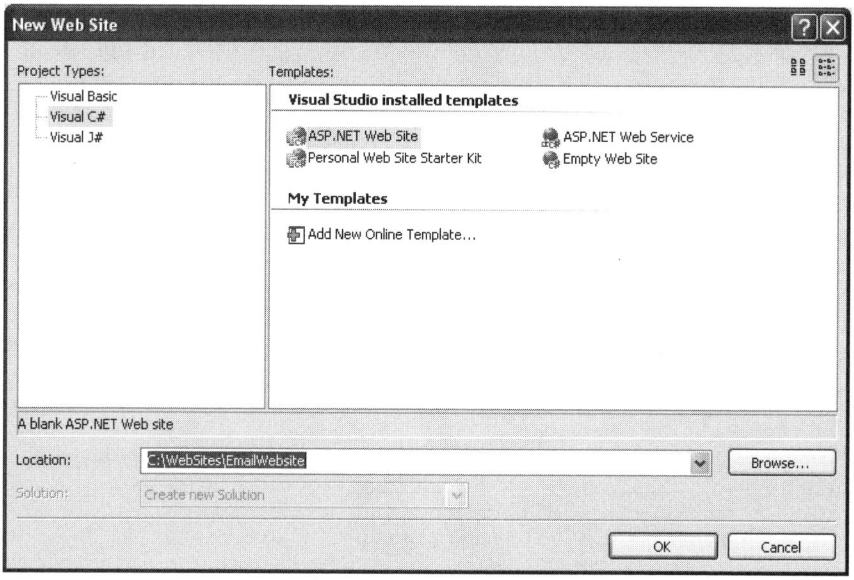

Figure 1-8. *Creating the EmailWebsite*

Your development environment should match Figure 1-9 (or look very similar).

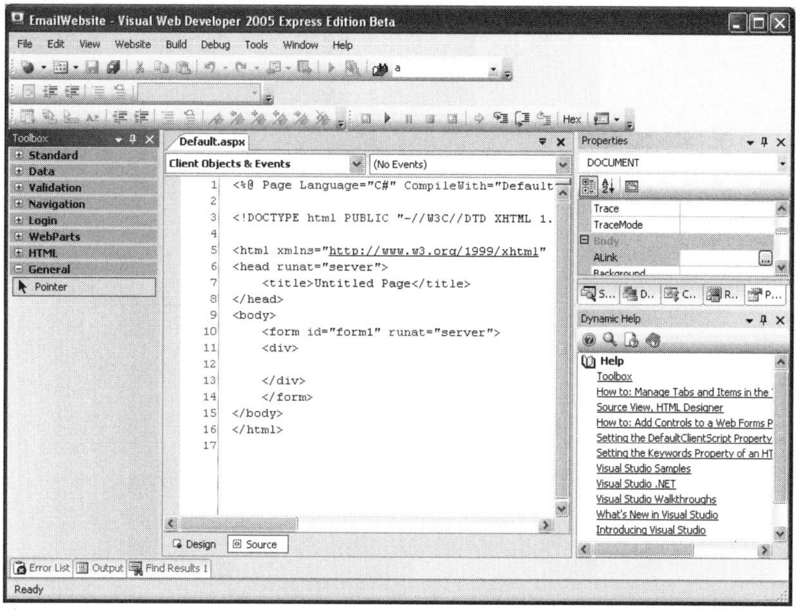

Figure 1-9. *The new EmailWebsite*

You have in front of you the HTML view of the Default.aspx. When a new website is created, the Default.aspx is included as a first page. You can use this page or delete it and start from scratch. You will use this page for your application. Click on the Design button at the bottom of the screen to go to the Web Form designer. This is where you will put your controls for the user to interact with. You will also require one more web page. When users submit their request to submit, you want to present them with another page to show them the information you have received and demonstrate their request has been accepted. You will add this page to your project after the next few steps.

On the left side of the development environment is a side window called the Toolbox. In the Toolbox, click the plus sign beside the word Standard so you can see all of the standard ASP.NET server controls. Now let's begin to add the controls to your web page.

1. From the main menu along the top, select Layout ➤ Insert Table.

2. In the layout section of the Insert Table dialog, select four rows and two columns and select Center Align.

3. Check the Caption check box so you can add a title to your table.

4. Ensure that your Insert Table dialog looks like the one in Figure 1-10 and click OK.

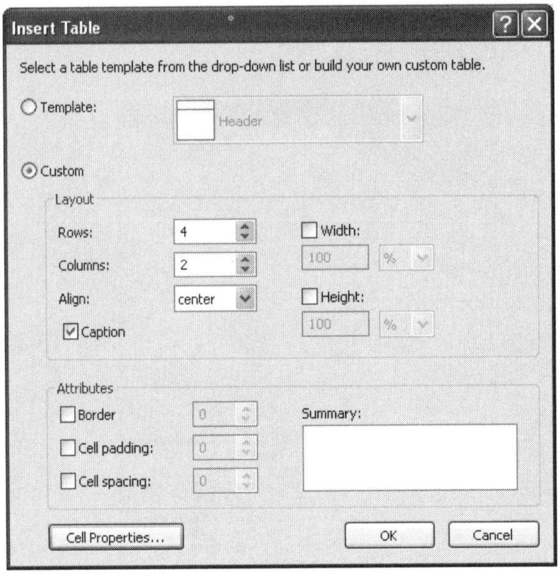

Figure 1-10. *Inserting a table*

This will draw a table on the designer. We will now run through the steps to set up your table so you can receive input from the users of your website.

1. Click in the top row of the table to give it focus and place the cursor in it. Enter the text **Sign-Up Now!** in the row.

2. Enter the text in the rest of the cells so it looks like Figure 1-11.

Figure 1-11. *Labels for the sign-up Web Form*

Now that your users know what to type, you must give them something to type it into and submit it to the server for processing. You will provide some controls for the user to interact with. You will need a few textboxes and a button to enable submission. You can find these in the Standard section of the Toolbox you just expanded. Drag and drop a textbox into each cell beside the text, and in the last row, drop a button into the right cell. Your form should now look like Figure 1-12 in the designer.

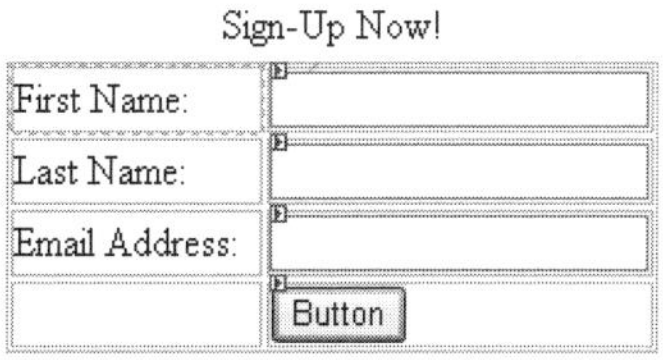

Figure 1-12. *The sign-up form with server controls*

You need to give your control some meaningful names so you can access them more easily from your code when users click the Submit button. Follow these steps to change the name of a control:

1. Select the textbox in the First Name row.

2. Right-click the textbox and select Properties.

3. When the Properties window appears on the right side, scroll to the bottom to find the ID property (Figure 1-13).

4. In the ID field, enter **FirstNameTextBox**.

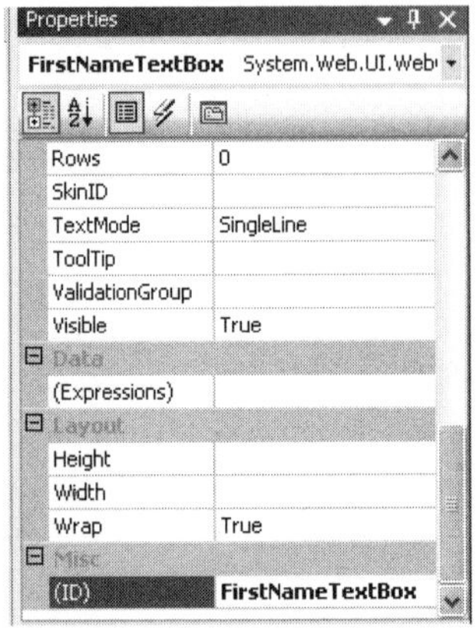

Figure 1-13. *Assign an ID to the first textbox.*

Repeat the previous steps for the other two textboxes and the button. Call the textbox in the Last Name row LastNameTextBox and the textbox in the E-mail Address row EmailAddressTextBox and the button SignUpButton. While in the properties for the button, change the Text property to **Sign Up**. Now you have all your controls just about set up. When your button gets clicked by the user, you want to submit the data to another web page. This procedure is called *cross-page posting*. To do this, first add the other page to your website. To add the new web page, follow these steps:

1. Under the main menu, select File ➤ New ➤ File. This gives you the dialog in Figure 1-14.

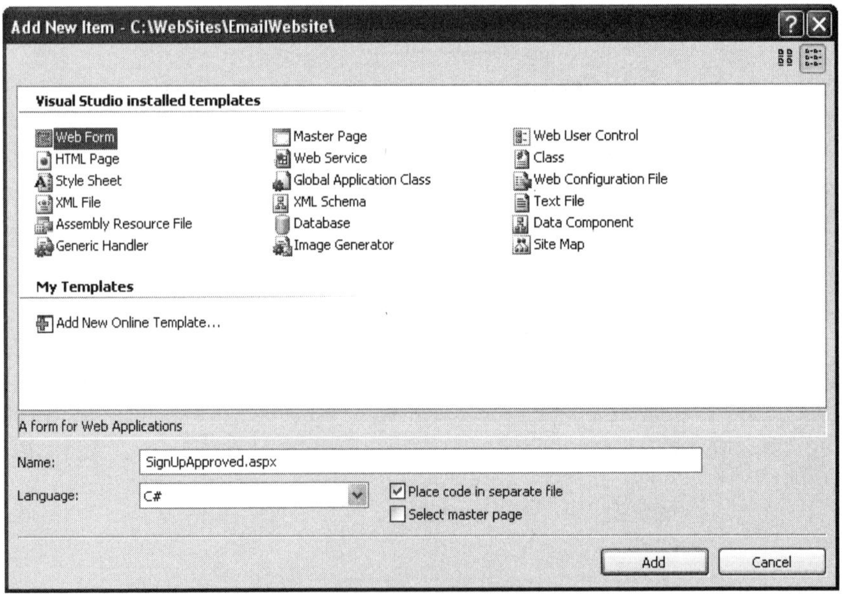

Figure 1-14. *Adding a new file*

2. Ensure that Web Form is selected.

3. Type **SignUpApproved.aspx** for the new file name.

4. Check the box to place code in a separate file.

5. Click Add to create the file.

Now that you have added a second web page, you see two tabs along the top. One tab has the name of your new file and the other has the name of your Default.aspx file. You need to go back to the Submit button and set up one last property called the PostBackUrl. This property will tell the page to submit the data from the Default.aspx page to the SignUpApproved.aspx page. To set up this property, follow these steps:

1. Go to the property called PostBackUrl for the Submit button. This is located in the behavior section.

2. Select the PostBackUrl property name. An ellipses button appears to the right.

3. Click on the ellipses button and select the new SignUpApproved.aspx page.

You need to put a few controls on the SignUpApprovedPage. Go to that page's designer just as we did earlier with the Default.aspx page, and follow these steps to set up the Web Form:

1. From the main menu, select Layout ➤ Insert Table. Add a table with two rows and one column, and align center.

2. Click the first row and enter the text **Congratulations!**

3. In the second row, drag and drop a Label control from the General section of the toolbox. Change the ID of this label to **SignedUpLabel**.

4. Next to the SignedUpLabel, type the following text: **has signed up**.

The SignUpApproved Web Form should look like the designer in Figure 1-15 (you may have to drag the side of the table to make it a bit wider).

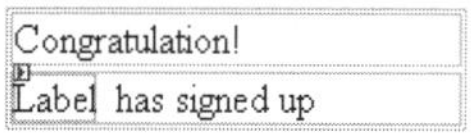

Figure 1-15. *The SignUpApproved page with controls*

We are just about done. There is one step left. You must add a little bit of code to the Sign-UpApproved.aspx page to read the values of the TextBoxes from the Default.aspx page. Right-click anywhere on the designer and select View Code. Ensure that the following code is in the file (add the Page_Load method):

```
Partial Class SignUpApproved
Inherits System.Web.UI.Page

Private Sub Page_Load(ByVal sender As Object, ByVal e As EventArgs) _
Handles Me.Load

Dim firstName As TextBox = _
CType(Me.PreviousPage.FindControl("FirstNameTextBox"), TextBox)
Dim lastName As TextBox = _
CType(Me.PreviousPage.FindControl("LastNameTextBox"), TextBox)
SignedUpLabel.Text = firstName.Text + " " + lastName.Text
End Sub

End Class
```

In this code, we are handling the Page_Load event. Events are covered in greater detail in a later chapter, but to help you understand what is happening here, we introduce them briefly now. An event is triggered or invoked as a response to something happening. For example, the user clicks a button and the button raises a click event that allows you to add code to handle the event in the manner you choose. In this case, you want to handle the event that is raised when the SignUpApproved.aspx page is loaded. This is conveniently called the Load event. By adding the method with the name just as you specified, the runtime knows you want that method to handle the Load event and calls this method when the Load event is raised.

Why do you want to handle the Load event? The Load event is raised closer to the beginning of processing the page (we will learn more about the lifetime and processing of web pages later). At this time you want to look at the information from the Defautl.aspx page that the user entered. In this event handler, you write the code to get a reference to the controls you added to the Default.aspx. The SignUpApproved page has the PreviousPage property, which gives you access to the Default.aspx page. With that you can get a reference to the FirstNameTextBox and the LastNameTextBox, output their contents to the SignUpApproved.aspx page as the full name of the user, and congratulate the user for signing up successfully.

To run your application, go back to the designer for the Default.aspx page, right-click any-where on the designer, and select View in Browser. This launches your Default.aspx page in the default web browser. Enter some information into the textboxes and click Submit. Your results should look like Figure 1-16 (of course, substitute the values with the ones you used).

■**Note** You may receive a warning that debugging is not enabled with an option to enable it now by adding a web.config file to your application. Click OK to add the file. The web.config file is an important file and we will cover it in great detail later on.

Figure 1-16. *Your first website in action*

That's all there is to it. Of course, if this were a real sign-up website, you would have stored the information in a more permanent location such as in a database. Some of the concepts just covered may seem a little fuzzy right now. Don't worry! By the end of this book everything will be perfectly clear. You will be whipping up professional-looking websites with ease.

Building Web Applications

In the last section, you learned exactly how easy it is to build a few web pages and have them interact not only with a user, but also intelligently with each other. But what exactly is happening when we access these web pages? For the most part, the inner workings of a web application are hidden from us. But as developers, we should know a little more than our users. Let's take a few moments to scratch the surface.

Web Application Architecture

Web applications have been around for a while now. Because you are reading a book on how to build web applications, we assume you have some understanding of how the Internet and web applications work, so this discussion is only a cursory exploration. However, if you find yourself thirsty for more information on this subject, numerous resources are at your disposal. In the meantime, let's take a quick look at a typical user interaction with a website (Figure 1-17).

Figure 1-17. *A typical user interaction with a website*

The diagram in Figure 1-17 is relatively straightforward. In fact, we would venture to guess you have interacted with dozens of websites. In this day and age, people are interacting with websites almost daily. But what is actually happening from a technology perspective when you do interact with a web page? On a client machine, perhaps your personal computer in your den, you open your favorite Internet browser and type `http://www.apress.com` into the address bar. This forms the beginning of a web request. Your request goes out onto the wires (or through the air in the case of a wireless network) through what may seem like a massive void of the Internet similar to outer space, and it somehow finds a computer that has the information you are requesting. However, it is not a massive void similar to outer space. It is very straightforward.

Ultimately, all requests go over physical wires that form the backbone of the Internet. These wires hook up to computers that know how to find the computer you are looking for in the URL you entered. This magic is done by a Domain Name Server (DNS) whose only job is to translate domain names (such as apress.com) to their respective IP (Internet Protocol) address and direct the request to the appropriate computer (or vice versa, which is known as a *reverse lookup*). The computer that accepts the request, commonly known as a *web server*, receives your request and serves back the information you have requested in HTML form (web requests can return different forms of data, including documents, XML, and images), so your Internet browser can display the information to you in the form of a web page and formatted in the way that the web designer wants you to see it. The process of serving the information back to the client is called a *web response*.

It really does not get any harder than this. In fact, the current development paradigm is such that all the below-the-service logic that occurs to make web applications work is hidden from us, and for the most part, we don't really care about it. The important thing to note is that there is a *request* and there is a *response*. These are two key elements in building ASP.NET applications. As we will see later, different things happen during the request phase and during the response phase that impact coding and design considerations.

ASP.NET Runtime

When we build applications for the web using ASP.NET, we need to have the ASP.NET runtime installed. This background process is constantly running on the web server listening for requests that require its services. You can see this process running in your task manager as aspnet_wp.exe (ASP.NET worker process). When the web server receives a request, that is, for an ASP.NET item such as an .aspx page or an .asmx web service, it forwards the request to the ASP.NET worker process because that is the process registered as knowing how to handle such requests. If you use Task Manager by right-clicking your program bar, you can see aspnetwp.exe in the list of processes. A program registered to handle web requests like this is known as an Internet Services Application Programming Interface (ISAPI). The worker process then parses the page being requested and processes any server-side script that is necessary to derive the final page output (the response), including any code associated with the page (e.g., C#, VB .NET, etc.). In the upcoming chapters, you will learn in more detail about the request and response and how ASP.NET allows you to interact with the request and response. This chapter has only really exposed the tip of the iceberg.

Summary

In this chapter, you learned the basics of Visual Web Developer 2005, and you built your first interactive web application. You also learned about object-oriented programming (OOP). As you progress throughout the book, you will quickly be building more advanced web applications including database applications. But first, you need to get more familiar with your development environment. Chapter 2 takes you on a guided tour of the IDE so you will be able to navigate around quickly and accomplish your tasks.

■■■

The Development Environment

The Integrated Development Environment (IDE) we will be using to build our ASP.NET 2.0 applications is Visual Web Developer (VWD). Throughout this chapter we will take a high-level guided tour of the IDE so you become familiar with most of the important tools available to build your applications more quickly and with less hassle. As you will see, building web applications with VWD is no hassle at all.

Although hundreds of pages could be written to encompass all the productivity tools available in such a powerful development environment, this chapter will focus on the high-level items you will want to know right away. A lot of the other wizards and tools available are covered throughout the book as we discuss the aspects of the technology we are dealing with. For example, we will discuss the wizards that are used to configure a data source in the chapters that discuss working with data.

In this chapter we will examine the following:

- How to use the key menu and toolbar buttons

- How to use the Help system

- How to work with the many available window panes

- How to work effectively in the code editor

- How to configure your development environment

Main Menu and Toolbars

Microsoft has been relatively consistent over the years in providing a common look when it comes to the main menu and toolbar options. Visual Web Developer is no exception, as seen in Figure 2-1. In this section we cover the main menu and toolbar options and what they do. Of course, VWD has menu items for Copy, Paste, Delete, and so on. We venture to assume you know what these do and focus the discussion around development-oriented commands.

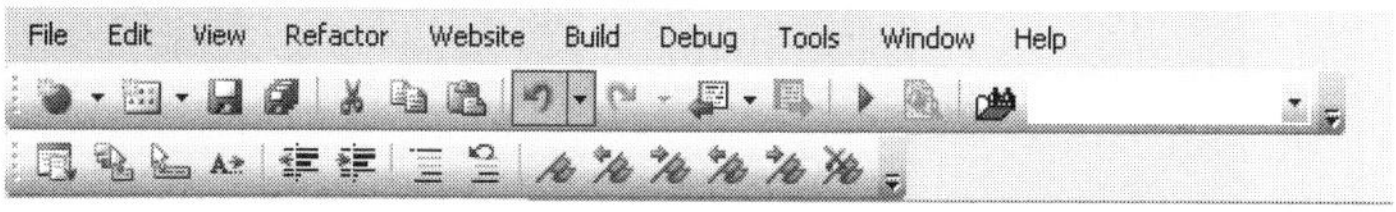

Figure 2-1. *The main menu and toolbar*

When you first launch VWD, the initial menu option will look different than what you see in Figure 2-1. The menu options that you do not see will become available once you begin a website. For now, let's just create one quickly so you can see the rest of the menu options. Navigate to File ➤ New Website under the main menu. In the New Website dialog, leave all values at their default and click OK (refer back to Chapter 1 for additional reference to this dialog). Now that you have created a website, all the other menu options and toolbars are available to experiment with. Let's start looking at them in more detail and tap out some code where the various options require it.

File Menu

Underneath the File menu is where you are provided all the options to do the tasks associated with core file operation. As you just saw, you are able to create new websites, open existing websites, add new files, and add existing files to websites. One of the nice features of this menu is the Recent Files and the Recent Projects items. If you find yourself working on a lot of files in many websites, these menu items keep a relatively extensive history of the files and projects you have been working in. Instead of having to use the Open command and navigate to the file manually, you may more easily find it in these lists and open it directly from there.

Edit Menu

Underneath the Edit menu you will find the most common text editing options, such as Copy and Paste. In addition, you have the Undo (one of our favorites) and Redo operations, which allow you to undo the last item(s) that you did or redo, which you can do after an undo. We have not tested exactly how many operations the Undo/Redo keeps in memory, but we have yet to be unable to recover from our worst situations.

Some of the handier menu items are located near the bottom of the Edit menu. These are the formatting options. A common scenario is the situation where you may find some code samples you would like to use in your project, but that code author does not format the code in the same fashion as you. The Format Document and Format Selection options give you the ability to have the IDE automatically format your code. You may specify formatting rules under the Tools ➤ Options menu item, which we look at in a later section. For now, to test this out, enter the following code in the Default.aspx file that should be open by default. The key here is the HTML for the table definition.

```
<%@ Page Language="VB" AutoEventWireup="false" CodeFile="Default.aspx.vb"
Inherits="_Default" %>

<!DOCTYPE html PUBLIC "-//W3C//DTD XHTML 1.1//EN"
"http://www.w3.org/TR/xhtml11/DTD/xhtml11.dtd">
```

```
<html xmlns="http://w ww.w3.org/1999/xhtml" >
<head runat="server">
    <title>Untitled Page</title>
</head>
<body>
    <form id="form1" runat="server">
    <div>
        <table><tr><td></td></tr></table>
    </div>
    </form>
</body>
</html>
```

Now go ahead and select the Format Document button on the Edit ➤ Advanced menu. The HTML for the table definition should now look like this:

```
<form id="form1" runat="server">
        <div>
            <table>
                <tr>
                    <td>
                    </td>
                </tr>
            </table>
        </div>
    </form>
```

The HTML has been automatically formatted to place each element on its own line with proper indention for easy readability. Now maintaining the code samples that you leverage may not be as daunting a task. This menu option will have the same effect on other code, including XML and your C# code.

Under the Edit ➤ Advanced menu option are a lot more options for formatting your code. We will leave you to experiment with these options to determine what you like and do not like. However, we will take a quick look at the Outlining options under the Edit ➤ Outline menu. These options provide the ability to collapse or expand areas of code. This is quite handy in large source files and especially with large HTML files. Try this out. Highlight the entire table definition from our previous example, and then select Edit ➤ Outlining ➤ Hide Selection. This will collapse the whole table definition down to one line with a plus sign on the left. By clicking the plus sign with the cursor, you will be able to expand the table definition again. This example was not very dramatic; however, imagine a page with multiple tables that all have a dozen rows and a half-dozen columns. This will provide you with a nice way to collapse all the tables down so you can be more organized in your source.

View Menu

The View menu is another one of the standard menu options that we see in all Microsoft applications. This menu has all the commands that will allow you to get at the majority of the panes you see along the sides and bottom of the IDE, such as the Solution Explorer and the Properties pane. If you ever accidentally close one of them, you can come here to open it again. We will be covering the majority of the panes available in more detail later in the chapter. In addition, the View menu contains a list of all the available toolbars that you can show. For the most part, the toolbars encapsulate common themes of functionality that are typically also available through the standard menu options. The toolbars do provide easier access if there are commands you do more often. Two such toolbars are the Debug and Text Editor toolbars. We will be looking at the commands on both these toolbars in Chapter 12 on debugging. If you enjoy having as much of your screen as possible available to you for coding, you may find the Full Screen option useful as well that hides all the toolbars and side and bottom panes. This mode provides you with the largest view of your source files.

Website Menu

The Website menu provides the commands that perform operations on the solution. The solution is a container for one or more projects. This means that you can, if you have multiple websites, hold them all within one solution and have them all available at the same time. This menu is sensitive to what is available in the Solution Explorer window. For example, certain items will show and hide based on whether or not there are multiple projects. To see these other items, repeat the steps you performed earlier, except instead of selecting File ➤ New Website, select File ➤ Add ➤ New Website. Now with two websites in the solution, you will see some additional options in the Website menu.

In the Website menu, you now have the ability to add new and existing files to websites. You will also be able to add References. Adding References is required when you need to use code provided to you in external assemblies. Assemblies are generated when .NET code is compiled. These are dynamic link libraries (DLLs). You can also add Web References if there are web services you would like to use in your project. When there are multiple projects in the Solution Explorer, you are also provided with the Project Dependency and Project Build Order options. These allow you to specify if any of the projects are dependent on one another. The build order is very important. If one project is referencing the output from another project, you had better be sure the output from the other project exists first. In turn, the IDE will ensure that they are compiled in the proper order. The Start Options menu item is a shortcut to the Start Options tab of the Project Properties dialog, which you will see in more detail in the Solution Explorer section later in this chapter. Finally, there is the Copy Website command, which gives you the ability to copy a website to a remote site, and the ASP.NET Configuration command, which you have seen a little bit of. In Chapter 10 we will get into the meat of this tool.

Build and Debug Menus

The Build menu provides you with options for compiling your website. When *compiling,* you convert all of your code into a format known as machine language so the computer understands the instructions it receives from your code. In .NET this is a two-part process. When your assemblies are first compiled, they are compiled into Intermediary Language (IL). Then, when the code is actually required to run, the .NET runtime compiles the IL into machine language. This is called *Just-In-Time* (JIT) compilation.

There are a variety of compiling options for ASP.NET applications that we examine a little later. For instance, after typing out a lot of new code, you may want to do a quick check to ensure there are not any compile errors. By selecting the Build Solution option under the Build menu, you will quickly receive feedback about build errors. This is also a menu where you will add and remove items depending on what you select in Solution Explorer. If you have the project node selected in the Solution Explorer, you will see options pertaining only to building solutions. However, if you select one ore more files within a project, you can also use the Build Page option. This option is convenient in cases where multiple pages may be causing compile errors and you want to be able to fix things up one page at a time.

The Debug menu provides commands necessary to run your application, including both the Start (F5) and the Start without Debugging (Ctrl+F5) commands. This menu also provides some other advanced debugging options that we cover in detail in Chapter 12.

Tools Menu

The Tools menu contains a few interesting items. From the Tools menu, you have the ability to customize the Toolbox. The Toolbox is a side pane that contains all the controls you have available to place on a web page. The Toolbox is one of the most important areas when building Web applications. We reserve our main discussion on this topic for a later section dedicated to the Toolbox. In addition to the Toolbox, the Tools menu contains the command to launch the Add-In Manager, where you can load environment add-ins. There are always a large number of tools available out there, known as *third-party tools*, that can do things that perhaps the product team at Microsoft did not think of or that someone just finds useful. You can install these add-ins and use this menu option to load the add-in into the environment to make it available for use.

The Tools menu also provides the Options command. The Options dialog is covered in great detail later. In essence, this dialog provides you the ability to configure everything to do with your development environment, from how you would like your HTML displayed to the color you would like the keywords in your code to appear. It truly is the one-stop shop for customizing your development experience. The last command to note here is the Customize button, which allows you to customize the organization of your toolbars and the functionality they provide.

Customize Your Toolbars

Under the Tools menu you have the ability to customize all of the menus and toolbars we have looked at so far. Essentially, every menu item we have described in the main menu bar can also be configured to be displayed on a toolbar. A slew of toolbars provided out of the box are available from below the View menu. If a toolbar and a command that you want to appear on that toolbar is not present, you can add it by going into Tools ➤ Customize. You may navigate around in this dialog, and when you see a command you want, simply drag it onto the toolbar. Take a look at Figure 2-2, which shows you how to add the Restart button to the Debugging toolbar. This will come in handy in Chapter 12.

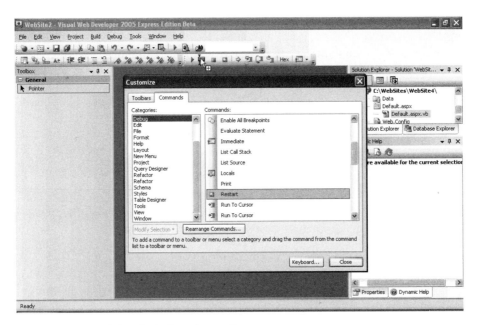

Figure 2-2. *Customizing the Debugging toolbar*

Window Menu

The Window menu is also one of the Microsoft standard menu items. In the case of the development environment, it does have a few useful items worth mentioning. One of the first buttons you will notice is the Split command. This is useful when working with larger code files. You can split the file into two so that you can see code at different areas of the file. Note the line numbers in Figure 2-3. The next section of commands is sensitive to whichever side/bottom pane is selected. You will see these commands in a little more detail in the coming sections. Next is the Close All Documents button, which closes all open documents such as Web Forms, code-behind, XML files, configuration files, and so on.

Help Menu

The Help documentation shipped with VWD can be very helpful. The Microsoft .NET Framework is just too large for any one person to master completely. As such, the Help files are a valuable resource. In this section we take a look at the documentation at the disposal of the developer.

Contents and Index

The Contents and Index are the typical Help file format that you are probably used to from most other applications. If you have ever seen the Help files from other applications that are in the format of .chm files or even some HTML help system, there are two tabs. One tab provides a high-level table of contents that you can drill through, and the other tab provides an index just like the index in the back of a book. The index provides an alphabetical listing of all the keywords available in Help. There is a textbox at the top where you can enter in the keyword you are looking for and the index list will navigate automatically to that topic. Both the contents and the index are available from the same menu option. Clicking on the Help ➤ Contents button or the Help ➤ Index button will provide you with the same Help dialog. Figure 2-4 illustrates the new window that contains the Help file system.

Figure 2-3. *Splitting a code file*

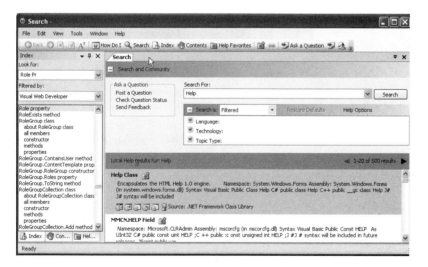

Figure 2-4. *Visual Web Developer Help file system*

In the bottom-right corner is a series of tabs. If you know the keyword you are looking for, you can switch to the Index tab and enter it there. If you prefer, you can drill through the Help files on the Contents tab. In either case, when you find content you are interested in, you can right-click and add the Help page to your Help Favorites for easy reference. These items will appear in the Help Favorites tab.

Dynamic Help

In addition to the standard contents and index help options, VWD offers Dynamic Help. This is a dockable side pane that will dynamically reload itself with the topics that pertain to the current selection. Let's use the website you built in Chapter 1 to demonstrate this. Open the code file for the SignUpApproved.aspx Web Form. In the code that we entered, highlight some of the keywords, such as FindControl and TextBox. Take a look at Figure 2-5 to see what happens when we select the PreviousPage property. The Dynamic Help is updated to reflect the selection. If we want to get help on the PreviousPage property, we can simply click the link provided in the Dynamic Help window pane and we will be brought to the documentation for the property. This can be a huge time-saver over trying to use the Help index and Help search engine.

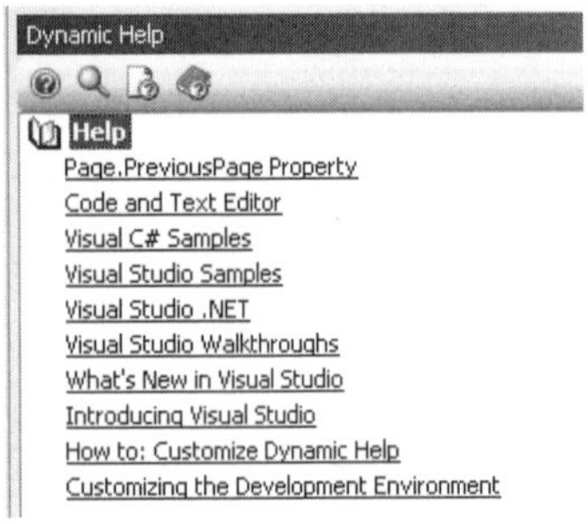

Figure 2-5. *Dynamic Help in action*

Dockable Windows

One of the key features of an effective development environment is easy access to common tasks. We saw this with the toolbars and menu structure. In addition to that, there is also a wide range of dockable side and bottom window panes. It is the fact that each and every window is dockable that makes these little panes so useful. This lets you place each window in an area of the IDE that fits most comfortably for you. To move a window around, you simply left-click the title bar and drag it to its new location. Once you begin to drag the window, the IDE will provide you with some icons to assist in the operation. See Figure 2-6. Once you begin the drag-and-drop operation, blue arrows appear at the top, left, bottom, and right of the IDE. If you release the window by moving the cursor on top of one of the arrows, the window will become docked to that side of the IDE.

As you drag a window around the IDE, you will notice a larger image with four arrows and a centerpiece that follows you around. Actually, this graphic will be centered over any other window where you are currently hovering. If you move the cursor right to the center of this while dragging a window, you will group this window with the one where you are currently hovering.

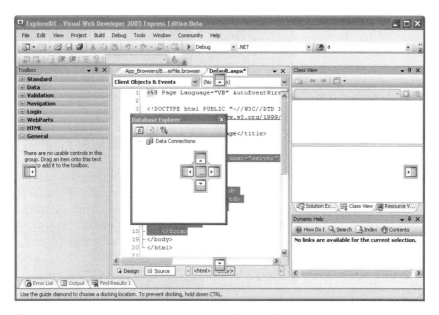

Figure 2-6. *Dragging and dropping a dockable window*

If you so choose, you may also convert any dockable window into a tabbed document. *Tabbed document* is the term used to describe any window that is open in the middle of the IDE. For example, when you double-click a code file in the Solution Explorer, it opens up in the middle of the IDE as a tabbed document. To try this, right-click the title bar of any dockable window and select Tabbed Document. To make the window dockable again, simply right-click and select Dockable. At this point, we will leave you to experiment with this.

Next, we'll take a thorough look at all the windows available within the IDE to understand the important role that each will play in our development. We'll begin with one of the most important windows, the Solution Explorer.

Solution Explorer

The Solution Explorer is the window where you will be able to see the structure of your projects. In this view, you will be able to see every file and folder that you have included with every project that is currently open. You will have the ability to add new files, delete existing files, rename files, add new projects, and so on. We will take a look at all the features provided by this window. By default, this window is located closer to the top on the right-hand side (shown in Figure 2-7). In this view of my Solution Explorer, we can see a website project. It is displayed as the path on the file system to where the website is located.

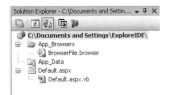

Figure 2-7. *The Solution Explorer*

The Solution Explorer does provide some shortcuts to some of the options we discussed earlier in the section on the Website menu. Place your cursor on one of the Website nodes in the Solution Explorer and right-click. You will be provided with a context menu that encapsulates all the functionality we saw on the Website menu, plus one more option called Property Pages. If you select this option you will see a dialog that allows you to configure aspects of the Website project's properties. There are additional options available depending on the type of item you right-click in the Solution Explorer. For instance, if you right-click Default.aspx, you are again presented with a context menu. This time, the menu contains all of the standard file operations such as Copy and Delete. However, you also have options to view this file in different ways. This is because the IDE is smart enough to know that you have selected a web page. As a result, it provides you the options to view the file at design time in various modes such as Design View or Code View; it also gives you the ability to view in the browser, in which case the page will be launched in your default browser or you can specify a different browser by selecting the Browse With option. There is also a toolbar across the top of the Solution Explorer window that provides shortcut buttons to some of the operations we have discussed and is context sensitive to what you select in the TreeView.

Now that you are familiar with the Solution Explorer, we can look at the next very important docking window, the Toolbox.

Special Folders

Within Solution Explorer, by default, you will see a data folder. You will also notice that this folder has a different icon in the TreeView than regular folders. There are a handful of folders that have special names and if included in your project will have special meaning to your application. Table 2-1 lists and describes those folders.

Table 2-1. *Special Folders*

Folder Name	Description
App_Assemblies	This folder contains all output assemblies and assembly references that your website project depends on.
App_Code	The runtime checks this folder for any code files. If any are found, it automatically makes them available to your applications and compiles them at runtime.
App_WebReferences	This folder contains all the web service references that the website is currently referencing.
App_Data	This folder contains files such as SQL Server database files or XML data.

Folder Name	Description
App_Browsers	This folder contains browser definition files.
App_GlobalResources	This folder provides a container for resources that are global to the application.
App_LocalResources	This folder contains the resources used to display text in the different locals for individual Web Forms.
App_Themes	This folder contains theme files that permit applying a common look across an entire website.

Toolbox

The Toolbox is the pane that contains all the controls the IDE knows about that you can use to build web pages. If you want to add a textbox, label, WebParts, login controls, or data controls, they are all grouped here in the Toolbox, as shown in Figure 2-8.

Figure 2-8. *The Toolbox*

The Toolbox automatically has items grouped into their logical sections. Only controls/components that pertain to the currently open document will be shown here. So, if you do not have a Web Form open, you will not see items in the Toolbox that pertain only to Web Forms. Table 2-2 lists the various groupings that are available out of the box.

Table 2-2. *The Toolbox Organization*

Grouping	Description
Standard	All standard ASP.NET server controls, such as textboxes, buttons, check boxes, wizards, and the Calendar, are listed here.
Data	This section lists the controls that are used for connecting to data sources. This section also contains the powerful grid-based controls for displaying data, such as the GridView and the Repeater.
Navigation	This section contains the controls that perform the common tasks related to site navigation, such as the Menu and SiteMapPath.

Continued

Table 2-2. *Continued*

Grouping	Description
Validation	This section contains the validation controls. These controls are used to provide both client- and server-side validation of a user's input. Examples are the Required-FieldValidator and the CompareValidator.
Login	This section contains the components necessary to build an authentication system into your Website, including the Login, LoginStatus, and LoginView controls.
WebParts	This section contains the necessary controls to build a user-driven dynamic web-site using the Personalization providers. These controls include the WebPartManager, WebPartZone, and the various types of WebParts.
HTML	This section contains all the standard HTML controls, such as the plain HTML Input controls.
General	This section contains any other items that you may add manually or that may not fit into any other logical group. By default, this section contains the pointer, which switches the context of the mouse cursor to the pointer for object selection.

Customizing the Toolbox

The Toolbox is also highly customizable. By right-clicking the Toolbox, you will be able to see all the options available. Let's walk through a few examples of how to customize the Toolbox.

Adding Tabs

By right-clicking anywhere in the Toolbox, you can select the Add Tab option. When you do this, you will see the new tab appear on the Toolbox with the cursor already in place awaiting the entry of the new tab's name. Call it My New Tab and it should look like Figure 2-9. You can now drag items for the other tabs onto your new tab.

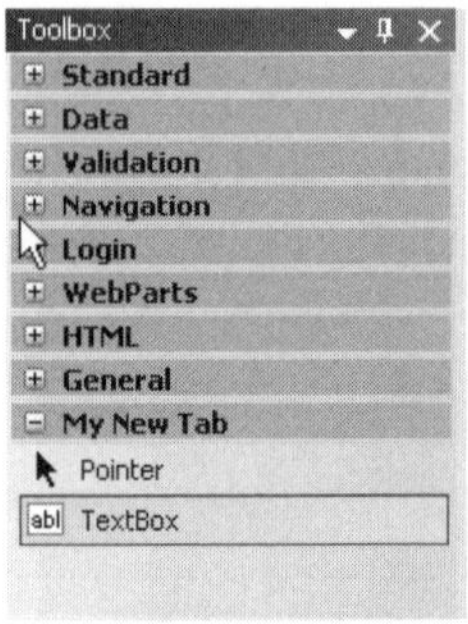

Figure 2-9. *Adding tabs to the Toolbox*

Now right-click on the new tab, and select Delete. This will permanently remote the tab from the Toolbox. You will notice that the Delete option is only available for custom tabs.

Adding Controls

There may be cases where the tool you are looking for is not available in the Toolbox. If this is the case, you may add the tool yourself. The menu option to do this is different depending on where you are. Under the Tools menu, the options is called Choose Toolbox Items, whereas if you right-click on the Toolbox, the options is simply called Add Items. Either one will bring up the dialog shown in Figure 2-10.

There are two tabs on the Choose Toolbox items dialog. One tab is called .NET Framework Components, and the other is called COM Components. The .NET Framework Components tab will display any .NET items that are configured to be viewable in the Toolbox that the IDE is aware of. If a component is not listed here, you can browse the file system for the assembly containing it and add it manually. The COM Components tab will display any components (e.g., ActiveX components) that are registered with the operating system. And again, if an item you are looking for is not here, you can browse for it. Most of the .NET components you see in the .NET Framework Components tab that are unselected are those that were brought forward into ASP.NET 2.0 to maintain backward compatibility with ASP.NET 1.x. When you add new components to the Toolbox, they will be placed in the tab that is active when the Choose Toolbox Items dialog is launched.

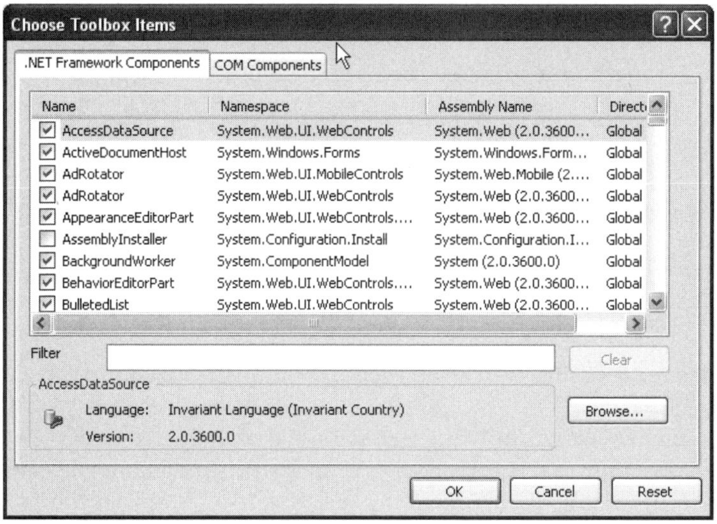

Figure 2-10. *Choosing Toolbox items*

Properties Window

The Microsoft .NET Framework is an object-oriented development platform. As such, it consists of many classes, each of which contains properties. This, of course, includes the controls you will be placing on Web Forms. The Properties window, as shown in Figure 2-11, is an area where you can configure the controls you use without typing any code. The IDE will take care of placing the appropriate code in the appropriate place.

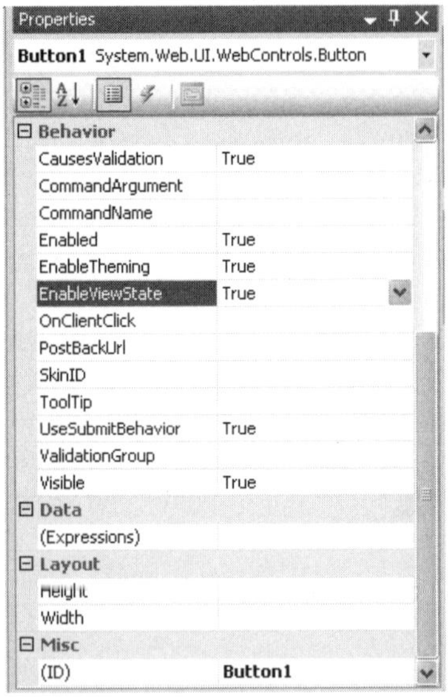

Figure 2-11. *The Properties window for a new button on a Web Form*

When you first drag and drop a button from the Toolbox onto the Web Form and then switch to source view, you see that the HTML the IDE rendered looks something like this:

```
<asp:Button ID="Button1" Runat="server" Text="Button" />
```

Using the Properties window, change the name to MyButton, change the text to My.Button, and change the BorderColor to some other color. Now look at the source. It should look similar to this (depending on what color you chose):

```
<asp:Button ID="MyButton" Runat="server" Text="My Button" BorderColor="Red" />
```

All these values have been set by using the convenience of the Properties window; you did not have to type any code.

There are a couple of ways to make a control's properties available in the Properties window. The first is to select the control on the designer, and the Properties window will automatically change to the selected control. The second is to place the cursor within a control's HTML source in the source view; again, the Properties window will automatically change to the selected control. Finally, you can manually find your control by name in the drop-down list provided within the Properties window itself. By changing the selection in the list, you inherently change the control whose properties the Properties window will be displaying.

The Properties window also has a little toolbar at the top that gives you the ability to configure how you would like to display the properties. The default is for the properties to be displayed in groups as you saw in Figure 2-11. However, by clicking the A-Z icon, you tell the Properties window to display its items in alphabetical order. The Properties window also provides a way to configure events for your controls. For example, if a user of your web page clicks a button, you may want to execute code based on the button clicked. By clicking the lightning bolt icon, you switch the window to display the events available to the currently selected control, and again, you may have these listed alphabetically or grouped by categories.

Database Explorer

The majority of web applications are driven by data in one way or another. The Database Explorer provides a nice, easy way to configure connections to various data sources and create new SQL Server databases. The Database Explorer is shown in Figure 2-12. We will explore this window in much greater detail when we introduce SQL Server 2005 Express in Chapter 3.

Figure 2-12. *The Database Explorer*

Output Window

Once our application is in a state where we are able to start compiling it, the Output window becomes very useful. This window, as shown in Figure 2-13, provides a drop-down list at the top with some predefined views.

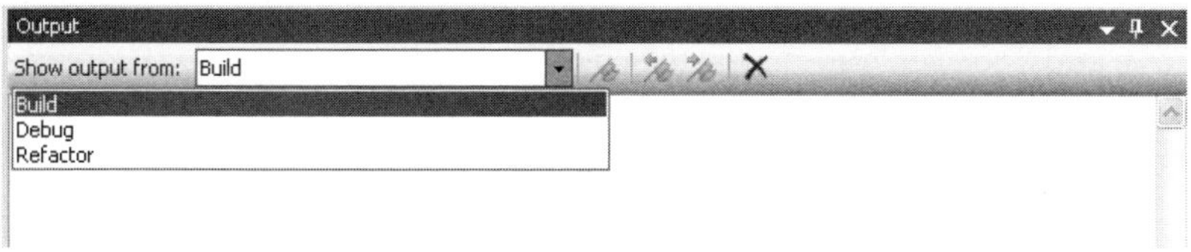

Figure 2-13. *The Output window*

The Build view provides information about errors, warnings, successes, and failures for each project and/or file that you selected during the last compilation. The Debug view shows much lower-level information about the last compilation. In this view you can see what files the runtime has loaded to complete the compilation. The Refactor view shows information about any code refactoring you have done recently. For example, in the earlier example when you renamed Button1 to MyButton, an entry was shown on the Refactor view in the Output window.

Error List

The Error List window's name is very self-descriptive. Any errors that exist in the current open documents are displayed here. The IDE is constantly scanning the open documents for errors. For example, say the following is typed into the code for Default.aspx:

```
Public Partial Class Default_aspx

    myInt

End Class
```

This code is obviously an error and will appear as an error in the Error List as shown in Figure 2-14. If you double-click on the item in the list, you will be brought directly to the proximity, if not the exact line, that is offending, so you can make any necessary corrections. As soon as you prefix that garble with a data type, such as int, and add a semicolon to the end, the Error List clears dynamically because the runtime now views that line as a legitimate variable declaration at the class level.

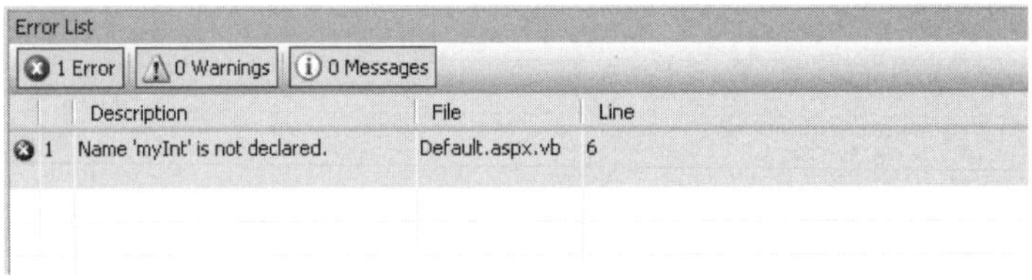

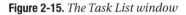

Figure 2-14. *The Error List window*

The toolbar at the top of this window shows three toggle buttons. If you are working in a large project, the number of messages shown in this list could get large. The Error, Warning, and Messages buttons toggle the visibility of the messages that fall into each respective category. You can also right-click the Error List and choose columns to be displayed and the sort order for the listed items. You can also change the column order by dragging and dropping the columns.

Task List

The Task List window, shown in Figure 2-15, provides a list of user-defined tasks you can create as well as items based on comments created throughout your code that begin with the appropriate token. The drop-down list at the top of the window lets you filter the list based on these two types of tasks. Note that the Comments view only appears if there are actually any comments defined using a valid token.

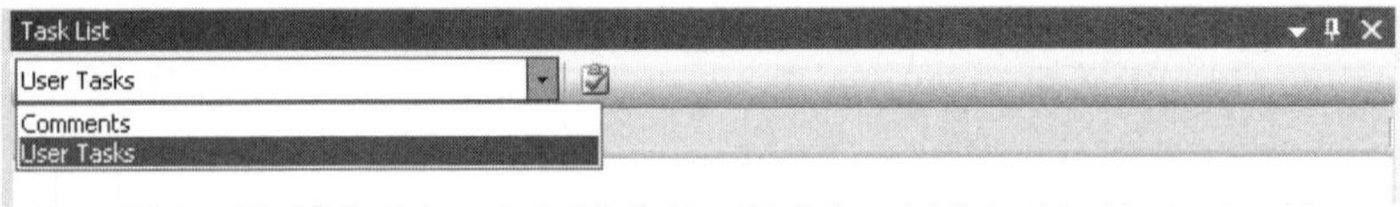

Figure 2-15. *The Task List window*

If you begin a comment line with a valid token that the IDE recognizes as a Task List comment, such as the word TODO, it will be picked up and displayed by the Task List. At any time, you can double-click an item in the Task List and be brought directly to that line of code and complete any necessary work. Using the previous example from the Error List, if you determine that now is not a good time to fix that error, perhaps because of the amount of work involved, you could simply comment on the line of code so your website would compile and mark it with a TODO comment and you do not forget about it.

```
Public Partial Class Default_aspx

    ' TODO Finish fixing this error
    ' crrrrrrbuuuuuu
End Class
```

This code results in the Task List being updated as shown in Figure 2-16. Other default comment tokens that are available are HACK and UNDONE. Of course, you may add your own tokens via the Tools ➤ Options, which we will see a little bit later.

Figure 2-16. *TODO comments displayed in the Task List window*

If you want to create your own Task List items without having to place comments throughout the code, you may be clicking the Create User Task button, the toolbar directly beside the drop-down list. When you click this button, you will see that the first available row in the list becomes editable. You can now type in your notes about the task and then press Enter to save the task. This task behaves much like the Task List in Microsoft Outlook. As you complete each task item, you can check it off as complete. The leftmost column in the list lets you assign a priority of High, Normal, and Low to the task. As your Task List grows, you can sort it by Priority, Complete, and Description. The Task List is shown in Figure 2-17.

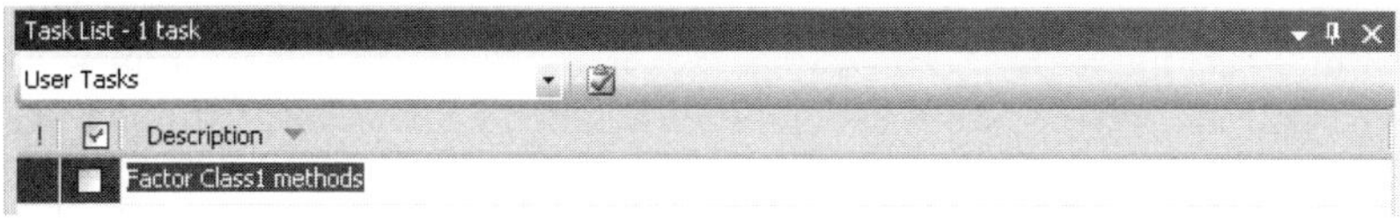

Figure 2-17. *User-created Task List*

Find Results View

The Find Results View displays the results of Find operations. Under the menu Edit ➤ Find and Replace are a variety of Find options that can be very useful when looking for specific items throughout your solution. Most of these options are self-explanatory. However, we will add that there is a second Find Results View that is available when performing many searches. You can specify that the results of your search be displayed in either Find Results 1 or Find Results 2. This gives you some flexibility so you do not wipe out previous searches in case you still need that information.

Class View

The Class View window, available from View ➤ Other Windows ➤ Class View, provides a mini object browser for your websites. You can use this view to traverse your own class hierarchy and view the organization of your code. In Class View, classes are called *symbols*. Figure 2-18 shows the Class View for a website.

■**Note** VB .NET and C# are object-oriented development languages. Terms such as *class, object, member variables, properties*, and *method* are going to be used throughout this book. In most cases, we provide a brief explanation of what each term refers to, but for the most part, it is assumed you have some familiarity with these terms and object orientation. If interfaces and object-oriented programming in general are new to you, we recommend reading some resources available on the topics to get familiar with the terminology.

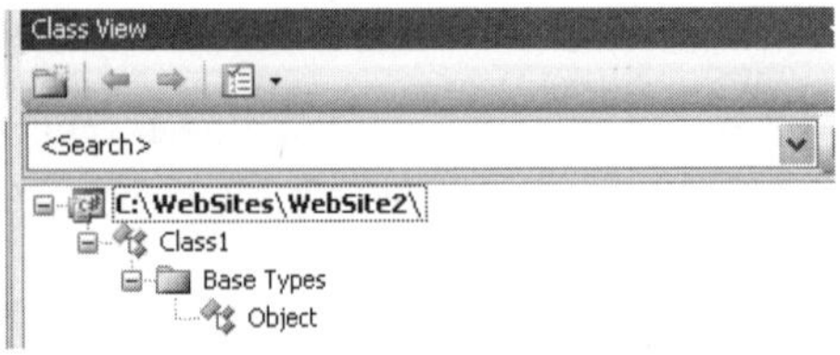

Figure 2-18. *The Class View window*

The Class View is handy in that you can drill through to find particular symbols, and once you find them, you can right-click and be brought to their definition. This will open the document containing the symbol itself so you can further examine its details. This view is especially useful for viewing your object hierarchy. Some classes may have specific interfaces implemented that you may be interested in knowing about, such as when working with various types of collection classes.

Code Editing

Code editing is where the power of an IDE, such as Visual Web Developer Express, really shines. In this section we take a look at the feature set built into the development environment to assist with writing code as effectively and efficiently as possible. We also take a look at the code-beside model, as well as other features such as event handling, code refactoring, using the clipboard, and, of course, IntelliSense.

Code-Beside

Typically, there have been two paradigms for where the code is placed. The code-behind model is one that was used by previous versions of ASP.NET and is still supported. In this model, all the code supporting a web page was in a code file that sits behind the .aspx file. This provided some separation from your code and your HTML and made it a lot cleaner to work with web pages.

The code-beside concept is very similar. The only difference is the amount of extraneous code placed in the file. ASP.NET 2.0 web pages are built on the new construct available to the .NET Framework called *partial classes.* In the code-behind model, the default behavior when adding a new Web Form to your website was for a code-behind file to be created. The Web Form itself used an attribute in the Page directive that told the runtime that the Web Form inherited from a class (page directives are special HTML tags at the top of the .aspx file that tell the ASP.NET runtime special information about the page). This class was the code-behind for the Web Form. The underlying architecture of this was such that the code-behind was indeed the driving force for the web page. It contained a great deal of Initialization code that you had better not touch or you could be in trouble.

However, the code-beside and partial class architecture greatly simplifies this problem set. When you add a Web Form, there is a check box option available to you. You can select to have your code placed in a different file. If you do not check this option, you will be placing all your code inline within your Web Form file. It is not the best way to organize your code, but it is fully supported. In the page directive of your Web Form, there are two attributes: CompileWith and ClassName. CompileWith tells the runtime what file contains the class that supports this Web Form, and the ClassName tells the compiler what class to use. By default, the class name will be <webformName>_aspx. You can change this to anything you would like, but just be sure to also change the class name in the page directive. If you forget to check the box off to put code in a separate file, you can always add this attribute by hand. The page directive for a new Web Form called HelloWebForm looks like this:

```
<%@ Page Language="VB" CompileWith="HelloWebForm.aspx.vb"
ClassName="HelloWebForm_aspx" %>
```

It produces a separate code file such as this:

```
Public Partial Class HelloWebForm_aspx

End Sub
```

Theoretically, with the way partial classes work, you could add as many files as you would like to your project and implement each method and property of the class in its own file. We think it is obvious that even though you would get full IntelliSense across the class, this is not desirable, but it is possible. The law of diminishing returns would apply to this scenario. Although it may be more manageable to organize a few files as partial classes for a particular class, the more you have, the more you have to manage, and debugging and maintaining could become troublesome.

■**Note** If you do decide after a Web Form is created to add a class file to work with as a code-beside file, it cannot be in the special Application_Code directory. You will receive compile errors if you try to do this.

IntelliSense

Ever since the earlier version of Visual Basic, there has been a really cool feature called Intel-liSense. We have already seen IntelliSense in action in some examples. IntelliSense is the feature that provides us with a list of available members for a class or namespace just by typing the period after it. For example, just by typing **System** followed by a period in the code editor, you get a list of all the subnamespaces, classes, enumerations, and types that are available at the System namespace level. With the use of IntelliSense, you can drill down a class/namespace hierarchy to find what you are looking for. This means you do not necessarily have to memorize what namespace every class lives in or memorize every method that is available for each class; it is often enough just to be familiar with what namespace and classes exist and generally what functionality they provide. From that much knowledge and the use of IntelliSense, it is very easy to find what you are looking for.

As cool as this feature was and still is, it has its limitations, such as only being available in the code editor. This has now changed. We now have an integrated development environment with fully featured IntelliSense. This means that we get IntelliSense for user controls, configuration files, JavaScript, HTML, Cascading Style Sheets, and more. IntelliSense is available in two forms: in-line IntelliSense and from the Context menu in the code editor, which provides various code snippets.

In-Line IntelliSense

As we described in the last paragraph, IntelliSense is available simply by typing in a period after the namespace or class. This is referred to as *in-line* IntelliSense, because you get the IntelliSense directly in line with what you are typing. This is a very powerful tool and can save you a lot of valuable time when coding your web applications. As mentioned briefly, this feature is available from just about anywhere in the IDE that you can type. It is also context sensitive. This means that if you have three script blocks in the Source view of your Web Form, where each is defined as using a different language and one has its runat attribute set to server, the IntelliSense engine will know exactly what to present you with in each block. In addition to this, you can specify a browser type in the HTML Editor toolbar and the IntelliSense engine will validate all client script against the document object model supported by that browser.

Another place where IntelliSense is now available that will make life a whole lot easier is in configuration files. Configuration files have an enormous number of options. To memorize all these options is hideous for the average developer. IntelliSense will now quickly show you what is available at each level of the schema and all the attributes available for each element. Setting up the web.config file has also been made easier with the ASP.NET administration tool, which we will examine more closely later on.

IntelliSense is really cool. It is not a completely new feature; it has been around for a while. But if you are new to this type of environment, just get coding and play around with it. It will not be long before you are reaping the benefits.

■Tip The keyboard combination of Ctrl+spacebar is a shortcut to make the IntelliSense drop-down menu appear on demand. Just place your cursor anywhere in a code file and try it out.

Inserting Code Snippets

Another feature built into the IDE is the ability to insert a code snippet. A *code snippet* in this context is a predefined set of code as provided by a Context menu in the code editor. As shown in Figure 2-19, the code snippets are available in a wide range of categories. There are far too many to elaborate on them all, but you can experiment and dig around in there to find out everything it has to offer.

Figure 2-19. *The Code Snippet menu*

Environment Options

As any powerful development environment should be, the Visual Web Developer environment is seemingly forever configurable. Everything from the color of each type of keyword to the background colors to the detailed formatting of HTML code is available for user customization. There are far too many options to cover here, but we will look at some of the key options available that will directly impact your development. The environment options are available by going to Tools ➤ Options. Here you will be presented with a dialog as in Figure 2-20 (you may need to select the check box in the bottom-left corner to show all options).

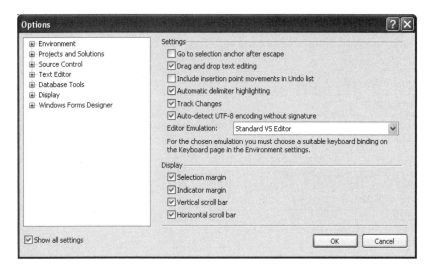

Figure 2-20. *Environment options*

As shown in the left TreeView, the options are broken down into categories. Each category provides its own subset of options. We will examine each of the main categories now.

Environment

Below the Environment node are a variety of subnodes. Again, each node divides the overall list of options into logical subsets. This is a common theme across all the nodes in this TreeView. Table 2-3 offers a brief explanation of the key features of each node under the Environment node.

Table 2-3. *Environment Options*

Option Subset	Description
General	Within this item you have the ability to configure options such as whether or not documents are displayed in a tabbed or MDI format, how many items are to be displayed in the Recent Files list, and how the IDE should appear at startup. This is useful for automatically opening the last website you were working on.
AutoRecover	This item is very important. VWD will save recovery information about your websites. In the event of data corruption or some other failure, you may be able to recover most of your work.
Fonts and Colors	In this section you can make your environment really feel like home. Change the colors and fonts of everything you can think of, including keywords, string constants, variable names, and so on.
Task List	This is the section where you can configure user-defined Task List comment tokens. Items such as TODO and HACK are already defined.

Projects and Solutions

The Projects and Solutions node offers some functionality that is useful for defining default behavior when creating projects and when running websites. Table 2-4 outlines the details.

Table 2-4. *Projects and Solutions Options*

Option Subset	Description
General	In this section, you define the default location where you want projects to be created.
Build/Run	In this section, you can tell the IDE to save all files when running the project. This is very important because if your environment crashes or becomes unstable for some reason while compiling or running, you want to ensure that your most recent work is saved to disk.

Text Editor

The Text Editor node provides options to define the characteristics of the code/text editors for all the various languages from C# to HTML. There are some options that can be applied to all languages and some that are specific to the individual language. For example, under Basic (Visual Basic) is a VB Specific node and under the C# node are a variety of options you do not see under the Basic node. When applying a particular setting to all languages, you can override it in the options for any specific language. For example, you can specify to show line numbers for all languages and then override this for VB .NET, so that when working in VB .NET you do not see line numbers. Under the HTML section there is a Format node, and within this node there is a button for Tag Specific formatting. When you click on this button, you are presented with a dialog that will allow you to define exactly how you want each specific HTML tag to be formatted in the IDE. If you remember the previous examples that demonstrated the Auto-Format functionality, this is where you can define the formatting. For example, you can specify that all HTML Anchor tags are followed by a line break. When you run the AutoFormat with this rule, you will see a <BR> tag placed at the end of all HTML anchors.

Database Tools

As you will see in Chapter 3, the IDE provides a very rich interface with SQL Server. In the Database Tools options, you can specify some default behavior that the IDE should respect. The IDE provides interfaces for creating database objects such as tables and stored procedures. With the Database Tools options, you can establish default field sizes for columns in a table based on data type, and you can limit the size of result sets that are returned from queries executed from the IDE.

Display

The Display node has options specific to the display of controls on the designer and the default view of .aspx files when they are double-clicked to open. You can specify that controls snap to the grid that is drawn on the form while in design mode or you can indicate that the controls should just be left where you put them. You can specify whether or not you prefer .aspx pages being displayed in source view or code view when you double-click them. This will depend on whether or not you are more of a *typist* or a *drag and dropper*. If you prefer to drag and drop the controls onto forms to build up your web pages, you can ensure that your pages are always defaulted to open in the designer. However, if you prefer to type HTML yourself to control the positioning of your controls, you may prefer to have the .aspx pages default to source view when opening them in the IDE.

Summary

In this chapter we have taken an up-close look at all the tools available throughout the Visual Web Developer IDE. We examined all the key menu options available and we took a look at how to customize the toolbars for easy access to key tasks. We discussed excellent features such as code refactoring, IntelliSense, and dockable window panes. As mentioned at the beginning of the chapter, it is not the most exciting material, but we think it's valuable to know, as you'll see later on in the book.

CHAPTER 3

■■■

Introducing SQL Server Express

Most applications require data in one form or another. Whether you are working in a Windows application environment or in a web application environment, there is usually the concept of a data store. A data store can be defined as any medium to which data is stored in order to be retrieved later for processing. Data stores are found in a wide variety of forms: files such as Microsoft Excel, XML documents, and even plain text files. More commonly, data is stored in a database management system such as SQL Server, Oracle, and even Microsoft Access. These are all great options for storing data depending on the requirements that you need to address and the type of data you need to store. One thing for sure is that all the options listed so far come at a price. With the exception of plain text files, all the options we have mentioned for data storage require you to purchase software. Access and Excel are components of the Microsoft Office suite of applications. SQL Server and Oracle are larger well-known database management systems.

Although the text file format is a free option, it is less than desirable when you have to store any amount of data that needs to be accessed quickly, and it certainly is not very scalable. For example, you would not want to use text files to store data for sales order processing for an e-commerce website that processes dozens of orders per hour. This system would quickly grind to a halt because the file operations and data scanning would be far too intensive. SQL Server is a very powerful database engine, but it can be very costly and mostly is geared toward enterprise-type applications. Fortunately, Microsoft's SQL Server Express Edition is both free and very scalable. SQL Server Express is ideal for applications where the requirements or the number of end users is smaller. In other words, if your web application is expected to grow in size and have thousands or hundreds of thousands of end users, perhaps SQL Server Express would not be best suited for the situation.

SQL Server integrates very nicely with Visual Studio 2005 and the Express versions. In this chapter we will take a tour of SQL Express as a stand-alone product; later in the book you will learn about integrating it with Visual Web Developer.

By the end of this chapter you will have an understanding of the following topics:

- The underlying design of SQL Server Express

- What database objects are and how to create them

- What T-SQL is and how the basic T-SQL operations work

- How to work with tools provided with SQL Server Express

- How SQL Server Express integrates with Visual Web Developer

The Visual Web Developer Integrated Development Environment (IDE) provides some very powerful tools, such as the Database Explorer window we saw in Chapter 2. We will explore that functionality in more detail later in the book. For now, it is important to have an understanding of the fundamentals when dealing with databases and SQL Server Express Edition. Although a full discussion of SQL Server and SQL Server Express Edition is outside the context of this book, after reading this chapter, you will be on solid ground when working with SQL Server Express. We refer to SQL Server Express as SQL Server throughout the book unless otherwise noted.

SQL Server Express

As already mentioned, SQL Server Express is the lightweight version of SQL Server 2005, which will become clear as you go through these next few sections. Before we get into writing code against the database engine, it is good idea to understand its limitations and abilities. Let's begin looking at these details.

What's Under the Hood?

People often believe that because SQL Server Express is free it must not be as good as SQL Server. But actually SQL Server Express Edition is SQL Server. Before getting into details, let's first establish that SQL stands for Structured Query Language. The database understands this language and allows you to manipulate the data and structures with it.

In this section, we outline the key difference between SQL Server Express and the other SQL Server versions. SQL Server is installed as a windows service, which is a piece of software running in the background. There are many services installed with an operating system that perform work in the background you may be unaware of. For example, the indexing service improves performance when searching for files on your computer, or you may have antivirus software installed on your computer that will also be running as a service in the background. In the same manner, SQL Server Express runs as a service in the background waiting for connections.

What makes SQL Server unique when compared to other software is that it may be installed multiple times on the same computer. There are very good reasons for this. With the full version of SQL Server, you can specify what central processing unit (CPU) the service should use. If you install multiple instances of SQL Server on a computer that has multiple CPUs, you can tell each instance to use a specific CPU and enhance performance. You will notice in that last statement we used the word *instance*. Each time you install SQL Server on the same computer, you install what is called an instance of SQL Server. In fact, you can install up to 50 instances on one computer. Each instance must be given its own name. When you install SQL Server Express Edition for the first time, you install the *default instance*. In previous versions of SQL Server, the default instance did not have a name; it was simply referred to as the default instance. However, in SQL Server Express, the default instance is called SQLEXPRESS. You refer to any instance of SQL Server by its fully qualified name, which is broken down as <computer name>\<instance name>. If you are dealing with a local machine, as you will be doing throughout this book, you can use a dot as the computer name.

Now that we have discussed SQL Server Express instances and SQL Server connections, let's put the two together. As we explained earlier, SQL Express runs as a windows service. It is simply running in the background while we are typing this chapter, minding its own business, waiting for a connection. Applications use some type of programming interface to communicate with SQL Server. A programming interface is nothing more than a library that you can use to establish connections with SQL Server. One such library you will see a lot of in this book is ADO.NET 2.0. ADO.NET provides a few different ways to talk to SQL Server; however, in all cases, it requires information about where SQL Server is, what database you wish to use, and what identity it should use to talk to SQL Server. All these items are put together in what is called a *connection string*. You will see more on this later in the book when we introduce ADO.NET 2.0. Here is a sneak peek at what one connection string could look like:

```
Server=.\SQLEXPRESS;Integrated Security=True;Database=MyDatabase.mdf
```

In this connection string we are saying that we want to connect to a server called localhost\SQLEXPRESS, we want to use Windows Integrated Security, and we wish to use the MyDatabase.mdf database. You will see more about the security options and what the database name consists of in the next few sections. For now it is important just to understand that SQL Server is running in the background as a windows service waiting for a connection to be established. Once a connection is established, what happens next?

It would not serve a great purpose if applications were to simply connect to SQL Server and remain connected. More often than not, a connection is going to be established because someone is using an application to request data, update data, or perform any number of other operations available against the data. ADO.NET 2.0 provides many mechanisms to accomplish working successfully with a SQL Server database, but in the end, the commands sent to the database itself must be in the form of SQL, the language that SQL Server understands and can interpret. It uses this language to determine which actions to take against which data. All database engines on the market understand SQL. Although SQL is an industry-standardized language, most of the larger database engines, such as SQL Server and Oracle, have their own proprietary extensions to the SQL. Oracle has PL/SQL, and SQL Server uses Transact-SQL (T-SQL). T-SQL greatly enhances the power of what you can accomplish when working with a SQL Server database. A full discussion of T-SQL is a large subject and certainly outside the scope of this book; however, in a later section, we take a look at the basic SQL syntax that will be required throughout the book as you build your application.

The inner workings of a database engine are extremely complex, and very large books have been written on the subject. This brief high-level explanation certainly does not do it justice, but for now, it is all you really need to know. At a high level, all versions of SQL Server work the same way. Of course, if they were all exactly the same, we wouldn't have so many different variations of it. Let's take a look now at the differences between SQL Server Express and the full Enterprise versions of SQL Server as well as the differences with Microsoft Database Engine (MSDE).

SQL Server Express vs. SQL Server 2005

The full-blown versions of SQL Server are a feature-rich enterprise database engine. There are a few variations of the product available for the enterprise level (e.g., Standard and Professional), but for the purpose of this discussion, we lump them all together under the heading of SQL Server Enterprise editions. SQL Server Express is also a feature-rich database engine. The design goals of SQL Server Express are twofold. First, it is designed to be an easy-to-use, scalable, and no-cost alternative for developers who want to use a very reliable database engine. Second, it is designed to be a client-side database engine for larger client server applications (e.g., a larger line of business applications that permit going offline and letting users work with a local copy of the data). In this book, we are more concerned with the first design goal. We want to build scalable web applications with a reliable database engine. With these design goals in mind, let's examine in more detail what SQL Server Express provides.

Application XCopy

SQL Server Express supports a new deployment model called Application XCopy. Since the dawn of the .NET era, we have heard the words XCopy deployment. This is simply the ability to deploy an application by copying the application files to the folder that you want to run the application from. This typically was a difficult task to accomplish with the database files. In previous versions of SQL Server, the files would always be locked by SQL Server. They would need to be detached and then reattached. The concept of attaching a database is how database files are installed to an instance of SQL Server. We discuss this further in the next section. The problem with detaching a database is that if the file is in use, it cannot be detached, so you would have to make sure all connections are closed, which in itself was never an easy task. In SQL Server Express, with Application XCopy deployment, the database is attached dynamically when the application connects to it and releases it when the application closes its connections. This dynamic attaching and detaching of the database happens with a new connection string parameter called AttachDBFileName. By setting this parameter to the relative path to the database file, SQL Server connects to the database and provides access to it for the duration of the connection.

■**Tip** A really useful technique for using Application XCopy is having two copies of the same database on the same machine. One is used for testing and the other is used for the live application. The database name is guaranteed to be unique because when attached in this way, the name defaults to the full path to the database file.

Management Tools

Full-enterprise versions of SQL Server ship with a suite of management tools with nice graphical interfaces. SQL Express has available a separate installation that provides management tools with a graphical user interface into the SQL Server Express. The tools, called Express Manager, are available as a different download. SQL Server Express also ships with a command-line utility called SQLcmd. You will see both these tools in action later in this chapter.

Performance Parameters

SQL Server Express comes with some limitations with respect to the amount of hardware it will take advantage of. SQL Express only supports one CPU, whereas MSDE supports two. It will only support up to 1GB of RAM for its data caching. Each database in SQL Server Express cannot exceed 4GB in size.

Common Language Runtime

One of the new features of SQL Server 2005 is its support for the Common Language Runtime (CLR). This support is also available in the Express edition. Using the CLR with the SQL Server means that in addition to using SQL to communicate and process the data, you also have the ability to use code that is written in a .NET-compliant or CLR-compliant language such as Visual Basic .NET or C#. To learn in greater detail about how this works, refer to a more in-depth book on the subject.

SQL Server Express Security Features

When building applications that depend on a data store, especially those containing sensitive data, securing that data is of utmost concern. It was not too long ago that the Slammer virus swept the world, raising a lot of concerns around the security of SQL Server. To address recent security concerns, Microsoft has increased the security features within its SQL Server products.

Windows and Mixed-Mode Authentication

SQL Server supports two authentication modes: Windows authentication and mixed-mode authentication. Windows authentication is always enabled. This is the most secure way to connect to SQL Server. As you saw in the sample connection string earlier, one of the parameters is Integrated Security. This means that we are telling SQL Server to take a look at who we are connecting as and validate that it is also a valid Windows user account that has been granted access to the database resources being requested. For someone to break into your data with only Windows authentication enabled, he or she would have to impersonate or act as if the connection belongs to another Windows user on your network.

With mixed-mode authentication enabled, you have two ways to connect to SQL Server: Windows authentication and custom SQL Server user accounts. Custom SQL Server user accounts are just like users for any other system. They require a user name and a password, and then they require access to be granted to them. When using mixed-mode authentication, you would specify the user ID and password parameters in the connection string instead of specifying Integrated Security. You can see that because the user name and password are part of the connection string, which is plain text, this method is already less secure. SQL Server best practices recommend using Windows authentication whenever possible. If you have to use SQL Server authentication rather than Windows authentication, use strong passwords that encompass letters, numbers, and special characters both uppercase and lowercase.

▐**Note** SQL Server has a special account called sa. The sa account is the system admin account. You cannot delete this account, and therefore you can guarantee that every SQL Server installation in the world has an sa account. That is half the battle; the other half is getting the password. You would be surprised how many installations we have come across that have a blank sa password. Although this is no longer possible in SQL Server Express, create a very strong password for this account or leave your installation in Windows authentication only.

Using Network Connections

Not only is it very important to know who is calling, it is important to know where they are calling from. For the most part, and at least in the samples in this book, SQL Server Express is going to be running on the same machine as the application. So, if this is the case, you may want to turn off the ability to connect over a network to the database server. In fact, this is the default setup for SQL Server Express. The ability to permit connections or deny connections over a network is the concept of configuring network protocols. By default, SQL Server Express only supports Shared Memory access, which means that any applications connecting must be running on the local computer. All other connectivity options, such as Transmission Control Protocol/Internet Protocol (TCP/IP), must be turned on by the administrator. This prevents unknowing access to the server from remote computers. These options are configurable from the Computer Manager tool you will see a bit later in the chapter.

SQL Server Databases

Now we'll discuss how data is organized in a database within SQL Server. It all starts with defining a database: a structured data store of a collection of tables, stored procedures, and functions of the related data. We probably all interact with databases every day, without realizing it in some cases. When an item at the grocery store is scanned, a database is accessed to retrieve information about the product being scanned, such as a description to print on your receipt and the price associated with the item used in totaling your grocery bill. An instance of SQL Server can contain very many databases. A database consists of database objects, which include tables, stored procedures, views, user-defined functions, and triggers. We'll say more on the database objects later, but for now let's concentrate on the database as a whole.

SQL Server is installed with four important databases, with each serving a very important role, as follows:

- *Master*: The master database is indeed the master. It contains all the information about the databases that the particular instance of SQL Server knows about, any user names, and security rights granted to users. A large number of system-stored procedures allow you to get information about the databases attached to the instance.

- **Tempdb*: The tempdb database is used for any temporary objects, which can include temporary tables used for short-lived operations.

- *Model*: The model database is the template database. When you create a new database, it will be based off what is in the model database.

- *Msdb*: The msdb database contains information about replication and maintenance plans. These features are not available in SQL Server Express.

What Is a Database in SQL Server?

A database in SQL Server consists of a minimum of two files: a main database file and a log file. The main database file has the file extension .mdf. The log file has the extension .ldf. For a database to be accessible via SQL Server, it must be attached to an instance. This is done with the Attach and Detach operations that you will see later when we look at the Express Manager. The main database file contains the actual database objects as well as the data itself. The log file contains all the history of the transactions that have occurred since the last full database backup. This is important to know about in planning database recovery; however, the details behind these concepts are outside the scope of this book.

Database Objects

In this section, we discuss the main objects used within a database to store data in an orga-nized fashion and the objects used to manage access to the data. For now, we define what each of the objects is, and in the next section we start to work with the SQL that is required to create the various objects.

Object Names and References

Objects in SQL Server have a four-part name, and each part is separated by a period. For exam-ple, if you want to refer to a table named Employee in the Store database that Jim created (so Jim is the owner), and the computer name is called Server1, you could refer to the table in this way: Server1.Store.Jim.Employee. There are some shortcuts to getting around this. For example, if you omit the computer name (Server1), the local computer is assumed. If you omit the database name, the default database for the connection is assumed. If you omit the owner name (in this case, Jim), then the owner will again be inferred based on connection parameters. It is all these conditions that permit you simply to refer to an object by its name alone. Not all four parts of the name are required, but at a minimum, you must specify the object name itself and then specify each name part in turn from right to left. In other words, Server1.Employee would not work. If you specify the name of the computer, you must also specify the name of the database and the name of the owner.

Tables

A *table* is what actually holds the data. A single table holds information about an entity. An *entity* is any object at all that you want to store information about. This could be employees, products, customers, or sales orders. Each entity has various *attributes*. For example, an employee has a name, an address, a phone number, and so on. These attributes create the col-umns of the table. Each column should only contain one attribute. Each table also consists of one or more rows where each row is a specific entity. For example, each employee would have his or her own row in the Employee table. When you have a table with many rows in it, you need a way to uniquely identity each one. You accomplish this by identifying what attributes exist that are unique to each row, for instance, a social security number. This column is the one you would select to be the primary key. The primary key must be unique so that you can retrieve individual records or rows from the table, and it also permits you to set up relation-ships with other entities.

   In designing a database, you must determine what information you need to store about each of your entities. Once you have all this information, you can then break out your required data into their respective tables and set up relationships between the tables. Relationships are established by defining a foreign key on one column of a table. For example, in the list of enti-ties just cited, you can say that a customer is related to a sales order. So, for each sales order, you would have a foreign key that references the primary key of the Customer table. This estab-lishes a relationship between each order and the customer who made the order. The process of organizing the tables in this fashion is called database normalization. *Normalization* is a term used when referring to databases where the structure of the data is designed to be the simplest but also the most stable. By normalizing the data, redundancy of data and data elements such as table relationships and keys are avoided. If you were to just use one table to store all the data to do with customers and orders, each row would have the same customer information over and over again for each order they have made. This results in duplicated data and a waste of space. By defining a table to hold customers and a table to hold sales orders, and then establishing the relationship with the use of keys, you eliminate the data redundancy and disk space. You will see all this in action in a little while when you build your database for your main application.

Views

Views are like tables. They exhibit just about all the same qualities. The key difference is that views are defined based on existing tables by using SQL. Let's say in the previous example that you only want customers to be viewed by employees that work in the same region as the customer. In this case, you could create a view for each region and only permit employees in each region to access their respective view. This may seem a bit confusing for now, but we clarify this concept later when we get into using the tools available to create the database objects. For now, it is enough to know that a view is based on one or more tables using SQL to determine what data the view should expose.

Triggers

Three basic operations can be executed against data stored in a table: insert, update, and delete. Sometimes, when one of these operations is executed, you want to be able to get in the middle and perform some additional logic or validation against the data. This can be done by using *triggers*, which can be defined for any of the three operations and can be defined to fire after the operation has completed or before the operation starts. Triggers can be defined on both tables and views.

Stored Procedures

Now that you know your data is stored in tables, you need a way to get at that data. Stored procedures are the preferred way to manipulate data in SQL Server.

    Stored procedures are SQL statements that are kept on the server and executed by a call from an application programming interface (API) such as ADO.NET 2.0. Stored procedures provide both performance enhancements as they are compiled and cached on the server and additional security from preventing SQL injection attacks. Within a stored procedure, you can leverage all the functionality provided by the T-SQL. Stored procedures accept parameters so you can better target the data being requested and the data that you return. We will be using a lot of stored procedures in our main application as we move throughout the book, so there will not be any shortage of examples, and you will see a lot of the anatomy of stored procedures.

User-Defined Functions

User-defined functions, a new object that was introduced in SQL Server 2000, provide you with the ability to move common logic from stored procedures to a function that can be called from a stored procedure. Using functions is useful to avoid repeating SQL from within stored procedures, where instead of repeating the SQL over and over, it can be wrapped into a function. Just as when you are creating applications, you want to make your code as modular as possible. You want to write the code once in one place and maintain it in one place. User-defined functions offer this same ability in SQL Server. Again, you will see examples of user-defined functions in your applications so you will certainly develop a clearer understanding of their role.

Using T-SQL

Now that you have an understanding of what a database is and all its objects, we can get to the innards of SQL and see how to create and manipulate these objects and the data they contain. In this section we examine the basic SQL used to perform the basic CRUD operations.

CRUD is a well-known industry acronym that defines the four operations performed against a database: *C*reate, *R*etrieve, *U*pdate, and *D*elete. Although tools such as Express Manager and the Visual Web Developer IDE provide an excellent graphical interface for creating CRUD-based SQL statements, it is very useful to know what these statements are made up of and how to tweak them manually when the need arises. In this section, we examine each of the major SQL statements.

There are two categories of SQL: the Data Definition Language (DDL), which is composed of the SQL used to define the database objects themselves, and the Data Manipulation Language (DML), which is composed of the SQL used to manipulate the data within the database. You will see real examples of all these in use soon. For now you just need an understanding of the main SQL elements. We know this information is not overly stimulating, but it is essential. Let's start by taking a look at the DDL.

Data Definition Language

The DDL includes the SQL statements required to define the structure of your database. Three main keywords make up the DDL: Create, Alter, and Drop.

Create

The Create statement is used to create database objects, including the database itself. You will use Create to create databases, tables, stored procedures, triggers, constraints such as primary keys and foreign keys, user-defined functions, and views. Here's an example of a Create statement to create an Employee table:

```
Create table Employee
(
    SSN int NOT NULL,
    FirstName nvarchar(30) NULL,
    LastName nvarchar(30) NULL
)
```

Alter

The Alter keyword is used to change the definition of any of the database objects. You will use it to change databases, tables, stored procedures, triggers, constraints, user-defined functions, and views. Let's say in the previous Employee table example that you wanted to add a phone number column. It would look like this:

```
Alter table Employee
Add PhoneNumber varchar(20) NULL
```

Drop

The Drop keyword is to remove objects. You will use the Drop statement to effectively delete any of the objects we have mentioned. Note that dropping a table while it contains data will result in the loss of the data. And dropping a database will result in the removal of the database from the file system. Following our example with the Employee table, you would delete the table with the following SQL:

```
Drop table Employee
```

Data Manipulation Language

Next we have the DML, which is the part of SQL used to manipulate the data in your database. Four main statements form the DML: Select, Insert, Update, and Delete.

Select

The Select statement is used to retrieve data from the database. You can use the Select statement to retrieve data from tables or views. The Select statement can be very complex; however, for our purposes, we can look at it like this:

```
Select <column1>, <column2> FROM <table> WHERE <condition1>
```

In this syntax you can see that the structure is very straightforward. Here is an example of a simple Select statement against the earlier Employee table example (assuming, of course, that it is not dropped).

```
SELECT SSN, FirstName, LastName FROM Employee
```

This Select statement is very functional. But for efficiency reasons, you may want a smaller result set because you know you are dealing with a particular employee and it helps to target the data. The previous statement will return all employees, but this one will return only the employee with the specified SSN:

```
SELECT SSN, FirstName, LastName FROM Employee WHERE SSN=123456789
```

We have shown you some relatively basic SQL here just to get you familiar with what it looks like. You will see more of this throughout the book as you build your applications. If it is a little confusing for now, don't worry; it will all be clear soon enough.

Insert

The Insert statement allows you to add new data to any table. Once again, we will use our Employee table to demonstrate the SQL required to add a new employee to the table. The syntax for an Insert statement is as follows:

```
Insert into <tablename> (column1, column2,…,column)
VALUES(value1, value2,…,valueN)
```

Let's look at a practical example now:

```
Insert into Employee (SSN,FirstName,LastName)
VALUES (123456789, "Richard", "Delorme")
```

Update

The Update statement allows you to make modifications to existing data. For example, if the employee you added previously were to change his name, you would use an Update statement to make the appropriate changes to his employee record. The Update statement syntax is as follows:

```
Update <tableName> SET <column1> = <value1>,…,<columnN = valueN> WHERE <condition1>
```

Now let's apply this to change the name of the last employee you entered:

```
Update Employee SET FirstName = "Rick" WHERE SSN = 123456789
```

You have just updated the name from Richard to Rick.

Delete

Finally, you have the mechanism to remove the data permanently. The Delete statement is very powerful. Once data is deleted, it is unrecoverable unless you have a good backup copy of the database. The syntax for the Delete statement is as follows:

```
DELETE <tableName> where <condition1>
```

Let's delete the employee from the database now:

```
Delete Employee WHERE SSN = 123456789
```

In both the Delete and the Update statements, the WHERE clause is very important. If you were to issue the last statement without a WHERE clause, which means without any conditions, all data would be deleted from the table. Likewise, from the Update example, all Employee names would be changed. Always ensure that you have the appropriate conditions associated to your Delete and Update statements or have adequate backups of the database or tables in the event you delete data by mistake.

> ■**Note** There is one more segment of SQL that is called Data Control Language (DCL). This encompasses the Grant, Deny, and Revoke statements that are used with respect to securing database objects. We will not be examining these in detail in this book.

This has been a rapid introduction to SQL. As we said earlier, you will get lots of practice in this chapter and throughout the book. Next, we'll take a look at the powerful tools available with SQL Server Express. Ideally, you will not have to write too much SQL by hand!

SQL Express Management Tools

The SQL Server enterprise editions come with an excellent suite of tools. SQL Server 2000 comes with the Enterprise Manager for managing databases, users, maintenance, and more, and it is available there. It also has the query analyzer for programming and testing SQL script and a few other very powerful tools. Here is a list of all the tools available to work with SQL Server Express:

- *Express Manager*: This tool provides a rich interface to manage databases on SQL Server Express.

- *Computer Manager*: This is a Windows-based tool to manage the configuration of the installed instances of SQL Express.

- *SQLCmd*: This is the command-line tool that replaces OSQL.

- *Books Online*: This is the help file system provided with SQL Server Express.

In this section we take a look at all the functionality provided by these tools, starting with Express Manager.

Express Manager

For the first time since Microsoft has shipped the lighter database engines (such as MSDE and SQL Express), we now have a graphical user interface (GUI) to accompany it. Express Manager (EM) is designed to be the lightweight database management tool to go along with its light-weight database.

Installing Express Manager

Installing EM is very similar to installing any other application. However, EM is not included as part of the SQL Server Express package. Microsoft provides these tools as a separate download. EM is dependent on there being a SQL Server Express instance installed to the same computer it is being installed on, and it is also dependent on the Microsoft .NET Framework version 2.0. If either of these components is missing, the install will fail. Because you have already installed Visual Web Developer along with SQL Server Express, you should not run into any problems when installing EM. Let's go ahead and do that now.

After downloading the installation from the link provided earlier, launch the .msi file that contains EM. You will be presented with a screen similar to that in Figure 3-1.

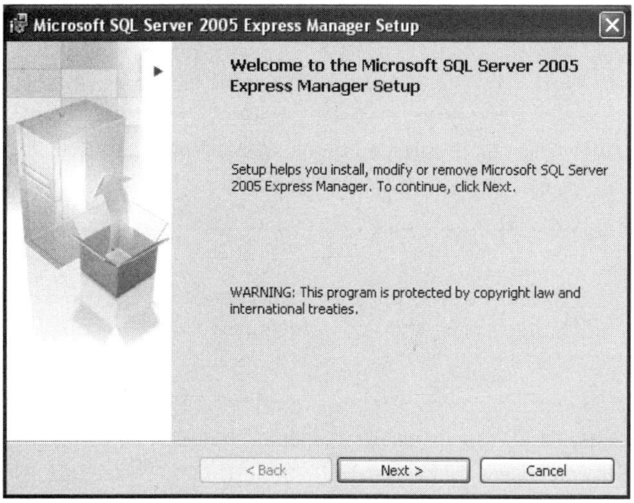

Figure 3-1. *Installing SQL Express Manager*

Click the Next button to begin navigating through the installation wizard. The next screen shows the standard End User License Agreement; read and accept it. Then you will be prompted with the component selection dialog as shown in Figure 3-2. For this installation, the default is to install everything, and as the dialog shows, there is not too much to choose from.

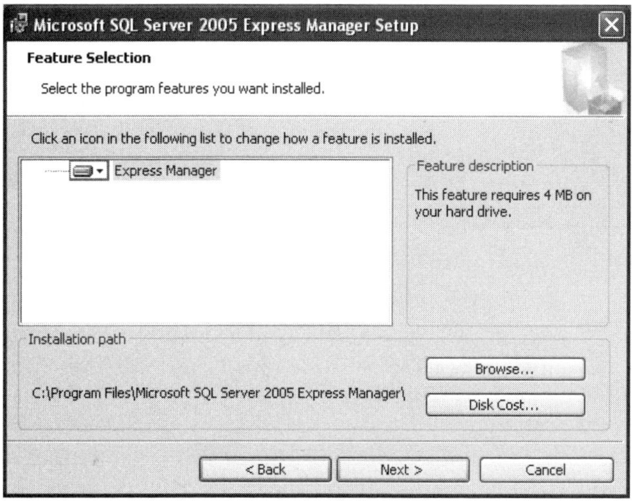

Figure 3-2. *Component selection for Express Manager installation*

After you click the Next button on the component selection screen, you will be at the last step of the wizard, and you can click the Install button to begin the installation. Once the installation is complete, there will be another shortcut in your SQL Server Express program group available from Start ➤ Programs. Go there now and launch EM, and we will now get into the cool features it provides.

■**Note** The first time you launch Express Manager, there will be a delay as some last-minute configuration is undertaken.

Once EM is configured and opens, you are shown the connection dialog in Figure 3-3. Enter the name of the local SQLEXPRESS instance as shown in the figure.

■**Note** As we mentioned earlier in the chapter, SQL Server runs as a windows service. By default, after installing SQL Server Express, the SQL Server service is not running. You need to start the service to be able to connect to it. Go to Start ➤ Run, and type this line: **net start MSSQL$SQLEXPRESS**.

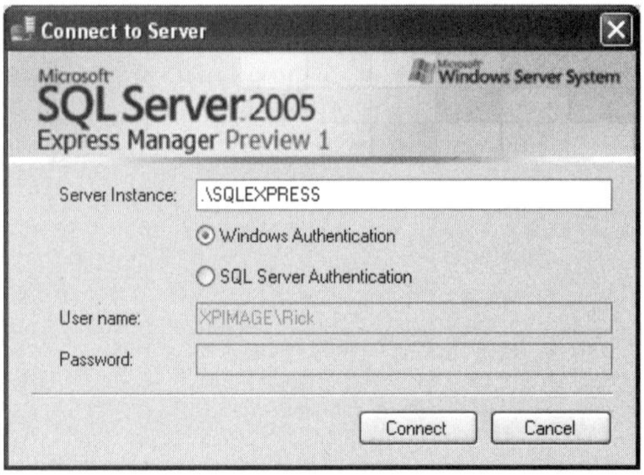

Figure 3-3. *Express Manager connection dialog*

Once EM establishes a connection with the SQL Server SQLEXPRESS instance, it opens up and looks like Figure 3-4 (we have expanded the treeview so we can discuss everything you see there).

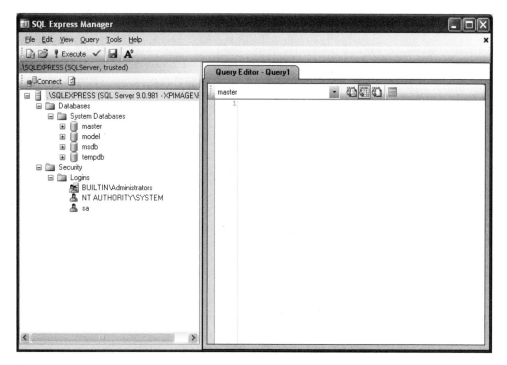

Figure 3-4. *SQL Server Express Manager*

When EM first opens, you see a treeview on the left-hand side that is somewhat similar to the Database Explorer pane you saw in the IDE in Chapter 2. This treeview lists all the objects that it knows about for the instance of SQL Server to which it is connected. At the root of the tree, you can see the actual instance name to which you have connected. Below that, you see two main tree nodes: one to group together all the system databases that it found (in order to distinguish them from user databases you will see in a short while), and the other to manage all the user accounts that have access to connect and manipulate objects on the SQL Server instance. Across the top of EM, you have a toolbar with some buttons available to perform the more common operations. Table 3-1 lists the buttons with their functional descriptions.

Table 3-1. *Express Manager Toolbar Buttons and Their Functionality*

Button	Functionality
	This button gives you the ability to open a new query in a new tabbed document.
	This button allows you to open a query from a file, just as the toolbar button with the floppy disk enables you to save a query to a file.
! Execute	This button allows you to execute the query in the active tab. A shortcut for this is to press the F5 key.
✓	This button allows you to verify the syntax of your query before executing it. It is a nice quick way to see if you have any errors in you SQL before putting the load against the server.

As always, all the toolbar button commands are also available from the main menu. Another important item to note in EM is the drop-down list provided within each Query tab. This drop-down list contains a list of all the databases for the instance of SQL Server express to which it is connected. The significance of this drop-down list is that the database selected is the one that the current query will be executed against. By default, it is showing the master database. If you wanted to execute a query against the master database, you could do so by entering the following text into the query window and then pressing the F5 key, or clicking the Execute button on the toolbar.

```
SELECT * FROM sysdatabases
```

If you leave the drop-down list with the master database selected and try to execute a query against one of the other databases, you will get an error indicating that the object does not exist. In this case, you would have to use the full three-part naming of the object or switch the drop-down list to the database you want to work against in order for the objects to be found and the query execute successfully.

Now that you have already executed your first query in EM, let's take a look at creating a database. (Later we create this same database using the command line to provide a clear comparison between using this tool and the SQLcmd.exe utility.) To create a database, follow these steps:

1. Right-click the Databases folder in the treeview and select New Database. You then get a tabbed document created, such as the one in Figure 3-5, where you can fill in the name and location of your database.

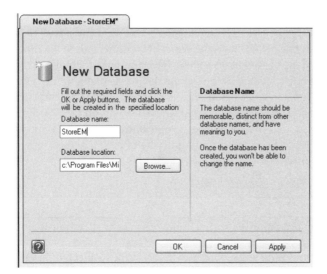

Figure 3-5. *Creating a database in Express Manager*

2. Type in the name **StoreEM** (as shown in Figure 3-5), and leave the default file location.

3. Now click the OK button to create your database. You should see the new database in the treeview below the System Databases section as in Figure 3-6 (you may need to click the Refresh button).

Figure 3-6. *A new database created with Express Manager*

Ideally, if your store is doing well, it has some customers and some orders. You will now create two tables in the database to represent each of those entities. Let's start with the Customers table. To create the tables, follow these steps:

1. Expand the treeview below the StoreEM database so that you can see the table's tree node.

2. Right-click the table's tree node and select New Table.

Working with the Command Line

In this day and age, we often wonder why we ever have to do anything on the command line anymore. We know there are some folks out there who live by the command line; we are just not part of this crowd. However, we have found tremendous value in being familiar with the command-line tools available to work with SQL Server.

Although it is nice to have Express Manager or the Visual Web Developer development environment, it may not always be available. It is a separate download, and there is a very good chance that it may not be installed on a production server. You will always be able to guarantee that the new command-line tools called SQLcmd.exe will be there. Anything you can do in EM, you can also do on the command line. Instead of right-clicking and selecting what you want with the mouse, you have to know the T-SQL commands to accomplish the same tasks.

If you are the type of developer that does not really see any need for the command line, you may want to skip this section and just know that it is here for future reference; however, going through this exercise will certainly help you develop a respect for the productivity enhancements afforded by EM. Others will find this an interesting topic. The command line is very powerful, and you will see how you could accomplish everything we did with Express Manager using T-SQL on the command line.

SQLcmd

The SQLcmd command-line utility can be found below the main installation directory of SQL Server. By default this will be located at C:\Program Files\Microsoft SQL Server\90\ Tools\binn\SQLcmd.exe. However, this path should already be added to your environment variables and be accessible from anywhere on the command line.

Let's go ahead and fire up the command line. Go to Start ➤ Run and enter **cmd.exe.** Just to test out that the environment variable is set up correctly, enter **SQLcmd.exe -?** on the command line and press Enter. If things work as expected, your screen should look like Figure 3-7.

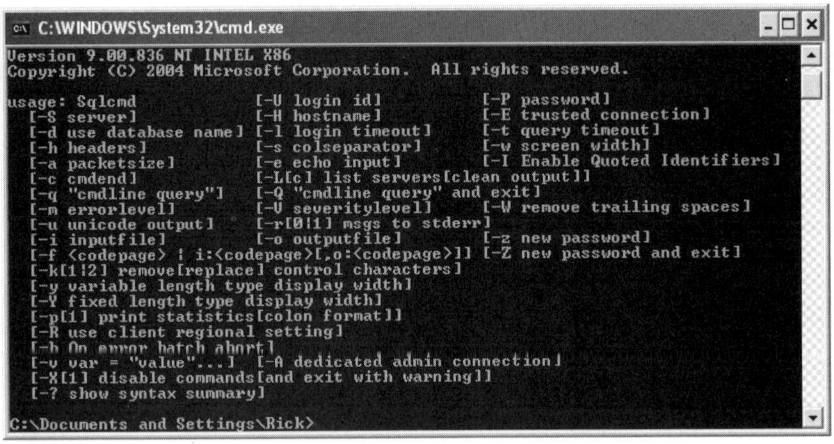

Figure 3-7. *SQLcmd command-line options*

Each of the items in the list that is displayed is called a command-line switch. These switches are passed into the SQLcmd utility when it is launched and provide it some instructions on how to behave. There are too many to look at here, and not all switches are relevant; however, Table 3-2 outlines the main switches and their uses.

Table 3-2. *SQLcmd Most Common Switches*

Switch	Description
-U -P	These two items are used together when connecting to the SQL Server using SQL Server authentication. -U specifies the user name and -P specifies the password. If you do not specify these parameters, Windows authentication is assumed.
-E	This option tells SQLcmd to connect to SQL Server using a trusted connection. This is using Windows authentication.
-S	This option tells SQLcmd to which server to connect. This is in the same format that you saw earlier when dealing with connection strings: <computername>\<instancename>.
-d	This option tells SQLcmd what the default database should be for the connection. This will assist in referring to the database objects by their name only.
-i	This option allows you to specify an input file. If you have a SQL script file, you can use this parameter to input it to the command line and execute the SQL within the file.
-?	This option outputs all the command-line options available as you see them in Figure 3-7.

Now that you are familiar with the options, let's try some out. Type the following on the command line to connect to SQL Server Express:

```
SQlcmd -E -S.\SQLEXPRESS -d master
```

This command tells the utility to connect to the SQL Server instance SQLEXPRESS running on the local machine using Windows authentication and to use master as the default database. We chose master because you have not yet created the database that you will use for the rest of the samples. Once connected, the command line turns into a prompt as shown in Figure 3-8. Every time you enter SQL into the command line, it will start with the prompt at 1>. When you press the Enter key, the prompt will move down a line and show a 2>. This is simply the line numbers of the batch. Once you type **Go** and press Enter, the batch will be executed and the command line will reset to 1>.

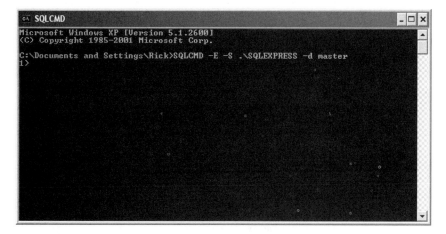

Figure 3-8. *The SQLcmd prompt*

Now you can go ahead and create your database. Type the following SQL into the command line:

```
1>CREATE DATABASE StoreCmd
2>GO
```

In this line, you create your database. Call it StoreCmd to differentiate from your StoreGUI database. You now have a database called StoreCmd. Now, to make life easier, you will change the default database of your connection by issuing the following SQL:

```
1> USE StoreCmd
2> Go
```

This tells the connection to now treat StoreCmd as the default database for all operations. You should see a message indicating that the database context has been changed to StoreCmd. Now let's go ahead and create the tables.

```
1> CREATE TABLE Customer
2> (
3>   CustomerId int NOT NULL IDENTITY(1,1),
4>   FirstName varchar(25) NULL,
5>   LastName varchar(25) NULL
6> )
7> CREATE TABLE Orders
8> (
9>   CustomerId int NOT NULL,
10>  OrderId int NOT NULL
11> )
12> GO
```

With your two tables created, you will create your primary keys and your foreign key (indentation is for readability only):

```
1> ALTER TABLE Customer
2>   ADD Constraint PK_CustomerID PRIMARY KEY (CustomerID)
3> ALTER TABLE Orders
4>   ADD Constraint PK_CustomerOrderID PRIMARY KEY(CustomerId, OrderID),
5>       Constraint FK_CustomerID Foreign Key(CustomerID)
6>           REFERENCES Customer(CustomerID)
7> GO
```

With your tables all set up, you can go ahead and create your stored procedures. Enter the following SQL into the editor:

```
1> CREATE PROCEDURE GetCustomer
2> (
3>      @CustomerID int
4> )
5> AS
6>      SELECT * FROM Customer
7>      WHERE CustomerID = @CustomerID
8> GO
1> CREATE PROCEDURE AddCustomer
2> (
3>      @FirstName varchar(25),
4>      @LastName varchar(25)
5> )
6> AS
7>  INSERT INTO Customer (FirstName, LastName) VALUES (@FirstName, @LastName)
8> GO
```

You now have a database with two tables and few stored procedures that you can use to add and retrieve data. To disconnect, simply type **exit** or **quit**. If you look in EM now, you can see what you have created (Figure 3-9).

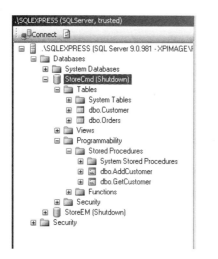

Figure 3-9. *Database created from SQLcmd*

Books Online

Books Online is the name of the help file system provided for SQL Server. This is an invaluable resource when working with SQL Server. Ensure that you have the latest version of all the documentation. It is available for download from the Microsoft website.

Visual Web Developer Integration

In this section, we take a look at how SQL Server Express integrates with the Visual Web Developer environment. It really is irrelevant what your data source is when working with data from the VWD environment because data connections of all sorts are acceptable. You can set up a connection to an OLE DB provider, an ODBC provider, an Oracle provider and, of course, of particular interest here, a SQL Server provider. Our attention will be focused on the SQL Server provider because you will be connecting to your instance of SQL Server Express.

The Visual Web Developer environment provides a very robust interface for working with SQL Server. We already briefly introduced the Database Explorer in Chapter 2. Now let's take a more detailed look at the options available from this window as we walk through creating the database for your Visual Photo Album application.

Connecting to a Database

Before you can work with a database, you need to be able to connect to it. Without a connection to the database, you will be unable to perform any operations against your data, which in essence will render useless any application that is dependent on the data. We will now walk through setting up a connection to your SQLEXPRESS instance of SQL Server.

Establishing a connection to the database is very simple. Go to the Database Explorer pane (if it is not visible, you can bring it to life by clicking on it under the View ➤ Database Explorer menu item available on the IDE's main menu) and click the Connect to Database button on the toolbar. You may also accomplish this by right-clicking the mouse over the Data Connection node in the treeview and selecting Add Connection. You will be presented with the dialog shown in Figure 3-10. Before rushing through to create your connection, let's explore all the options here.

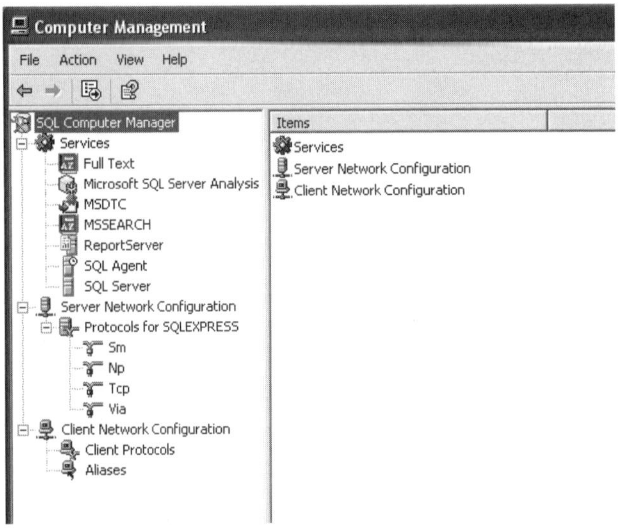

Figure 3-10. *The Connection Properties dialog*

By default, you are presented with the options for connecting to a SQL Server database. As we were saying earlier, there are other options for data sources that you can connect to. To see these, click on the Providers button. You will see a screen as shown in Figure 3-11.

You can see here that you can specify OLE DB, ODBC, and Oracle as alternatives to the SQL Server provider; however, you will select the SQL Server provider for your purposes here. The All button along the left navigation bar is the standard properties viewer that you saw earlier in the Properties window. The properties available are dependent on what provider is selected. Figure 3-12 shows the properties available for the SQL Server provider.

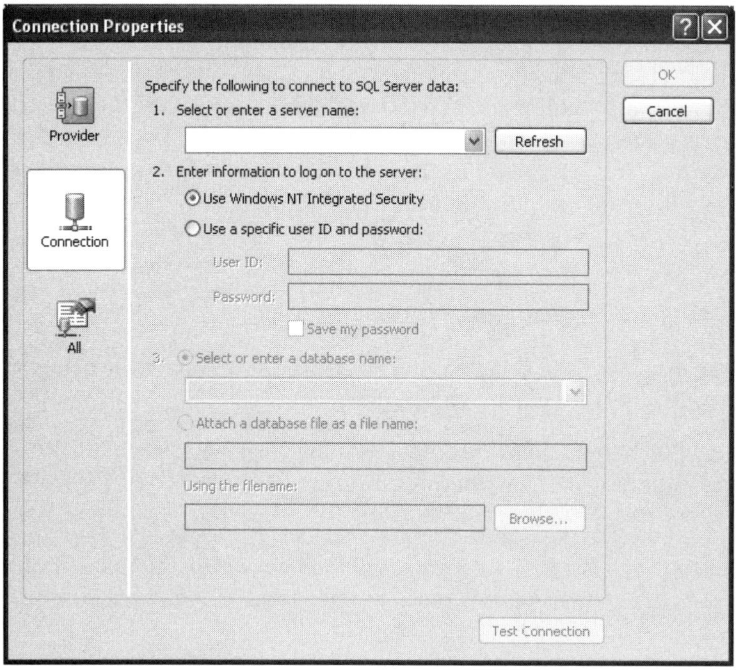

Figure 3-11. *The providers available in the Connection Properties dialog*

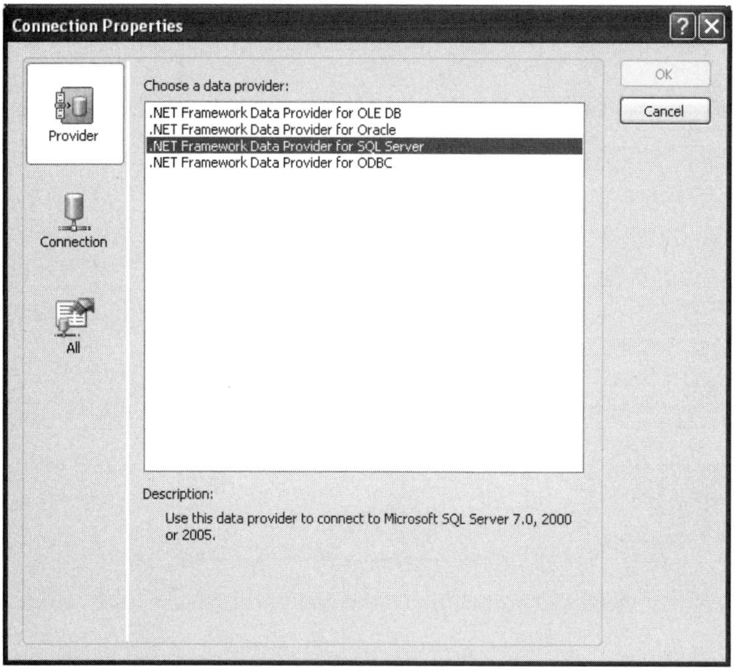

Figure 3-12. *Properties available for the SQL Server provider*

In the All properties view, you can configure your connection. There are a number of properties you just do not need to worry about; their default values will suffice. This is why the connection properties dialog defaults to the Connection tab. It provides you with the ability to specify the minimum amount of information necessary to establish a connection. You can always access all the properties later if you need to make some modifications. For now, let's establish a connection to your default SQL Server Express instance. Follow these steps as they coincide with the step numbers on the Connection tab:

1. Enter **.\SQLEXPRESS** to connect to your default instance of SQL Server Express.

2. Leave the default of Windows authentication selected.

3. Leave the option to select or type in a database name, and enter the database name **VisualPhotoAlbum** directly in the database drop-down list.

4. Click the Test Connection button to ensure that everything is set up properly. Click OK on the message box, indicating that the test was successful.

5. Finally, click the Done button. The database connection will be added to the Database Explorer window as shown in Figure 3-13. If you encounter a problem, double-check that the SQL Server service is running, and repeat the steps again.

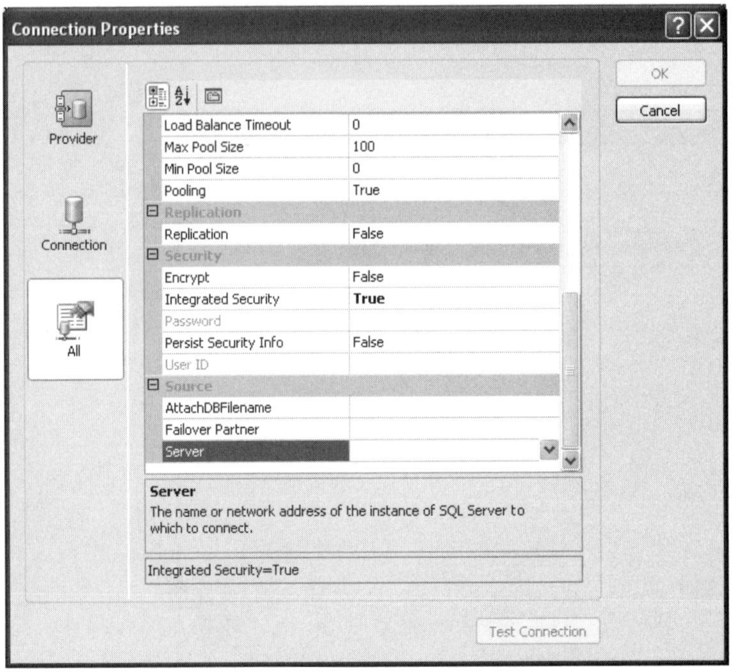

Figure 3-13. *Connection to the VisualPhotoAlbum database*

Now that you have established a connection to the VisualPhotoAlbum database, you can begin to create your database objects that will help drive your application.

Creating Database Objects

As you saw in Figure 3-13, when you expand the node that is displaying the connection to your database, there are folders displayed that group each of the database object types mentioned earlier in the chapter. The objects that you create are not actually stored in SQL Server in folders, but this organized treeview makes it easier to find objects that you want to work with by placing them in logical groupings by type. The ability to create new objects is only a click away.

If you right-click over the Tables folder in the treeview, you are presented with a context menu that offers a few choices:

- *New Table*: This option provides you with the ability to create a new database table.

- *New Query*: This option provides you with the ability to create a new query against your database tables or views.

- *Refresh*: This is more important than it may seem at first. The treeview of your database objects is loaded once and then cached. If any changes are made to the database from a source outside the IDE, you will have to invoke Refresh to see the latest changes.

- *Properties*: This option displays the objects properties in the Properties window.

■**Note** That database you will be creating for your Visual Photo Album application will consist of a large number of objects; for demonstration purposes, we will create some of them here. A full script to create the entire database is available with the source code for the book at www.apress.com.

You can now go ahead and start creating some database objects for your application. You will start with creating two tables as shown in the entity diagram in Figure 3-14.

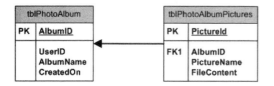

Figure 3-14. *Entity diagram of the VisualPhotoAlbum database tables*

Before jumping in and creating the tables, we will first explain what Figure 3-14 means. Each square item in the figure represents a table (also known as an entity). The arrow between the tables represents a relationship between the tables. Relationships can be *one to one* (a row in one table is only related to one row in the other table); *one to many* (one row in one table can be related to one or more rows in the other table); or *many to many* (many rows in one table can be related to many rows in the other table and vice versa). Let's take a look at the tables for your database.

In your database, one table is called tblPhotoAlbum. The tblPhotoAlbum table will contain all the information about the photo albums that the users of your application create. This information includes the name of the photo album and the date it was created. The date it was created is for informational purposes, and the name provides a descriptive way for users to identify their photo albums. You will also see a UserId column. This column will establish a relationship with the user who created the album. And finally, you see an AlbumID field. This field will be a system-generated unique identifier commonly known as a Globally Unique Identifier (GUID). This field will server as the primary key. Each table in a database must have a way of uniquely identifying each row in a table. This is the purpose of the primary key.

In the second table, tblPhotoAlbumPictures, you will store all of the pictures that go in each photo album. This table has a field for the name of the photo and the actual photo itself. This will be stored in the database as binary data.

You also see a field for the AlbumID. This establishes the relationship or link from a photo to the album that it belongs to. Once again, you add a PictureID column that will provide a GUID value to uniquely identify each picture in the table. Now that you know what you have to create, you can go ahead and create it.

Creating Tables

Let's jump right in and right-click the Tables folder in the treeview of the Database Explorer and follow these steps to create your first table:

1. Select Add New Table from the context menu. Your IDE will create a tabbed document like the one in Figure 3-15.

2. Begin by entering the first column for the table, **AlbumID**, by typing directly into the table designer.

3. Right-click the AlbumID field and select Set Primary Key from the context menu. This will establish this field as the unique identifier for rows in this table. Now, in the Properties window for this field, find the Default Value or Binding property and enter the text **newId()** (**newId()**, which is a SQL Server function that will return a GUID value.

4. Enter the rest of the columns in the table designer as shown in Figure 3-15, and be sure to uncheck the Allow Nulls check box because you want to ensure that all columns have a value for each row inserted.

5. Select the Name column in the designer. In the Properties window for this column, ensure that the length is set to 50. This will only allow a maximum of 50 characters in the column.

6. Once you have set up all your columns as shown in Figure 3-15, click the Save button on the toolbar to save the table to the database. You will be prompted for a table name. Enter **tblPhotoAlbum** and hit OK.

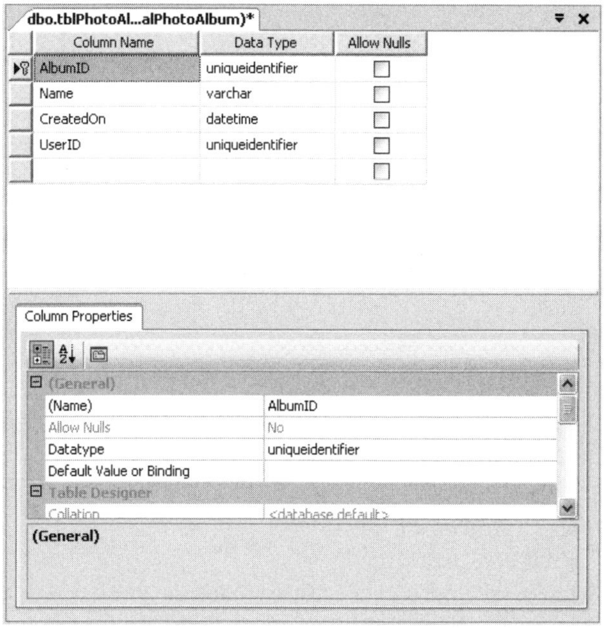

Figure 3-15. *Creating the tblPhotoAlbum table*

You will now repeat similar steps to create the tblPhotoAlbumPictures table. Here they are:

1. Right-click the tables folder in the treeview within the Database Explorer and select Add New Table.

2. Enter in all the columns as shown in Figure 3-16. Ensure the length for the Name column is 50, and ensure that newid() is specified as the Default Value for the PictureID column.

3. Right-click the PictureID field, and set it as the primary key.

4. Now save your table and give it the name **tblPhotoAlbumPictures**.

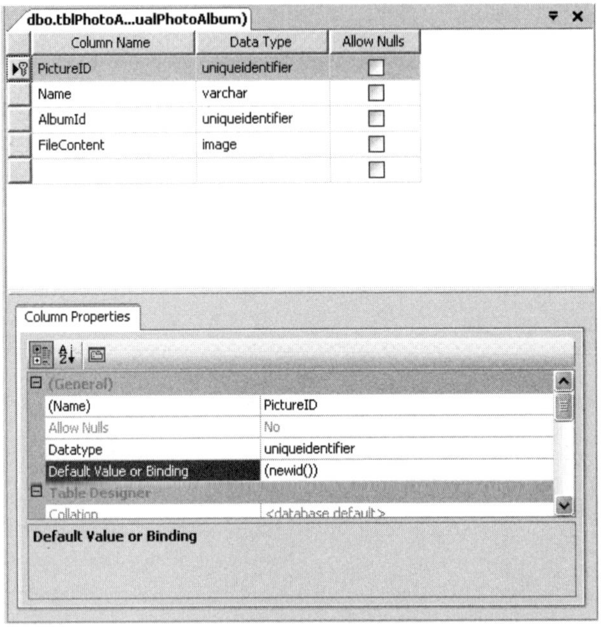

Figure 3-16. *Creating the tblPhotoAlbumPictures table*

Now that you have the two tables created, you need to establish the link between them by defining a relationship. In your case, the relationship is one to many. This means that one photo album can have many pictures associated to it; however, a single picture can be associated to only one photo album. This relationship is accomplished by the addition of the AlbumID column to the tblPhotoAlbumPictures table. By defining this relationship in SQL Server, you force SQL Server to validate every picture row that is inserted that is associated to a valid photo album. Let's walk through the following steps to create the relationship:

1. Right-click the Table Designer and select Relationships.

2. In the Relationships editor, as shown in Figure 3-17, click the Add button. The Relationship object will be added to the list and given a default name beginning with FK_.

3. Scroll down in the properties and select the Tables and Columns Specification. This is where you will be able to define what columns make up the relationship. Click on the ellipses button in the textbox beside the property name. You now have the dialog in front of you (shown in Figure 3-18).

4. On the left-hand side of the Tables and Columns editor, select tblPhotoAlbum as the Primary key table, and select the AlbumID column as the primary key.

5. On the right-hand side of the Tables and Columns editor, select tblPhotoAlbumPictures as the Foreign Key table. In fact, it should be selected by default and read-only as it is the only possible relationship that can be defined. Select the AlbumIDcolumn as the Foreign Key.

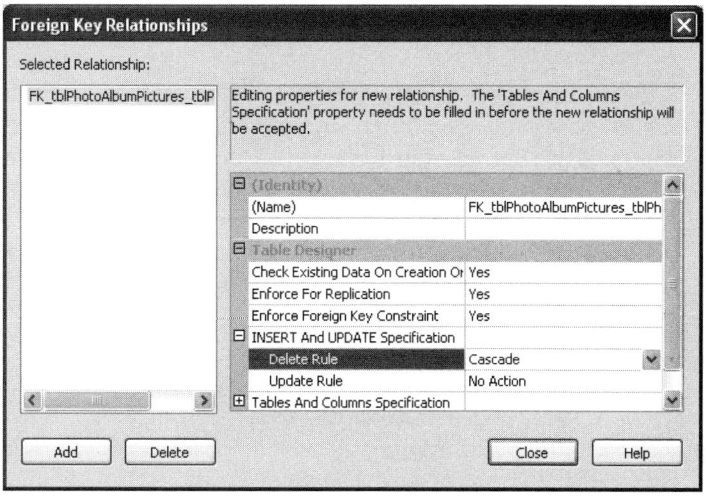

Figure 3-17. *Working in the Relationships editor*

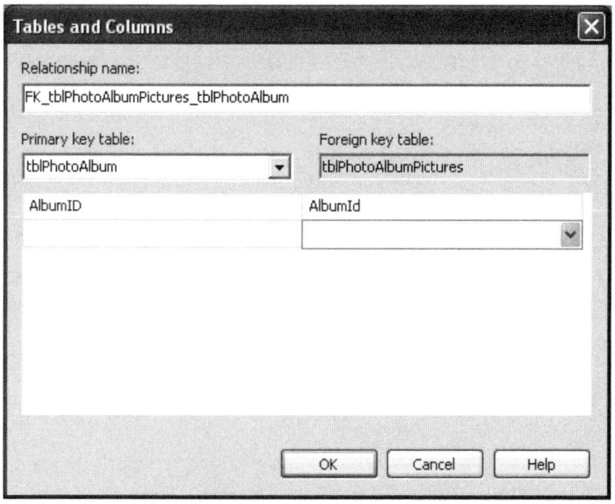

Figure 3-18. *Defining tables and columns for a relationship*

6. Ensure that your screen looks like that in Figure 3-18, and then click the OK button to save the Tables and Columns settings.

7. Back in the Relationships editor, scroll to find the Inserting and Updating options in the Properties window. Change the Delete Rule to Cascade. This setting tells SQL Server to automatically delete rows from this table when the parent row is deleted. Essentially, you want all the pictures associated to a photo album to be deleted when the photo album row is deleted. By setting a Cascade Delete Rule, you get this without having to type any code.

8. Now you have our relationship set up as shown in Figure 3-17, you can click Close on the Relationships editor to go back to the table designer.

9. Save the table so the new relationship will be persisted to the database. You may be presented with a change confirmation dialog box warning what database objects will be affected. You did not see this dialog before because you are always only affecting the single table. But now you have a relationship that affects other tables, and this warning lets you know that you are affecting more than just this current table. Although you can deselect the check box on this dialog to turn it off, we recommend leaving it on because it can prove very useful when your database has many more objects in it.

Having tables defined in a database is great, but you also need a way to insert, update, and delete data in these tables. Although it is possible to use SQL in your application and pass those in, it is more common practice to use stored procedures. In the following walk-throughs, you will create a stored procedure for each of those operations on the tblPhotoAlbum table (the rest of the stored procedures will be created from the database creation script). Stored procedures provide a few advantages.

- *Compiled execution*: Stored procedures in SQL Server are compiled after the first time they are executed so as to increase performance on subsequent request.

- *Security*: Stored procedures help prevent against SQL injection attacks in the way that parameters are passed in to them.

- *Maintenance*: Stored procedures can usually be more easily updated than application code.

Let's get down to creating some *sprocs* (a common acronym for stored procedures). To create your first stored procedure, right-click the Stored Procedure folder in the Database Explorer treeview for the database, and select Add New Stored Procedure. In the new tabbed document created, you have some SQL entered for you like this:

```
CREATE PROCEDURE dbo.StoredProcedure1
/*
    (
        @parameter1 datatype = default value,
        @parameter2 datatype OUTPUT
    )
*/
AS
    /* SET NOCOUNT ON */
    RETURN
```

The purpose of this code is to give you a quick starting point to building your stored procedure. Modify the SQL to look like this:

```
CREATE PROCEDURE dbo.AddPhotoAlbum
    (
        @Name varchar(50),
        @UserID uniqueidentifier,
        @AlbumID uniqueidentifier
    )
AS
    SET NOCOUNT ON

    SET @AlbumID= newid()

    INSERT INTO tblPhotoAlbum
    (Name,UserID,AlbumID)
    Values
    (@Name,@UserID,@AlbumID)
    RETURN
```

This stored procedure, which we have called AddPhotoAlbum, will insert a new row into the tblPhotoAlbum table. It has three parameters. Two are passed into the stored procedure and will provide a name and userID for the photo album. The last parameter is the unique identifier for the photo album. This value will be generated in code as a GUID and passed into the procedure. To create the stored procedure to update a photo album, click to create a new stored procedure and use this code for the procedure:

```
CREATE PROCEDURE dbo.UpdatePhotoAlbum
    (
        @Name varchar(50),
        @AlbumID uniqueidentifier
    )
AS
    SET NOCOUNT ON

    Update tblPhotoAlbum
    SET Name = @name
    WHERE AlbumID = @AlbumID

    RETURN
```

The UpdatePhotoAlbum accepts two parameters. One is the name of the PhotoAlbum, the only field that can be updated. The other is the AlbumID to update. Here you see the importance of having a primary key unique identifier on a table. If you did not have that in place, you would not be able to provide an adequate WHERE clause to ensure that only the single photo album you want to update gets updated. As you will now see, the same importance applies to the Delete operation. Create one more new stored procedure and enter the following code into it:

```
CREATE PROCEDURE dbo.DeletePhotoAlbum
    (
        @AlbumID uniqueidentifier
    )
AS
    SET NOCOUNT ON

    DELETE FROM tblPhotoAlbum
    WHERE AlbumID = @AlbumID
    RETURN
```

Again, you'll see that without the AlbumID column, you would have trouble knowing which row to delete and could potentially risk deleting all data from the database.

This wraps up the discussion on how to create and manage databases from within Visual Web Developer. The task of creating stored procedures can become quite repetitive, so for the purpose of demonstration we have created a few here, but be sure to run the script from the code downloads to ensure you have all the database objects that will be used throughout the application.

Summary

This chapter discussed SQL Server Express and how it works. You learned what a database is and the various objects that can exist within it: tables, views, stored procedures, user-defined functions, and triggers. You learned the basic SQL syntax dealing with both Data Manipulation Language (DML) and Data Definition Language (DDL). You took a thorough tour of the Express Manager, the SQLcmd command-line tool, and the Visual Web Developer integration with SQL Express. In Chapter 4 we look at creating websites in Visual Web Developer.

CHAPTER 4

■ ■ ■

Server Controls

When using ASP.NET and .NET Framework 2.0, there are many controls that are built in to accelerate development efforts; one of these is the *server control*, a component that is included within the Integrated Development Environment (IDE). In this book, we are referring to the Visual Web Developer (VWD). When developing web applications from within VWD, these controls are presented to the engineer within the Toolbox, enabling rapid development. The server controls represent pieces of functionality. If they were not present, the developer would have to repeat a great deal of code over and over again to achieve a specific result. Therefore, the server controls are available to perform these actions and minimize the development time as well as to create a standard on how to do so.

At the completion of this chapter, you will have a clear understanding of the following topics:

- Standard controls

- Data controls

- Validation controls

- Security controls

- Navigation controls

- Custom controls

- How to implement multiple controls to a web page

All of the controls have a very specific function to accomplish. Every control consists of an individual class that allows you to extend the class or even develop your own class or custom control. The functionality of the different controls comes in the form of displaying data or information, navigation, security, and validation. Throughout this chapter, we will discuss many of the main server controls and show how to use them within web applications.

Many times within a development project, there will be an instance where none of the included server controls meets the needs of your requirements. In such cases, you also have the ability to create your own custom server controls, thus giving you the flexibility you need.

Standard Controls

To begin working with the controls, first browse through the entire Toolbox within the Visual Web Developer IDE as shown in Figure 4-1.

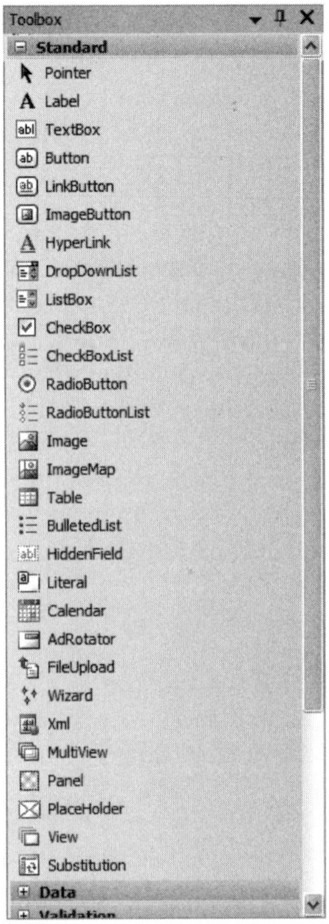

Figure 4-1. *The Visual Web Developer Toolbox*

The Standard controls can be classified into a group that you will use most often, enabling the end user to choose an option or provide a mechanism in which a specific event will occur. To be more specific, these server controls are named Label, TextBox, Button, LinkButton, ImageButton, Hyperlink, DropDownList, ListBox, CheckBox, CheckBoxList, RadioButton, RadioButtonList, Image, ImageMap, Table, BulletedList, HiddenField, Literal, Calendar, AdRotator, FileUpload, Wizard, Xml, MultiView and View, Panel, PlaceHolder, and Substitution.

We'll briefly discuss the server controls included in the Standard group in the sections that follow, and then we'll move on to present an exercise (Exercise 4-1) that will show many of the controls in action and working together.

Label

The Label control allows you to display text on a web page in a specific location. As opposed to a static piece of text, the Label control has a Text property that can be set programmatically.

TextBox

The TextBox control enables the end user to enter text. This text can then be extracted and evaluated.

Button

The Button control is used to initiate some type of action. When the button is clicked, the web page that it is placed on posts back to the server.

LinkButton

The LinkButton control is the same as the Button control except that instead of seeing a rectangular object on the web page, the LinkButton resembles a hyperlink. This is best used when a hyperlink needs to be displayed visually but a post back to the server is also desirable.

ImageButton

The ImageButton control is also the same as the Button and LinkButton; however, the button will display an image that is set from the control's property.

HyperLink

The HyperLink control allows navigation from one web page to another.

DropDownList

The DropDownList control provides the end user with a defined set of options from which to select, where only one selection can be made at a given time.

ListBox

The ListBox control is similar to the DropDownList control, where the end user can make a selection, but it also allows for selecting multiple items.

CheckBox

The CheckBox control accepts input in the form of a Boolean value or, in other words, true or false.

CheckBoxList

The CheckBoxList provides the end user with a series of check boxes and allows for multiple selections.

RadioButton

The RadioButton control is used within a series or group of RadioButton controls and is designed to allow the end user to only select one of the choices.

RadioButtonList

The RadioButtonList control provides a series of RadioButton controls at runtime. However, it still is designed for situations where only one selection is permitted by the end user.

Image

The Image control is used to display a defined image on a web page by specifying the ImageURL property of the control.

ImageMap

The ImageMap control is used when one image has defined regions or "hot spot" areas. When these defined regions are selected or clicked, a post back to the server occurs, and navigation to a specific URL can be performed.

Table

The Table control builds an HTML table programmatically by adding TableRows to the Rows collection of the table and TableCells to the Cells collection of the row.

BulletedList

The BulletedList control is used to show a list of items that are formatted with a bullet in front of each.

HiddenField

The HiddenField control is used to store a value or object that needs to persist across web pages or post backs to the server. The value stored within a HiddenField is rendered as an element. Using this method to persist a value is an alternative to using ViewState or Session.

Literal

The Literal control is used to display text and apply styles when placed within a web page.

Calendar

The Calendar control displays the current month and allows the end user to navigate to past as well as future months and allows selection of a specific date.

AdRotator

The AdRotator control displays a series of predefined images that rotate in a random fashion. When clicked on, it navigates the end user to a specified location or web page.

FileUpload

The FileUpload control displays a TextBox and a Command Button to the end user, and allows the end user to browse his or her local computer for a file and upload it to the server.

Wizard

The Wizard control provides the end user with navigation through a predefined series of steps in which to perform actions or enter in information incrementally.

Xml

The Xml control enables the display of rendering an XML document and its contents to the web page.

MultiView and View

The MultiView and View controls allow for displaying content or other controls and act as a container to hold these different views.

Panel

The Panel control is a container to hold other controls or content. It is useful when the desired effect is to hide the content and then make it visible again.

PlaceHolder

The PlaceHolder control is also used as a container to hold other controls or content but is best used to add other controls programmatically.

Substitution

The Substitution control is related to caching data within a web page. It allows content within a web page that is being cached to remain dynamic, in that the control and its string values are never cached.

Exercise 4-1. Working with the Standard Controls

The following example using the Standard controls will demonstrate how to retrieve the text property values from a TextBox and set the text property of a Label to that value along with adding an item to a DropDownList.

1. From the Toolbox, add a Label control named labelDisplay, a TextBox control named textDisplay, and finally a Button control named buttonCopy to the web page as shown in Figure 4-2.

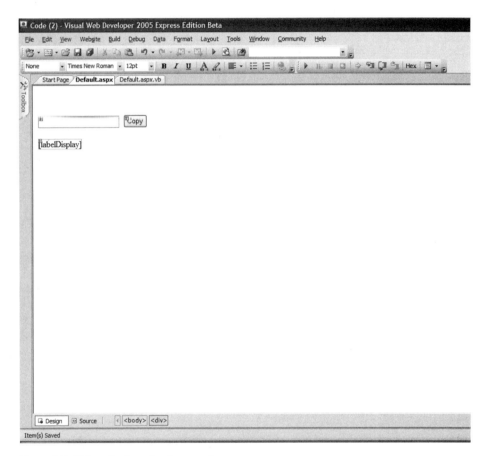

Figure 4-2. *Using the Standard controls*

2. Double-click on the Button control to switch over to the code. Upon switching to the code view, you are going to set the text of the Label control to that of the TextBox control when the Button control is clicked. The following code will allow this to happen:

```
Protected Sub buttonCopy_Click(ByVal sender As Object, ByVal e
As System.EventArgs)
    Handles buttonCopy.Click
labelDisplay.Text = textDisplay.Text
End Sub
```

3. After entering the code, build and run the web project to test. Within the TextBox control, enter **This is a test**, and then click the Button control. You should now see that the text entered into the TextBox is copied to the Text property of the Label control as shown in Figure 4-3.

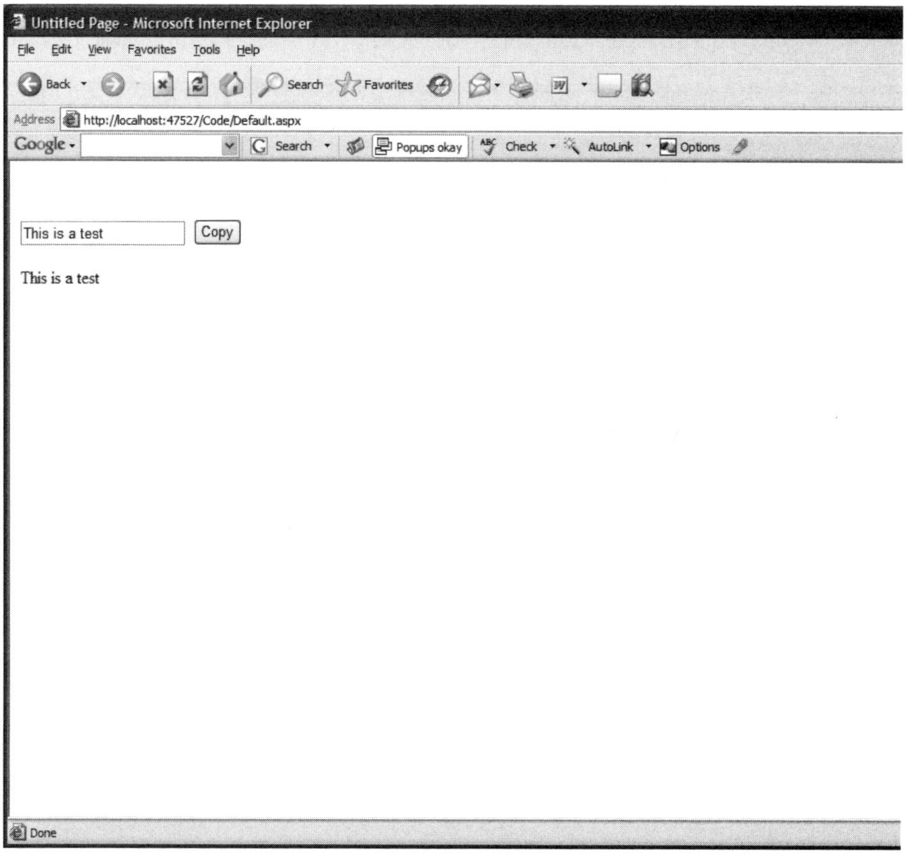

Figure 4-3. *The Standard controls during runtime*

We have just examined a simple demonstration of the Standard controls and used three different types. Let's take our example and expand on it by utilizing some additional Standard controls.

4. Add a DropDownList control from the ToolBox to the web page and place it near the Label control. Name the DropDownList control **dropdownlistDisplay** and proceed to the code view. Keep the same code as in the previous example; however, comment the line of code that sets the text of the TextBox to the Label and add code to add the text from the TextBox to the DropDownList control.

```
Protected Sub buttonCopy_Click(ByVal sender As Object, ByVal e As
System.EventArgs)
     Handles buttonCopy.Click
'labelDisplay.Text = textDisplay.Text
dropdownlistDisplay.Items.Add(textDisplay.Text)
End Sub
```

The code that adds the text from the TextBox to the DropDownList control centers around the Items of the DropDownList in that the control consists of a collection of Items and includes a method called Add( ). Therefore, the text entered within the TextBox control is added to the DropDownList control with the following code:

```
dropdownlistDisplay.Items.Add(textDisplay.Text)
```

Now that we have examined the Standard controls, let's move on to the next group of controls: the Data controls.

Data Controls

The controls that are grouped within the Data controls have a specific purpose: they are used to display data on a web page or more likely a series of data or results from a data store, such as a query from a database or even an XML file or stream.

The Data controls consist of the GridView, DataList, DetailsView, FormView, Repeater, SqlDataSource, AccessDataSource, ObjectDataSource, XmlDataSource, and the SiteMapDataSource. After we briefly describe these controls, we present an exercise (Exercise 4-2) that shows some of the Data controls in action.

GridView

The GridView control is used to display a result set or series of data. Functionality to sort columns of data, page through the results, and edit and delete rows is built into the control and easily implemented.

DataList

The DataList control displays results from a data store in a repeating list. Each item has the option to be selected or edited.

DetailsView

The DetailsView control is a data-bound control in which a single item is rendered from the associated result set.

FormView

The FormView control is similar to the DetailsView control in that it is a data-bound control where a single item is rendered from the result set; however, the difference is that the FormView control requires the user to define the rendering of each item.

Repeater

The Repeater control displays items from a result set or data store in a repeating list. It is similar to the DataList control; however, unlike the DataList control, the Repeater control has no built-in layout or styles to utilize.

SqlDataSource

The SqlDataSource control is a data source control that represents a connection to an ADO.NET SQL database. Examples are SQL, OLEDB, ODBC, or Oracle providers.

AccessDataSource

The AccessDataSource control is similar to the SqlDataSource control, except it is designed to connect to an Access database.

ObjectDataSource

The ObjectDataSource control is a generic data source control that can be used with a variety of underlying data stored, such as a SQL database or XML data.

XmlDataSource

The XmlDataSource control is a data source control designed to be used with XML data. The XML data can be a stream or an XML file.

SiteMapDataSource

The SiteMapDataSource control gives you the ability to declaratively bind data to site navigation data within the entire web application. For more detail on this control, see Chapter 7.

Exercise 4-2. Using the Data Source Controls

This exercise will show the GridView control working in conjunction with the SqlDataSource control.

1. Within the same web project, add a new Web Form and then add a new SqlDataSource control. When adding the control to the Web Form, you will be presented with the wizard (see Figure 4-4) after clicking on the option to Configure Data Source.

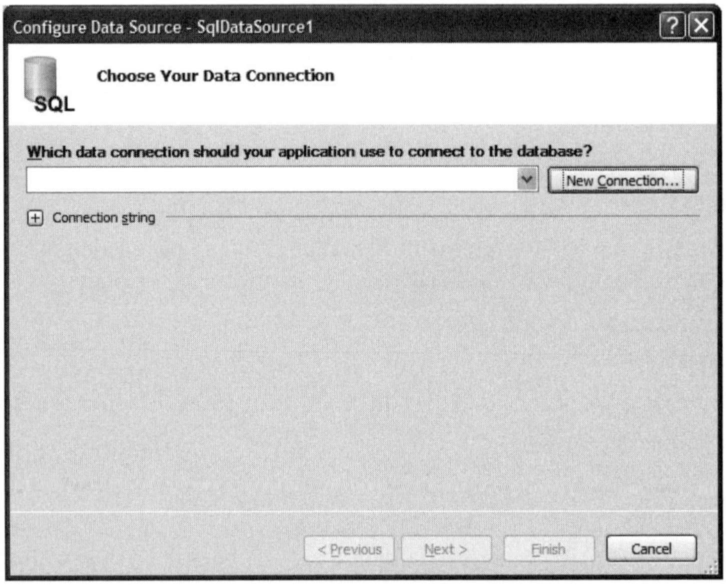

Figure 4-4. *Establishing the SQL connection*

2. Next, click on the New Connection button, and the window shown in Figure 4-5 appears.

3. Enter the server name or instance, add the login information, and select the Northwind database, which is included as an example of a database with SQL Server Express. When you are finished entering the information, test the connection with the settings by clicking the Test Connection button. If all is well, you will be alerted as shown in Figure 4-6.

Figure 4-5. *Configuring the SQL connection*

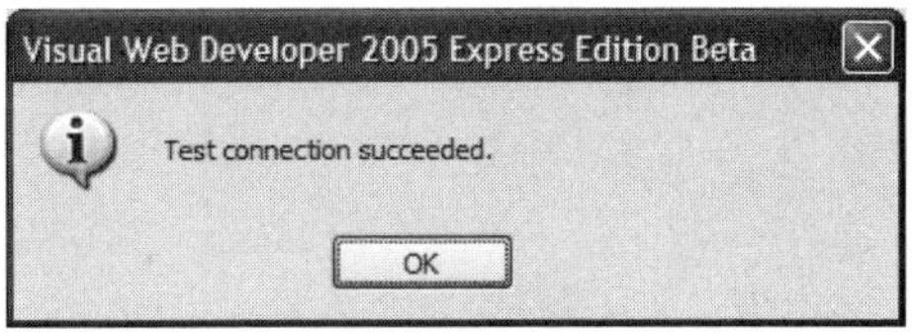

Figure 4-6. *Testing the SQL connection*

4. Click OK to proceed back to the original window in the SqlDataSource wizard. Click Next when asked to save the connection string name (Figure 4-7).

5. Within the next window, you will configure the SELECT command for your data to be retrieved (as shown in Figure 4-8).

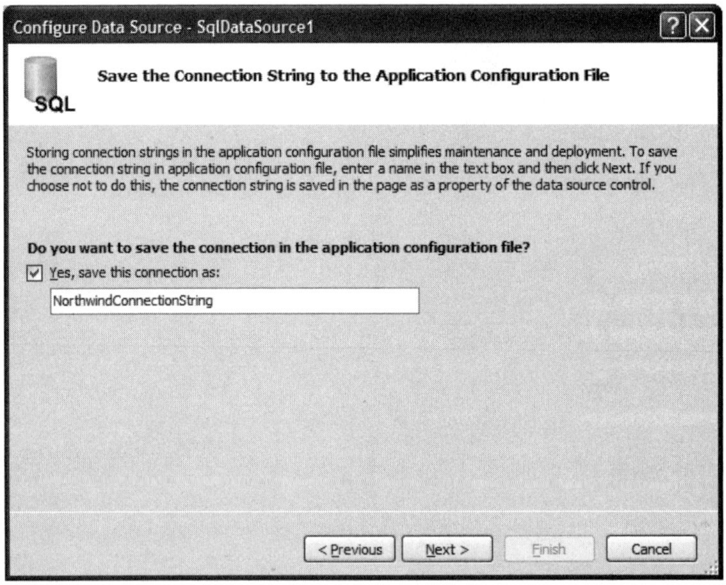

Figure 4-7. *Saving and naming the SQL connection*

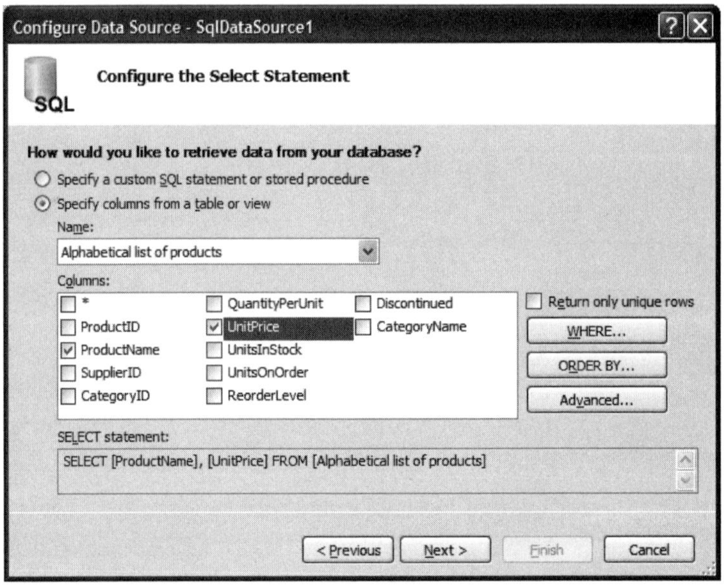

Figure 4-8. *Configuring the SELECT Statement*

6. Choose the option to Specify columns from a table or view, and check the ProductName and UnitPrice items from the Columns choices. When finished, click the Next button.

7. After clicking the Next button, click the Test Query button to test the SELECT statement configured in the previous step. The results will then resemble Figure 4-9.

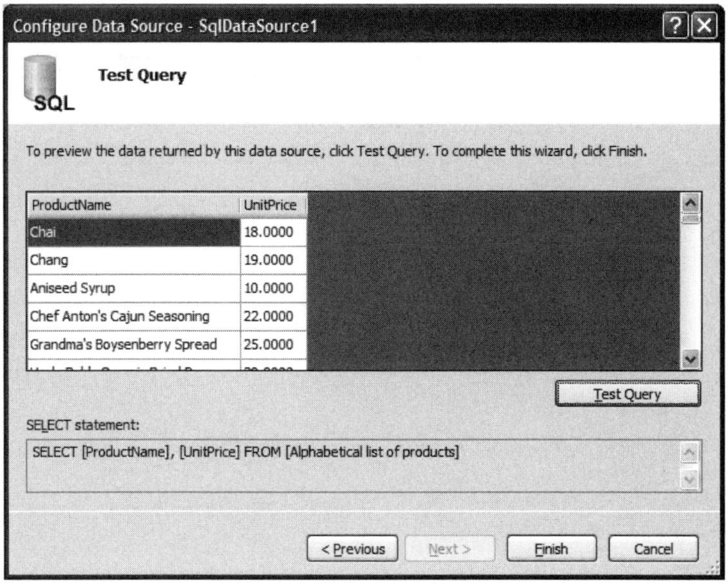

Figure 4-9. *Testing the SQL Query*

8. Finally, click the Finish button, which will close the window and take you back to the web page.

9. Now that you have the data source structure set up, you have to add the visual representation to the web page by adding a GridView control. From the ToolBox, add a GridView control, and upon doing so set the data source property of the GridView to the previously added SqlDataSource control via the window that will appear (Figure 4-10).

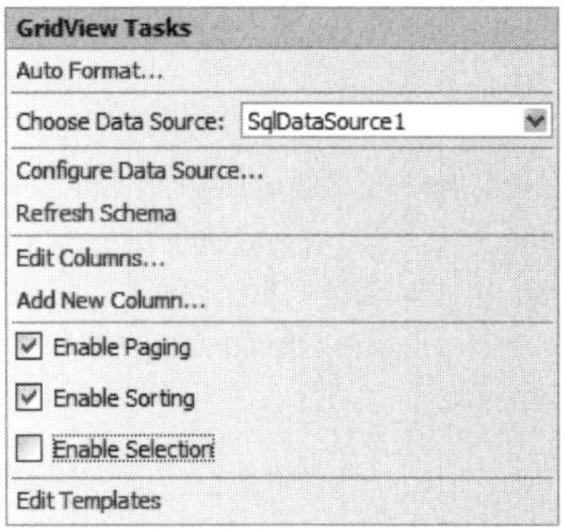

Figure 4-10. *Configuring the GridView control*

10. Also check the Enable Paging and Enable Sorting options.

11. The Web Form will now resemble Figure 4-11 and even show the results of the SELECT statement that was configured.

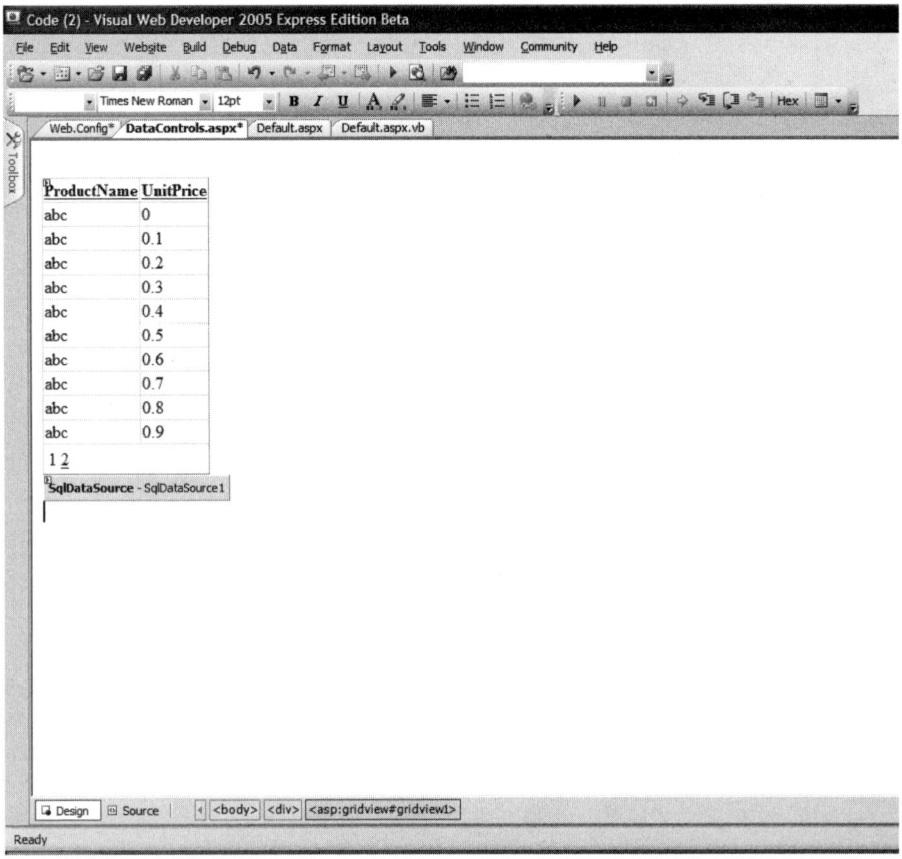

Figure 4-11. *The GridView and SqlDataSource controls*

12. Build and run the web project. When the web page is displayed, the GridView will render with the results of the SELECT statement previously configured, showing the ProductName and UnitPrice columns as specified. Also notice that the column headers are rendered as links, and at the base of the GridView there are numbered links. These are for sorting the data in ascending and descending order as well as paging through the result set. See Figure 4-12 for the end result.

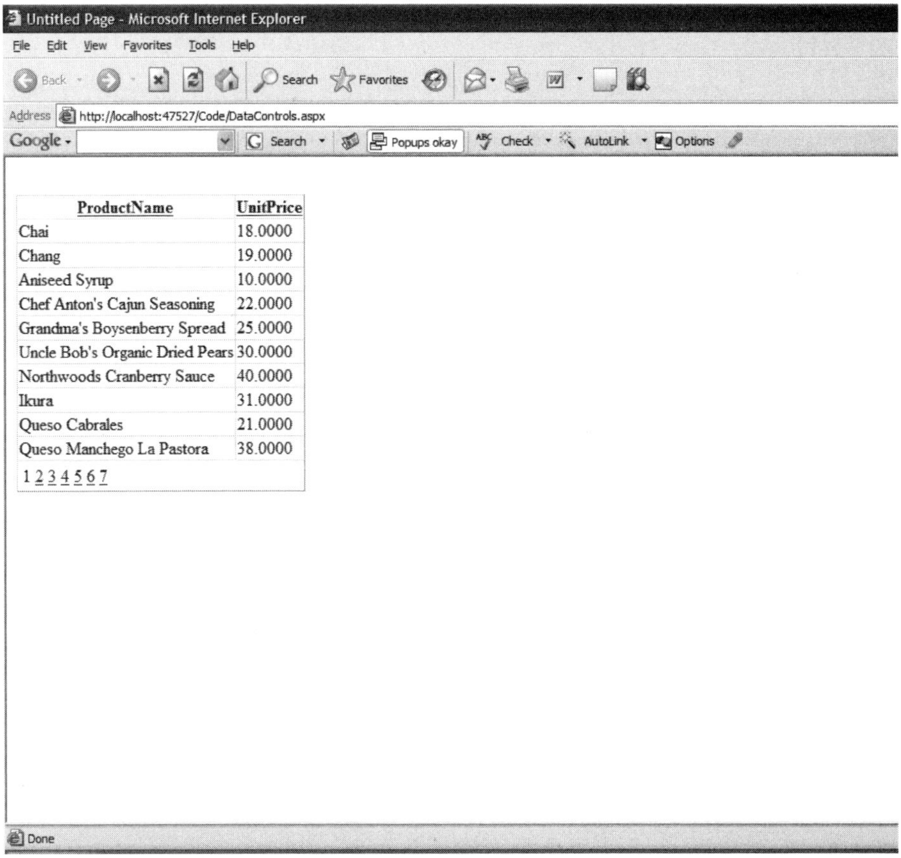

Figure 4-12. *The end result*

13. Practice clicking and navigating through the sorting and paging options within the result set.

We have now examined the Standard controls as well as the Data controls. The next section deals with validating the input and end user submits.

Validation Controls

Many of the controls discussed up to this point have given the end user the ability to enter values or text for the web application to capture and process. Many times, these values entered need to be a specific format, either within a certain range or simply requiring the end user to enter any value before proceeding.

Ensuring that values are the specific type of format is called *validation*, and the .NET Framework 2.0 makes much of this implementation simple by providing a set of controls grouped in a category called Validation controls.

Validation is a critical aspect to deal with when designing software applications. It is true that additional validation can be performed or handled at the database level; however, it is best to validate the information at the user interface (UI) level. When validation occurs at the UI or client level, it is the earliest possible time for this to occur, thus greatly reducing the risk of invalid information being entered in your system.

The Validation controls consist of the RequiredFieldValidator, RangeValidator, Regular-ExpressionValidator, CompareValidator, CustomValidator, and the ValidationSummary. We'll discuss these controls in the sections that follow and then present an example exercise (Exercise 4-3), in which you will practice using the Validation controls.

RequiredFieldValidator

The RequiredFieldValidator control ensures that the end user does not omit entering information or data into a specific control, usually a Textbox control. If end users do not enter information within the control, they will be prompted to do so.

RangeValidator

The RangeValidator control prompts the end user if a control's value does not fall between a predefined value. If the value is outside of the range specified, the end user will be alerted.

RegularExpressionValidator

The RegularExpressionValidator control confirms that the entry within the specified control will match a specific predefined pattern. This pattern can be that of an email address, telephone number, or a postal code. The pattern is verified by a regular expression.

CompareValidator

The CompareValidator control validates the value of one control to another.

CustomValidator

The CustomValidator control calls a user-defined function to perform validations that the standard validators cannot perform. This is typically used when a number of different and custom validations need to be performed before allowing the end user to proceed.

ValidationSummary

The ValidationSummary control displays the errors or the omitted values entered to the end user. It will give end users a description of what they need to address before proceeding.

Exercise 4-3. Using Validation Controls

This exercise uses the RequiredFieldValidator control along with the RegularExpressionValidator control to ensure that the end user will enter an email address as well to ensure that the email address is a valid address before submitting.

■**Note** The RegularExpressionValidator control only validates the actual format of the input specified. For our example, validating an email address, note that if an end user enters an email address such as x@x.com, the email address is actually valid because of the formatting. However, in all probability, it is a nonfunctioning email account.

---

1. Within a new Web Form, add a TextBox control named textEmail along with a Button, a RequiredField-Validator, and a RegularExpressionValidator control. Right-click on each of the Validation controls, and set the ControlToValidate property to the TextBox control textEmail. Also set the ErrorMessage property to **Please Enter a Valid Email Address** for the RegularExpressionValidator control and **Please Enter Your Email Address** for the RequiredFieldValidator control. One last property to add to the RegularExpressionValidator is the ValidationExpression. Click on this property and the dialog window in Figure 4-13 will appear.

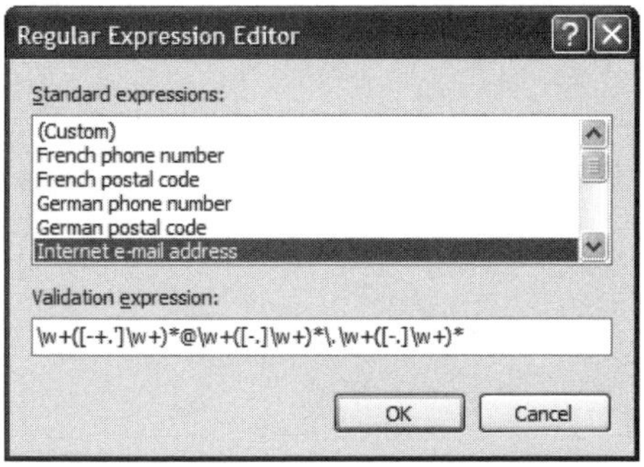

Figure 4-13. *The Regular Expression Editor*

2. Choose the Internet email address option from the list and click OK. Figures 14-4 and 14-5 provide further explanation.

Properties
RegularExpressionValidator1 System.Web.UI.WebControls.RegularExpressic
(Expressions)
(ID) RegularExpressionValidator1
AccessKey
BackColor
BorderColor
BorderStyle NotSet
BorderWidth
ControlToValidate textEmail
CssClass
Display Dynamic
EnableClientScript True
Enabled True
EnableTheming True
EnableViewState True
ErrorMessage Please Enter a Valid Email Address.
Font
ForeColor Red
Height
SetFocusOnError False
SkinID
TabIndex 0
Text
ToolTip
ValidationExpression \w+([-+.']\w+)*@\w+([-.]\w+)
ValidationGroup
Visible True
Width
ValidationExpression
Regular expression to determine validity.

Figure 4-14. *The RegularExpressionValidator control properties*

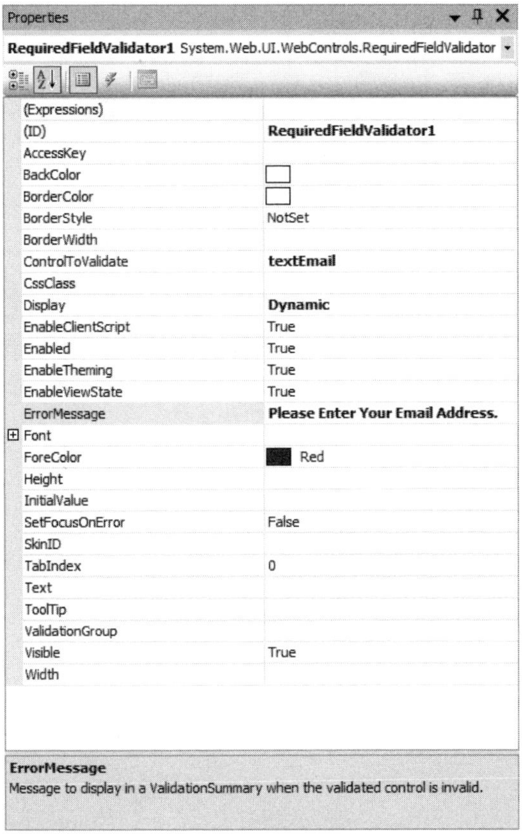

Figure 4-15. *The RequiredFieldValidator control properties*

3. The Validation controls are now set to the textEmail TextBox control, so when the submit Button is clicked and if the entry is omitted or does not contain a valid email address, the end user will be prompted and prohibited from proceeding.

4. Now you must deal with the Button control, so that when it is clicked the validation will occur. The property within the Button control to be addressed is the CausesValidation property, and luckily the default value for this is set to True, so nothing more needs to be done.

5. Your Web Form will now resemble Figure 4-16.

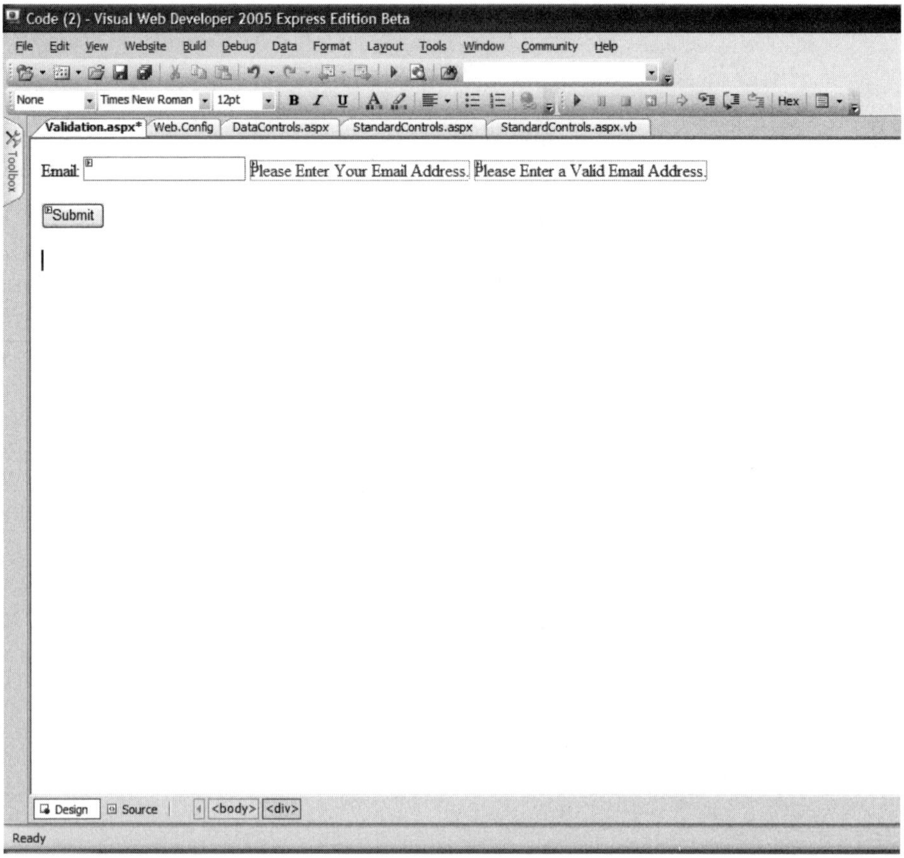

Figure 4-16. *The controls during design time*

6. Build and run the web project.

7. When the web page loads, click on the Submit button. Because nothing was entered into the textbox, you will be prompted to enter an email address as shown in Figure 4-17.

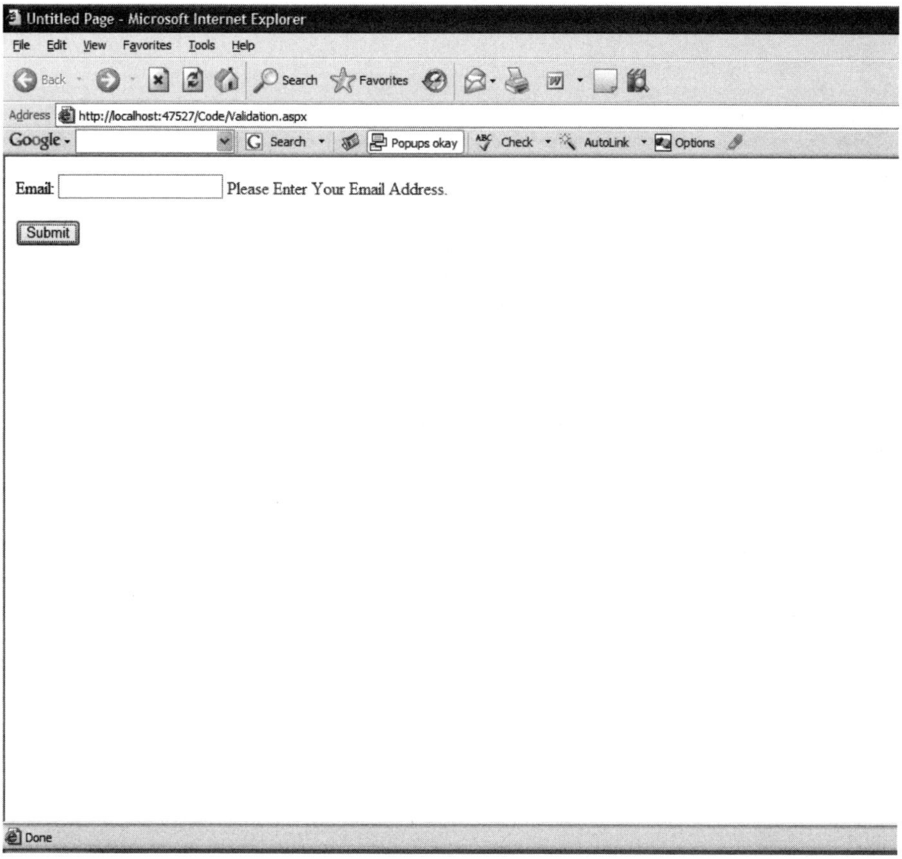

Figure 4-17. *The end result*

8. Now that we have tested the RequiredFieldValidator control, let's test the RegularExpressionValidator control so the entry within the textbox is a valid email address. Enter the text **abc** into the textbox, and click Submit. Because this text is not a valid email address, an error message will be displayed (Figure 4-18).

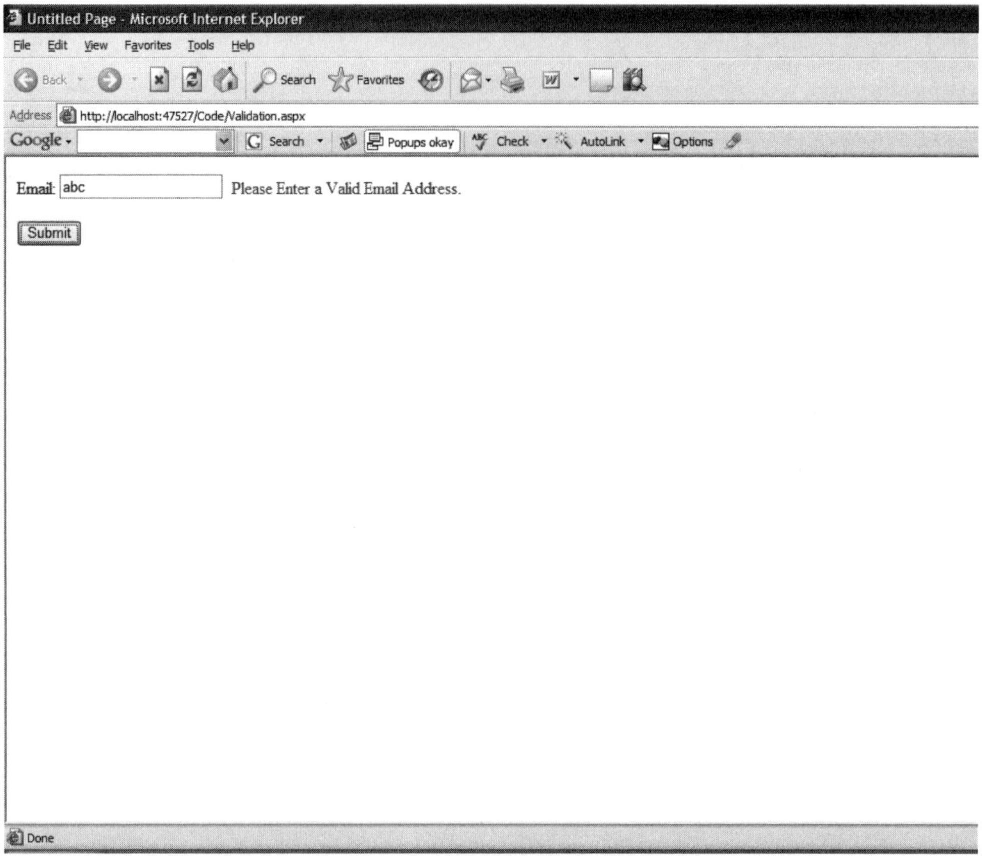

Figure 4-18. *Validating an email address*

This exercise shows that you cannot always trust what the end user will enter, and therefore you always need to implement validation to prevent the end user from entering invalid or bogus data.

Login and Security Controls

The Login controls, or what can be grouped into the Security controls, refer to entering credentials to be validated. Many web applications require end users to enter their account information or credentials, and undoubtedly you will encounter the need to add this type of functionality to one of your applications. For instance, an application will require end users to log in before they can view their bank account.

One of the last sets or groups of controls are the Login controls, which relate directly to the security of a given web application. The Login controls consist of Login, LoginView, PasswordRecovery, LoginStatus, LoginName, CreateUserWizard, and ChangePassword.

Login

The Login control provides the end user with a standard login interface that includes a textbox for the username as well as the password. There is also a login Command Button and some optional features, such as a Remember Me check box that will use a persistent cookie on the end user's machine.

LoginView

The LoginView control detects the status of the end user's authentication and role within the authentication and then will display the appropriate information to the end user.

PasswordRecovery

The PasswordRecovery control gives end users the functionality to recover or reset their password based on their username. This control is typically used on the login page of the web application.

LoginStatus

The LoginStatus control detects the end user's authentication status and will display the appropriate login or logout option.

LoginName

The LoginName control displays the authenticated user's name on the web page.

CreateUserWizard

The CreateUserWizard control extends the Wizard control with additional functionality that is built on the Membership services to create a new user within the membership data store.

ChangePassword

The ChangePassword control allows end users to specify their current password and then execute the changing and confirmation of a new password.

Navigation Controls

Up to this point within the chapter, most, if not all, of the controls have mostly been used for displaying data or groups of data from a result set. The controls that can be grouped together within the Navigation controls do not have a main purpose of displaying data, but they give the end user an easy way to navigate from one web page to another from within the web application.

Chapter 7 is dedicated to navigation and includes detailed examples of each of the controls. We briefly outline these controls here.

SiteMapPath

The SiteMapPath control displays a link to the end user's current page and a hierarchal path back to the root of the web application. This functionality is oftentimes referred to as a *breadcrumb trail* for the end user.

Menu

The Menu control consists of one or more MenuItems that are organized into different levels within the hierarchy.

TreeView

The powerful TreeView control aids in the navigation of a web application. It resembles the look and feel of Windows Explorer.

Custom Controls

To this point within the chapter we have discussed many different types of controls. Undoubtedly, there will come a time when one of the included controls will not be sufficient to meet your development requirements. For example, let's say your web application needs to use the GridView control and you want specific colors or styles associated with it. In such situations, you can extend the GridView control as a custom control, so you do not have to repeat adding the colors and styles throughout. Luckily, when presented with such a challenge, .NET Framework 2.0 allows you to build your own custom control.

To explain in greater detail how to build your own custom web server control is beyond the scope of this book and unfortunately cannot be accomplished with the Visual Web Developer. To do so, you will have to use Visual Studio .NET 2005. Therefore, if you would like to proceed with experimenting with custom controls, refer to the Help files included or research the topic within the Microsoft Developer Network (MSDN).

Summary

This chapter discussed all of the server controls that are included within .NET Framework 2.0 and also within Visual Web Developer. All of these controls will greatly aid in developing your web applications in terms of speed, efficiency, and consistency.

The best way to master and gain the most thorough understanding of how the server controls work is to practice and experiment with each of them in what we term a *dummy project*, where the only purpose is to experiment, in this case with each of the server controls.

Master Pages, Themes, and Skins

When designing and building a website application, the one critical element we all always strive for is to maintain a consistent look and feel across the entire site. Typically this comes in the form of a header, footer, or a navigation bar or section. The .NET Framework 2.0 offers some powerful features to accomplish these items. These features come in the form of master pages, themes, and skins.

Master Pages and Content Pages

Master pages are very similar to a normal page or Web Form. They can contain markup, controls, code, or any combination thereof. The distinguishing element with master pages, however, is that they can contain a special type of control called a ContentPlaceHolder control. This control defines a region within the master page that when rendered can be substituted with different content from associated pages to that master page. The ContentPlaceHolder control can also have default content in the cases where this is the desired display. The other main difference is that master pages have a file extension of .master as opposed to .aspx.

The ContentPlaceHolder control is implemented into the master page in the same way any other server control is placed onto a Web Form. It has the same elements, such as the `id` and `runat` declarations. Nested within the ContentPlaceHolder control can be any other server controls.

Overall, the benefit of using master pages is that your website can contain one specific template that holds graphics, images, and even some text that needs to be displayed on every web page. Implementing this functionality also allows the adding and maintaining of content to the web pages within the project. Exercise 5-1 shows master pages and content pages in action.

Exercise 5-1. Using Master Pages and Content Pages

This exercise demonstrates how master pages and content pages work together to achieve a consistent look and feel for a web application.

1. Within a newly created web project, add a master page file named Site.master as shown in Figure 5-1.

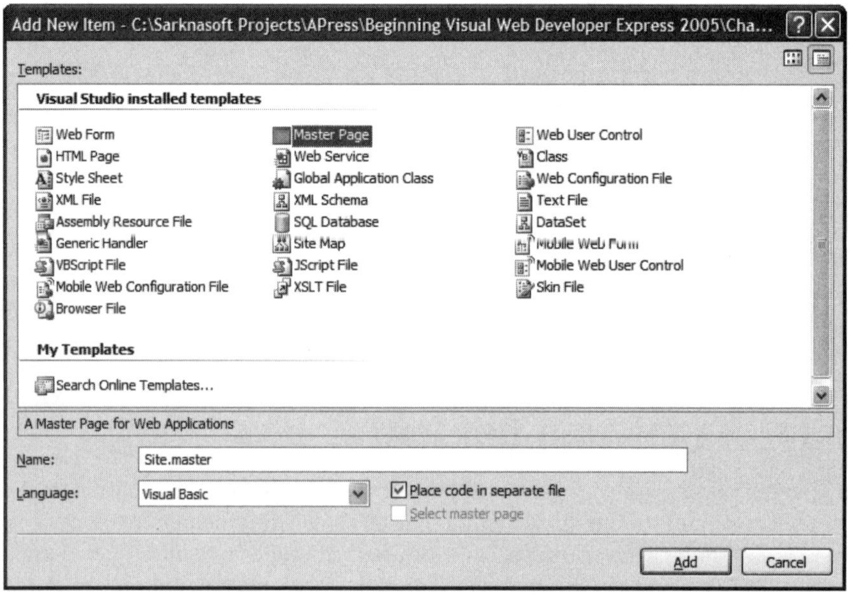

Figure 5-1. *Adding a master page*

Notice the page declaration at the top of the page and also the ContentPlaceHolder control that was automatically added.

```
<%@ Master Language="VB" CodeFile="Site.master.vb" Inherits="Site" %>

<!DOCTYPE html PUBLIC "-//W3C//DTD XHTML 1.1//EN"
"http://www.w3.org/TR/xhtml11/DTD/xhtml11.dtd">

<html xmlns="http://www.w3.org/1999/xhtml" >
<head runat="server">
    <title>Untitled Page</title>
</head>
```

```
<body>
    <form id="form1" runat="server">
    <div>
        <asp:contentplaceholder id="ContentPlaceHolder1" runat="server">
        </asp:contentplaceholder>
    </div>
    </form>
</body>
</html>
```

2. Click on the Design tab to examine the ContentPlaceHolder control in Design Mode view (Figure 5-2).

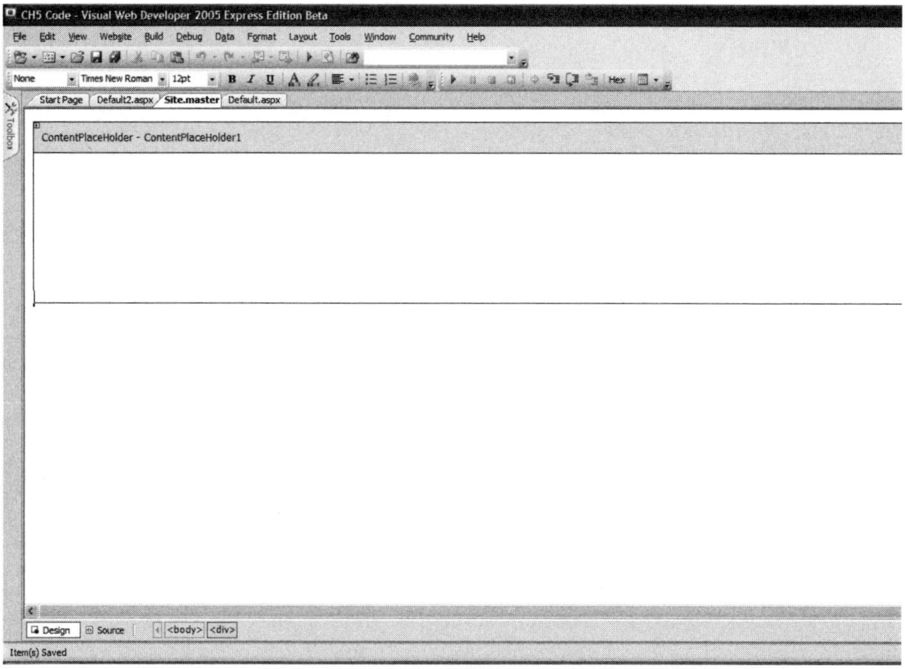

Figure 5-2. *ContentPlaceHolder control at design time*

You can see that the control looks like a large container; hence the word *content* in the name. You now have a master page within your web project that will act as the base for your design and layout throughout the application.

3. At the very top of the master page, add three different hyperlink controls and label the text properties Home, Account Summary, and Contact Us, respectively (Figure 5-3). Then set the `NavigateURL` property of the Home hyperlink to Default.aspx, Account Summary to AccountSummary.aspx, and finally Contact Us to ContactUs.aspx. These pages are not yet included in the web project, but we will address adding them in the next step.

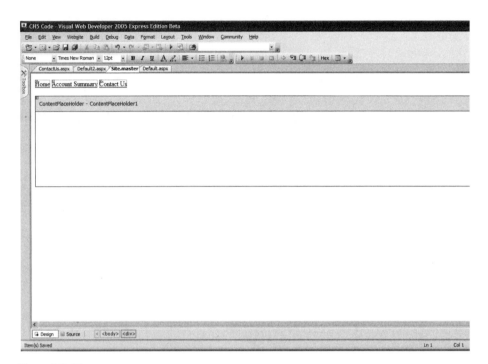

Figure 5-3. *The master page*

4. Now that the master page is set, you have to add the associated content pages. To do so, right-click on the web project and select Add New Item from the menu list. The window in Figure 5-4 will be shown.

   a. Select a Web Form to be added, name the Web Form Default.aspx, and make sure the check box for "Select master page" is checked. When finished, click the Add button. Because you selected the option to select a master page, you will be presented with a window to select a master page as shown in Figure 5-5.

   b. Select the Site.master file and click the OK button. You have now added a content page that is associated to the master page within the web project.

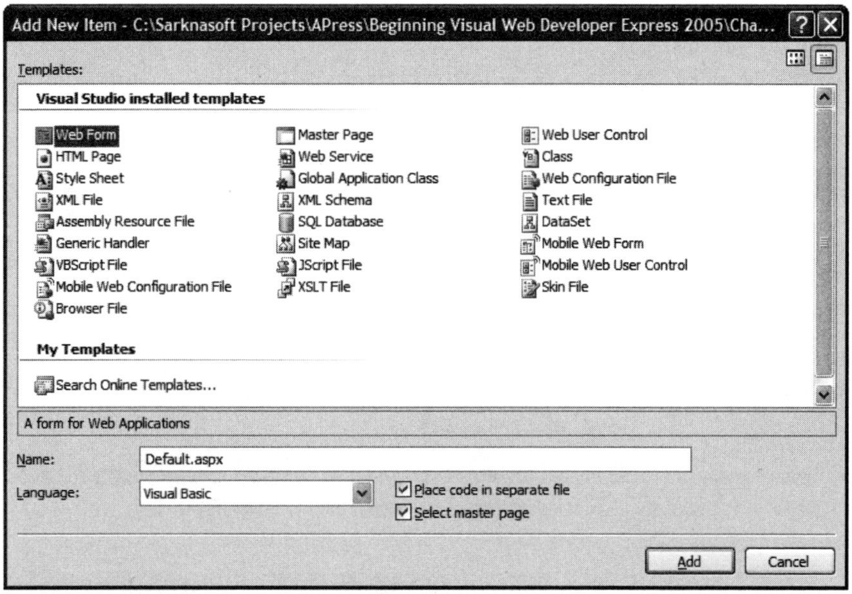

Figure 5-4. *Adding a content page*

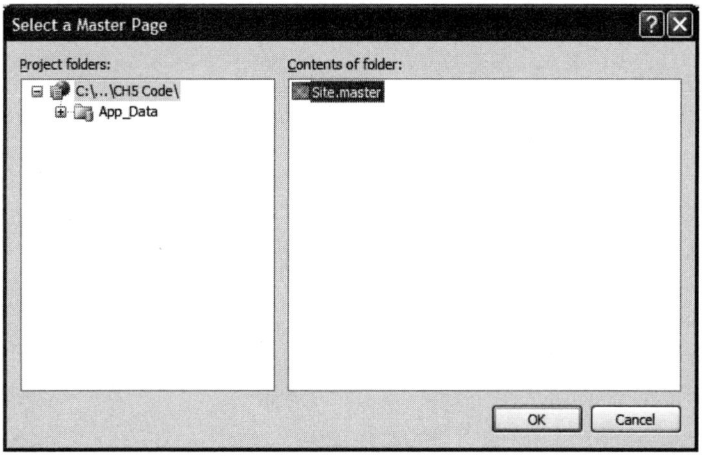

Figure 5-5. *Selecting a master page*

5. Take a look at the HTML markup of the new page, especially the page declarations at the top.

```
<%@ Page Language="VB" MasterPageFile="~/Site.master"
AutoEventWireup="false" CodeFile="Default.aspx.vb"
Inherits="_Default" title="Untitled Page" %>

<asp:Content ID="Content1" ContentPlaceHolderID="ContentPlaceHolder1"
Runat="Server">
</asp:Content>
```

Notice that the page declarations include a MasterPageFile attribute that includes a path to your master page file, Site.master.

6. Repeat steps 4 and 5 to add the other content pages, AccountSummary.aspx and ContactUs.aspx, that you set the hyperlink NavigateURL properties to.

7. Now you have the content pages as well as the master page. Let's add some content to the content pages. On the Default.aspx page, add some text welcoming the user (Figure 5-6).

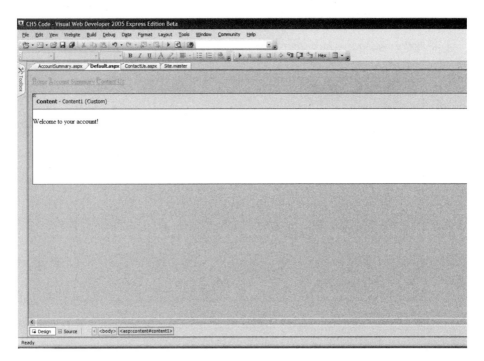

Figure 5-6. *Viewing the ContentPlaceHolder*

Add some fictitious account data on the AccountSummary.aspx content page (Figure 5-7) and some textboxes and a command button to the ContactUs.aspx content page (Figure 5-8).

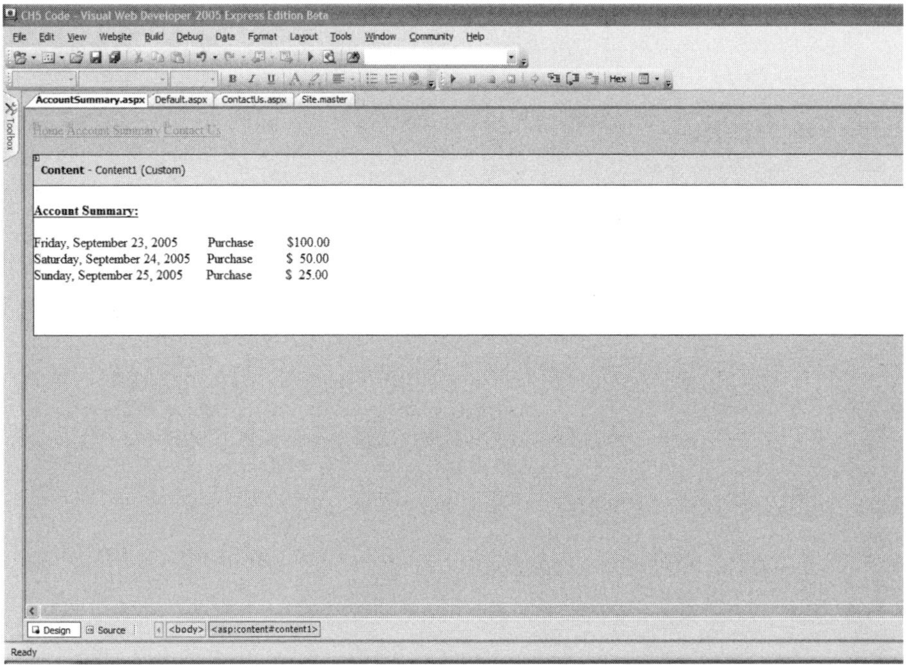

Figure 5-7. *Adding some account data*

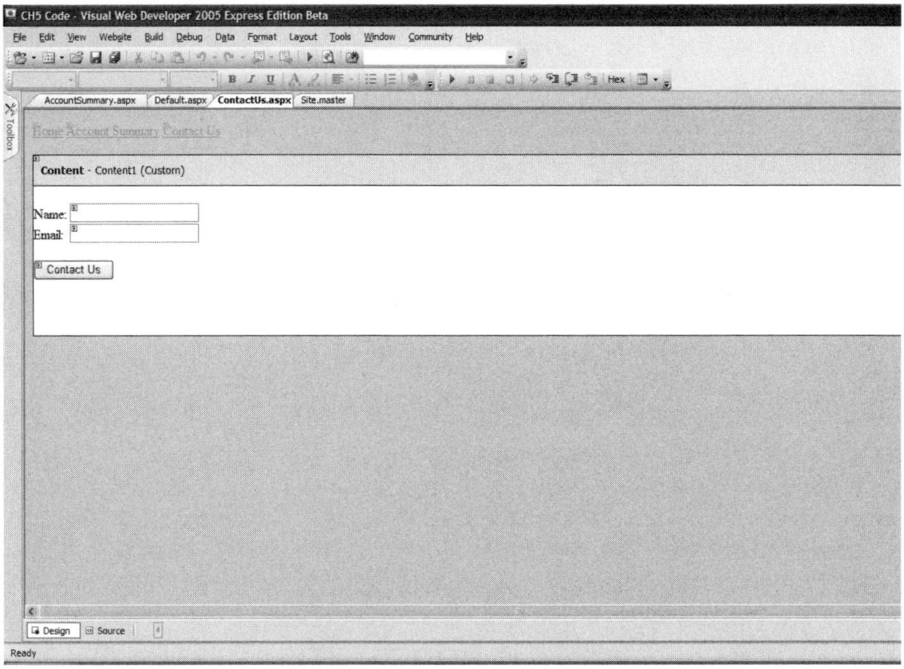

Figure 5-8. *Adding some textboxes and a command button*

8. Finally, build and run the web project to see the results of your work. Click on the hyperlinks at the top of the page to navigate throughout the content pages you created (Figures 5-9, 5-10, and 5-11).

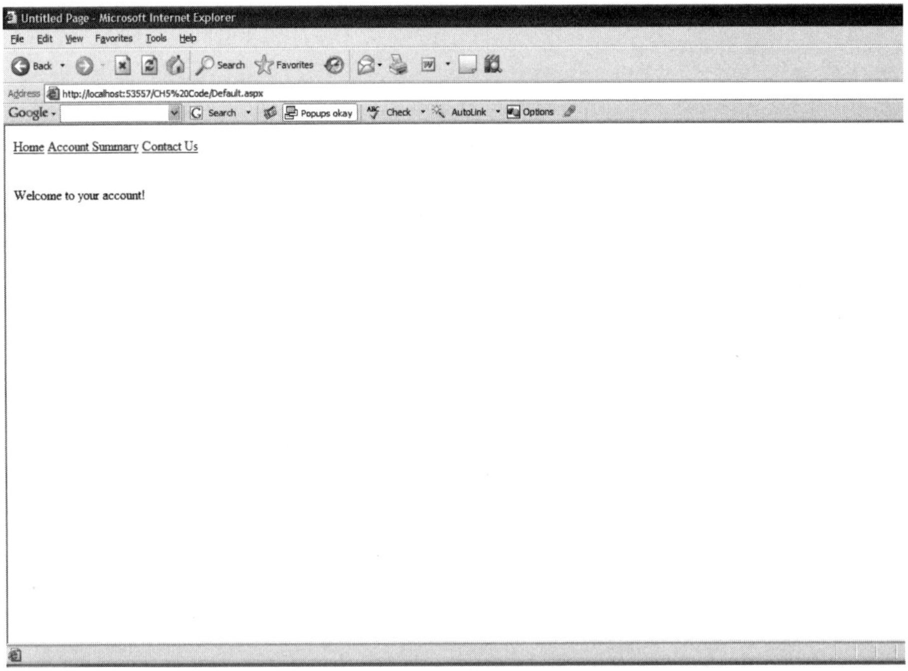

Figure 5-9. *Master pages at runtime: welcome page*

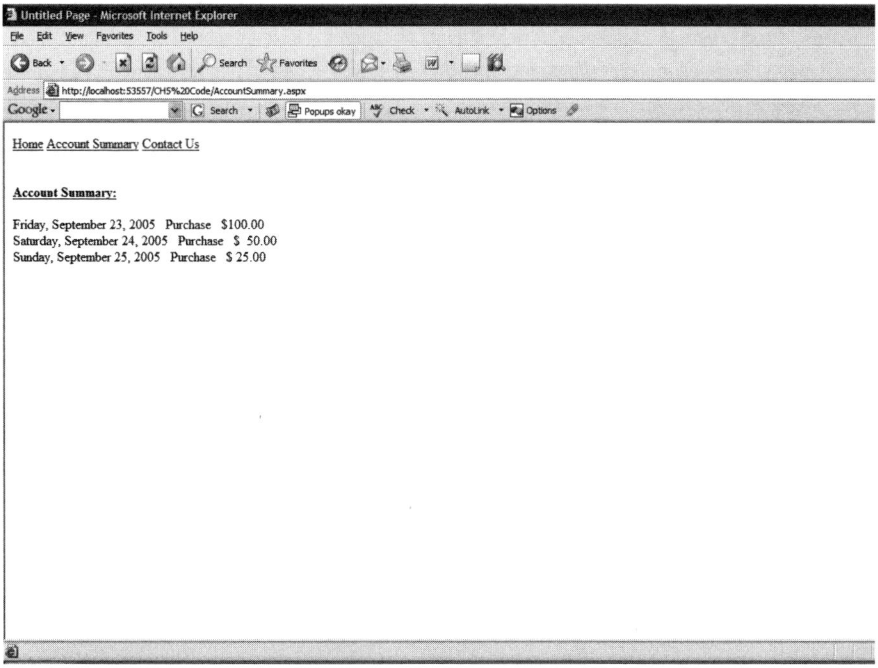

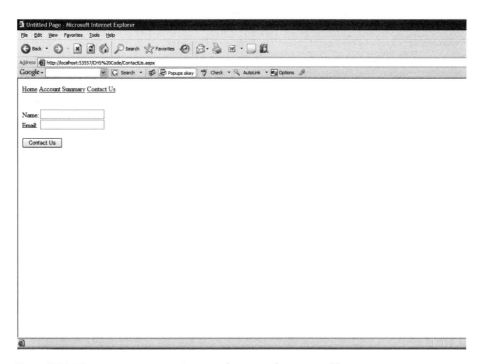

Figure 5-10. *Master pages at runtime: account data*

Figure 5-11. *Master pages at runtime: textboxes and command button*

Throughout this exercise, you learned to take a simple website simulation of an online account and give it a consistent look and feel by utilizing a master and content page. Although the look and feel was consistent, it could be said that the layout was not all that pleasing to the eye. After all, it was plain and had no color. We address this in the next two sections when we discuss themes and skins.

Themes

When developing a website, as mentioned previously, it is always important to have a consistent look and feel. In our previous discussion regarding master and content pages, you learned how to provide the consistent structure. A web application also needs to maintain a consistent color, fonts, and font sizes, as well as the styles for the server controls.

The .NET Framework 2.0 includes functionality to manage this challenge by using the functionality of themes. Themes are very similar to .css files (Cascading Style Sheet files) in that they allow you to define the visual layout for your web pages. The main difference between themes and Cascading Style Sheets are that themes or theme files allow you to take it a step further, in that they allow you to apply styles, graphics, and even .css files themselves to the web pages of your applications. ASP.NET themes have the ability to be defined at the application, page, or server control level, giving enhanced flexibility.

Adding a Theme

Regardless of whether you would like to apply a theme at the page or application level, you will first have to add the actual theme file to your web application project. The first order of business is to actually add the folder or directory in which the themes will reside. The .NET Framework 2.0 has a special directory in which to place the theme content.

This special directory is called the App_Themes directory, and it can be added by right-clicking on the web project, selecting the Add Folder menu item, and finally choosing the Theme Folder submenu item (Figure 5-12).

After choosing these items, you will see that within the Solution Explorer you have two new directories: the App_Themes directory and a subdirectory named Theme1.

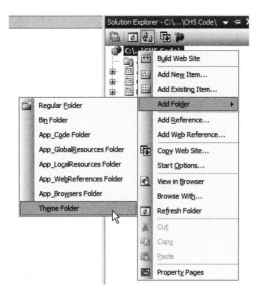

Figure 5-12. *Adding a Theme folder*

Figure 5-13. *The Theme1 subfolder*

At this point, you have the underlying structure of where you will place the themes for your web application. The next step is to add the theme content. This is going to come in the form of adding a .css file, or Cascading Style Sheet. Right-click on the Theme1 folder, choose Add New Item, and select a Style Sheet file named MyStyle.css. Within this style sheet you just added, you are going to add an element for the text or body color that will be blue. The following is the code for the style sheet added:

```
BODY
{
    color:Blue;
}
```

You have now configured and added a simple theme for your web application. Next we demonstrate how to implement the theme at the page and application levels.

Applying a Theme at the Page Level

When the requirements you are working with call for having a theme only to be used or applied to a single page, there is a way to accomplish this within your Web Forms or content pages. For any single web page to include or use a theme, turn your attention to the page declarations. Earlier in our example, you saw that the page declarations for the content pages included an element specifying the master page; similarly, you will specify the theme being used as shown here:

```
<%@ Page Language="VB" MasterPageFile="~/Site.master"
AutoEventWireup="false" CodeFile="Default.aspx.vb"
Inherits="_Default" title="Untitled Page" Theme="Theme1"%>
```

The last element names the theme desired for use: Theme1. When finished, run the project, and you will see that the text for this specified page will have a color of blue; however, none of the other pages will be affected (Figure 5-14).

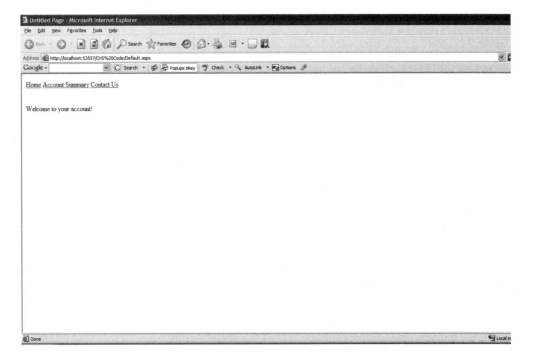

Figure 5-14. *Blue theme at runtime*

Applying a Theme at the Application Level

In most cases, when applying a theme to your web application it will be more common to apply the theme to the entire web application. When this is the case, it is true that every web page can include a page declaration for the theme; however, this will be very cumbersome to manage as the project grows in size and has many different web pages. A much easier and more efficient method is to specify the theme in one location and have the effects propagate throughout. Luckily, you can specify such information within the web.config file:

```
<?xml version="1.0" encoding="UTF-8" ??>

<configuration>
   <system.web>
      <pages theme="Theme1" />
   </system.web>
</configuration>
```

You can see that the declaration is almost identical to the individual web page specifications except that the web.config will include the directions to use the theme for the web pages regardless of how many web pages are used within the project. Notice when you run the web project now, all text is blue, as opposed to only the single web page used in the prior example (Figures 5-15, 5-16, and 5-17).

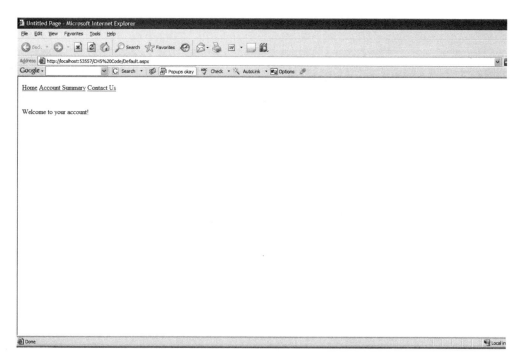

Figure 5-15. *Default page with theme at runtime*

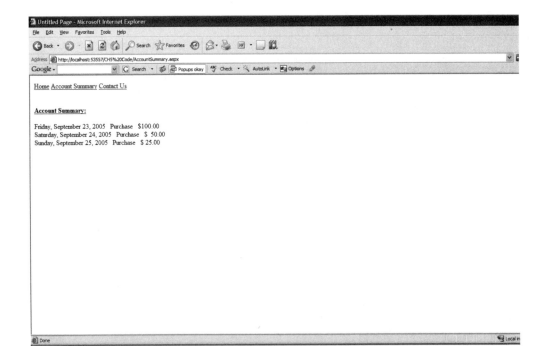

Figure 5-16. *Account Summary page with theme at runtime*

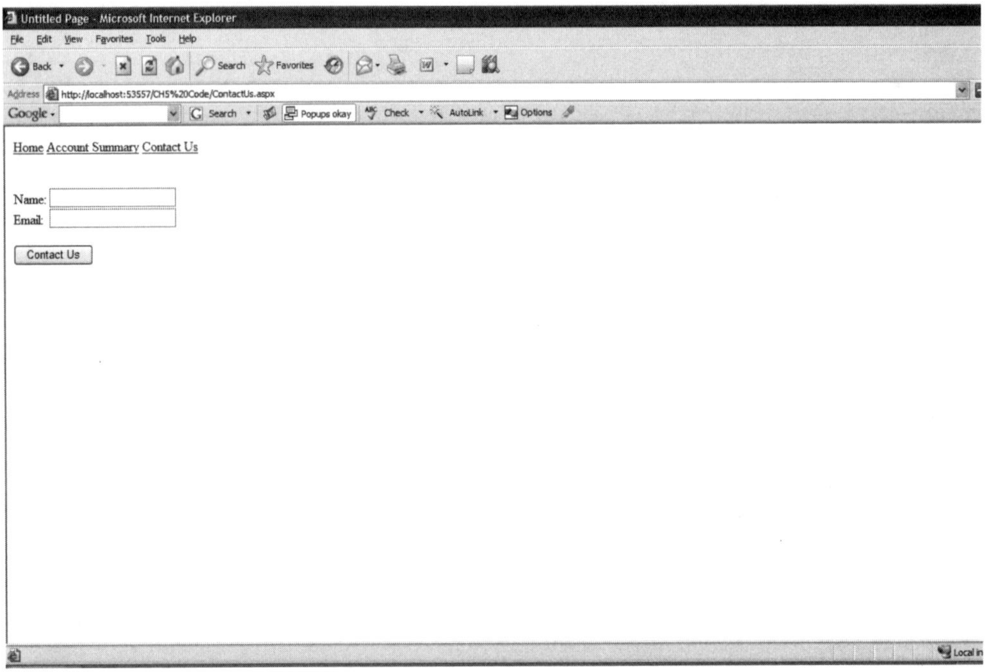

Figure 5-17. *Contact Us page with theme at runtime*

By utilizing themes within your application, you will be successful in maintaining a consistent look and feel. We have one topic remaining that you can add to your arsenal to help you in this ongoing challenge.

Skins

Skins are similar to themes in that they aid in the visual layout and consistency of a web application. The main difference is that a skin refers to the server controls that are being used. Skins can be used in conjunction with .css files or images. To demonstrate using a skin within your application, we are going to continue to build on the code and examples used thus far.

Creating a Skin

Creating a skin is very similar to creating a theme. Just as you created a theme, right-click on the Theme1 folder and choose Add New Item. From the Add New Item window, select a skin file and name it MySkin.skin (Figure 5-18).

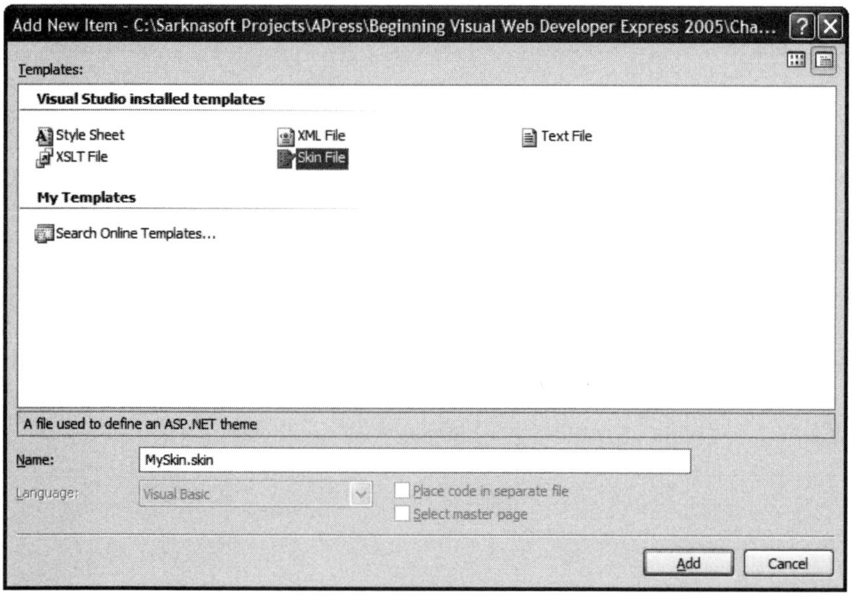

Figure 5-18. *Adding a skin file*

After the skin file is added to the web project, it will look similar to the .css file when you added themes. Again, the main difference is that with a skin file you are going to address the server controls in your application. For this example, we focus on the Button control by adding the following to the skin file:

```
<asp:Button Runat="server" ForeColor="#004000"
            Font--Names="Verdana"
            Font-Size="Small" BorderStyle="Solid"
            BorderWidth="1px"
            BorderColor="#004000" Font--Bold="True"
            BackColor="#FFE0C0"
            />
```

Notice that we define the forecolor, font name, font size, border width, border color, and back color of all the Button Server controls. At this point, your code is still enabled with the Theme1 at the application level from the previous example, so all you need to do is run the web application again. When the web page is displayed, navigate to the only page where you have a Button control, ContactUs.aspx, and let's look at the style difference (Figure 5-19).

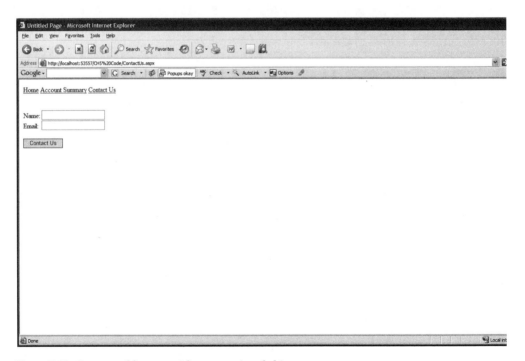

Figure 5-19. *Command button with an associated skin*

Notice the Button control with its new style (Figure 5-20).

Figure 5-20. *Command button*

Summary

In this chapter, you have learned through demonstration how master pages, themes, and skins will help in your overall development of websites and keep a consistent look and visual structure. As web applications grow in size and complexity, it is more difficult to maintain this consistency. However, using master pages with themes and skins will greatly aid in efficiency and time to completion.

CHAPTER 6

■■■

Working with Data Using ADO.NET

At the core of any software application, whether it is a Windows application or a web application, is the data, which is possibly the most vital element. The data is key because of the need for data-driven web applications with dynamic pages. It is the data itself that gives the pages their dynamic feature, in that what they display is the actual data in some type of format. When you design these types of web applications, it does not make much sense for you to have redundant code to extract or add data to the data store. The .NET Framework 2.0 provides a complete library to help you manipulate the data.

This chapter discusses all the fundamental aspects of data access and ADO.NET and will give you a vital understanding of how data should flow in your web application. We cover the following topics:

- Data access architecture

- Data controls

- Data binding

Data Access Architecture

Prior to a discussion of any details regarding ADO.NET and examples of communicating with the data in your applications, let's take a look at the fundamental structure of the entire picture.

The data access architecture relies on two primary layers, or tiers. The first layer consists of the included components or mechanisms within the framework of .NET, called the *data providers*. Data providers are components specific to the data store or data source. They act as a bridge to the data source in that they are optimized for the specific type of data. For instance, a data provider can come in the form of SQL Server, Oracle, or XML.

The second layer is the section where you will utilize the controls, or components, to provide the data access functionality, called the *data access layer* and the *web application layer*. Within each of the layers of the architecture reside different components that work together, ultimately to provide the entire system with a methodical way to manipulate the data from the presentation or web pages to the data store and then back again in a cycle. To better understand this concept and architecture, refer to Figure 6-1.

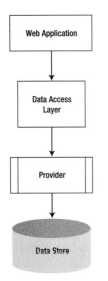

Figure 6-1. *Data access architecture components*

Data Access Layer

The data access layer is usually a section, or tier, within the architecture of a web application that ultimately connects the presentation layer to the data structure. Within this layer, ADO.NET utilizes the provider and transitions the data from the data store to the presentation.

Data Providers

The section, or layer, directly before or on top of the data store is called a data provider. It is a set of predefined classes, interfaces, and class integration points. These provide the storage and retrieval functionality against the specified data source.

As mentioned previously, the most common types of data providers are SQL Server and Oracle because they are included providers with .NET Framework 2.0 that supply the optimized connections to the given data source.

Data Stores

At the end of the line in the data access architecture, the data stores provide the container in which the actual raw data are stored. The data stores can range widely, allowing a web application to access data from relational databases such as SQL Server and Oracle, XML files, web services, and flat files such as text or comma-separated values, or even from spreadsheet programs such as Microsoft Excel.

Web Application Layer

At the very top of the chain is the presentation, or web application, layer. In this area you will find the web pages along with the contained server controls that ultimately will display some type of data to the end user.

Typically there are two different types of server controls. The first type comes in the form of grids, menus, lists, drop-down lists, or even labels. The second type is the data source controls. These controls are not visible to the end user because they do not show data, but they provide the mechanism the other controls use to consume the data from the data store. We discuss this topic in more detail next.

ASP.NET Data Controls

Within the .NET Framework 2.0 lies a number of specific sets of data controls designed to manage the connection or construct the bridge to the data source. As mentioned earlier, there are two different types of data controls: data source controls and controls that display data. We discuss each type separately (see Exercise 6-1).

Exercise 6-1. Using ASP.NET Data Controls

In this exercise, you are going to use the GridView data control to display information on the web page. The GridView control will use a SqlDataSource to connect to the data source that holds the information being displayed.

1. Within a web project, add a SqlDataSource control from the Toolbox panel located under the data controls to the Web Form as shown in Figure 6-2.

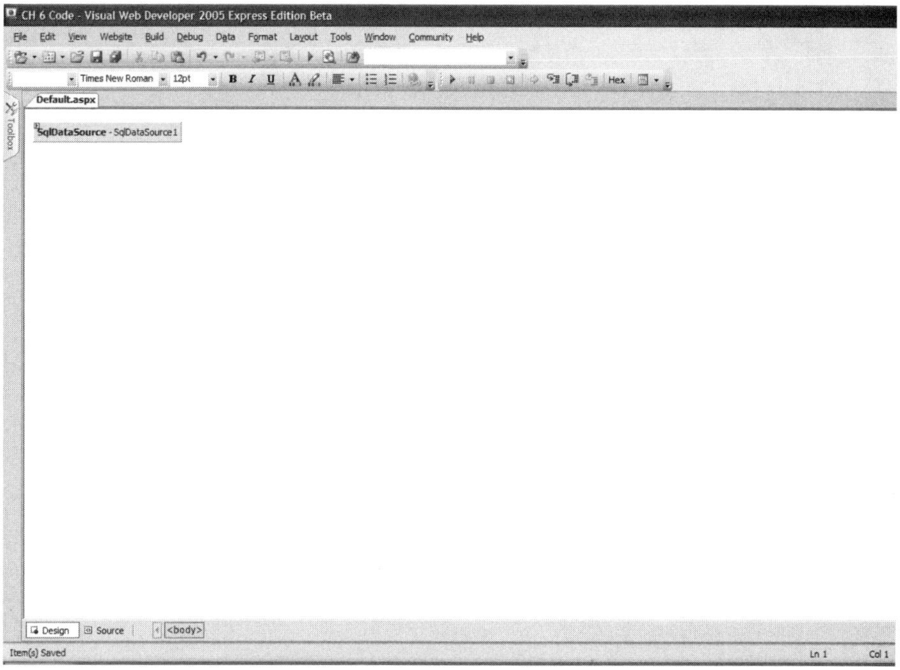

Figure 6-2. *Adding a SqlDataSource control*

2. The next step is to configure the SqlDataSource. To accomplish this, right-click on the SqlDataSource control, and choose the Configure Data Source menu item (Figure 6-3).

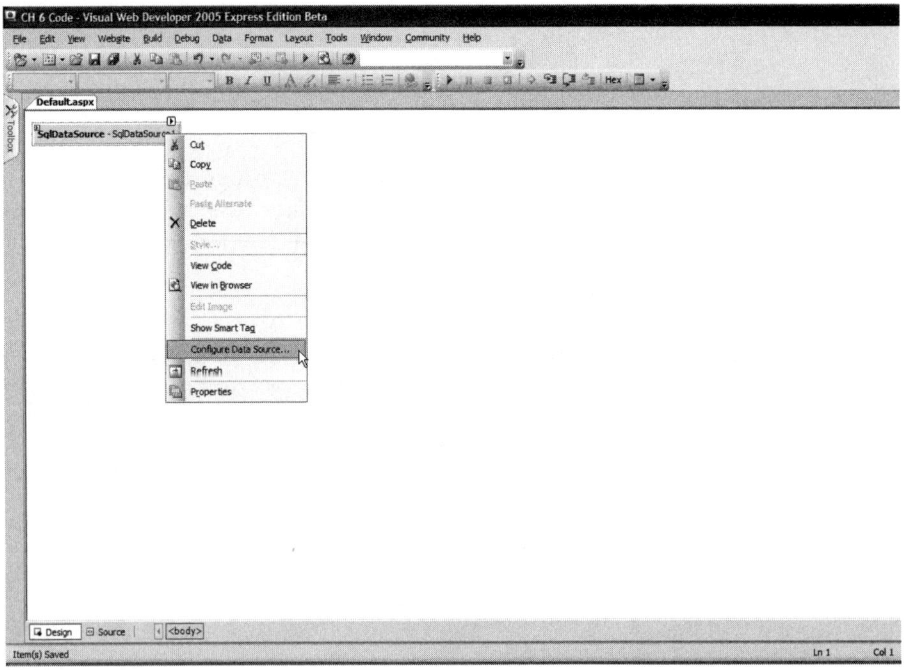

Figure 6-3. *Configuring the SqlDataSource control*

3. After choosing this menu item, you will see a wizard that will walk you through the task of setting up and configuring the data source you will use (Figure 6-4).

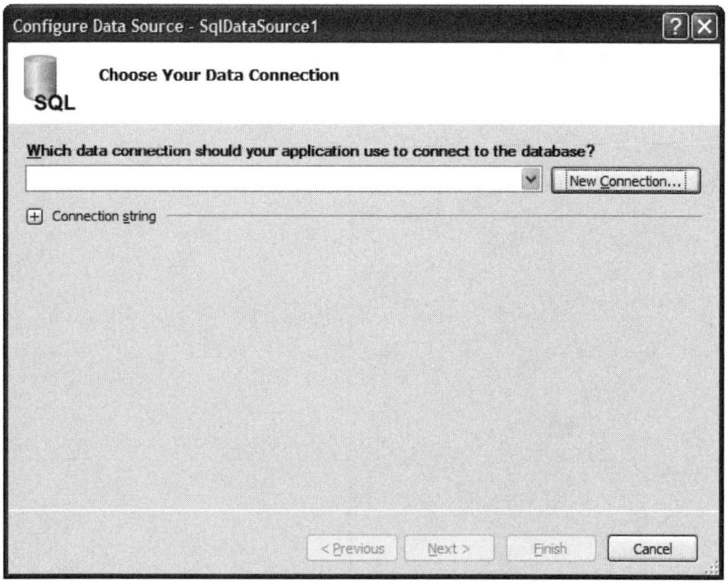

Figure 6-4. *Choosing the data connection*

From the Configure Data Source dialog window, click on the New Connection button to set up a connection that does not presently exist. The next window will ask you for the database information, such as the server name or instance, how to log on, and what database to use (Figure 6-5). For our purposes here, you will use the local machine with Windows authentication and the sample database provided, which is called Northwind.

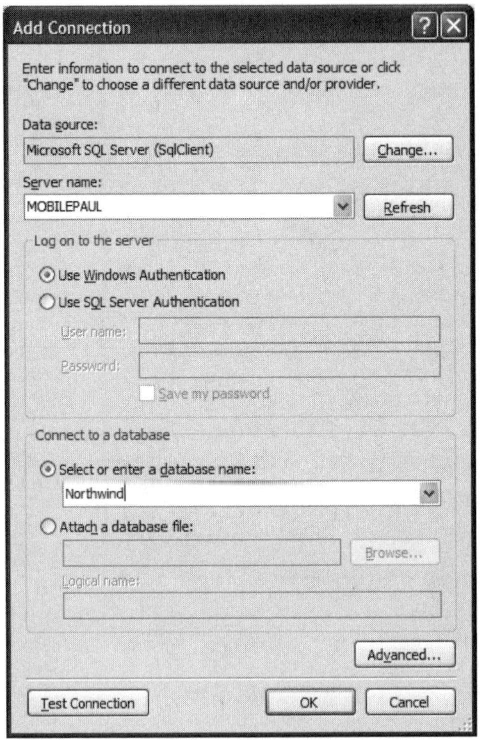

Figure 6-5. *Adding a connection*

Click on the Test Connection button, and if all is well, you will be prompted with the message in Figure 6-6.

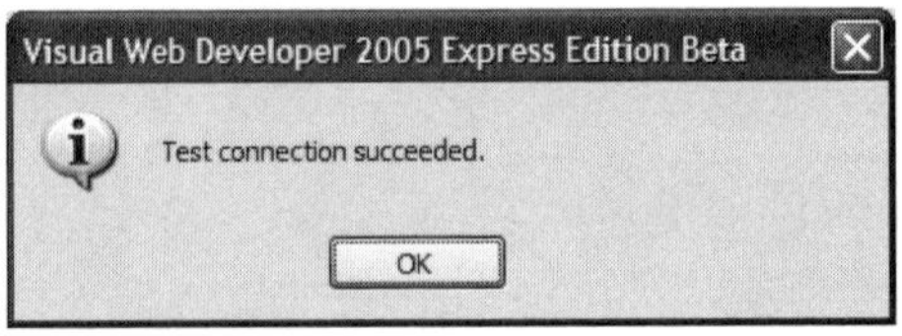

Figure 6-6. *Testing the connection*

Finally, click the OK button on the dialog box, and then click the OK button on the Add Connection window. You will arrive back at the original dialog window (Figure 6-7).

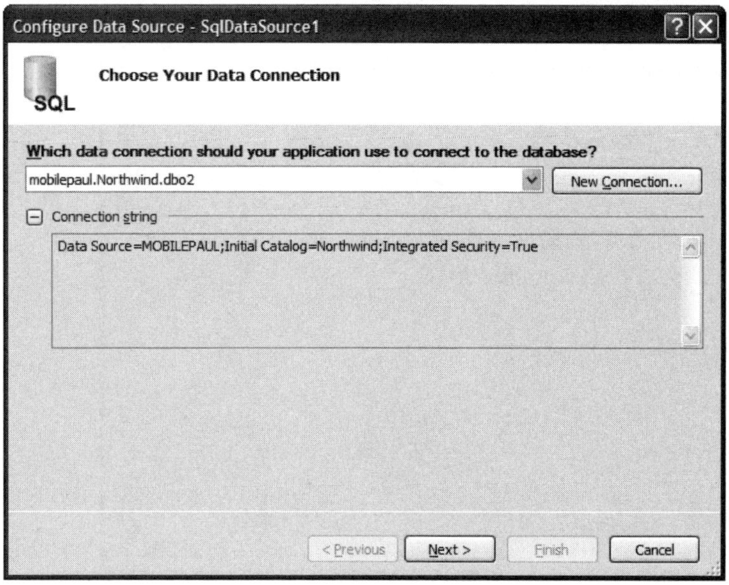

Figure 6-7. *Examining the newly created connection string*

4. Now that you are back at the Configure Data Source window of the wizard, notice that the drop-down list is populated with the new connection that was just configured, and you can see the connection string. The connection string that is displayed will be placed into the web.config file. Click the Next button.

5. The next step asks you to name the connection string. It gives a default name, NorthwindConnectionString, which will be sufficient for your purposes. Click the Next button again (Figure 6-8).

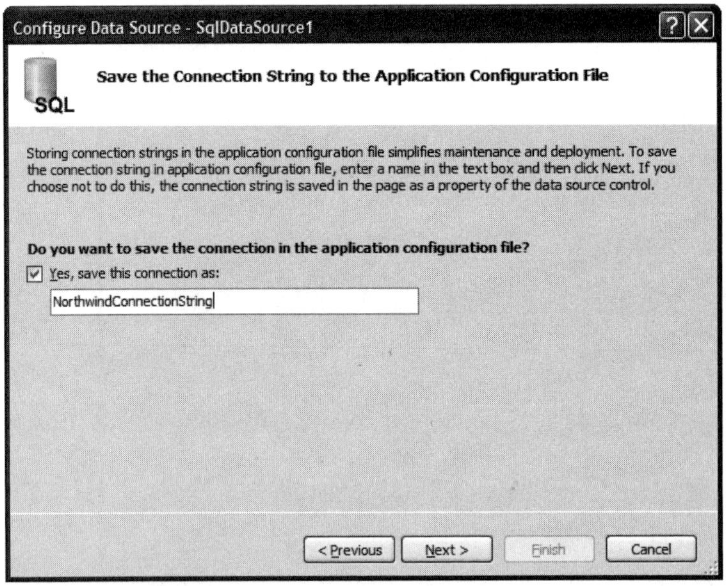

Figure 6-8. *Naming the connection string*

6. You will now arrive at the next step of the wizard that will help you configure the SELECT statement, which will specify what data and information to return. From the drop-down list, choose the Products table and check the field names for ProductName and UnitPrice. The information being returned will be all of the product names along with their respective prices (Figure 6-9).

Notice the SELECT statement that will be placed in your code:

```
SELECT [UnitPrice], [ProductName] FROM [Products]
```

Click the Next button, and you will actually test the SELECT statement.

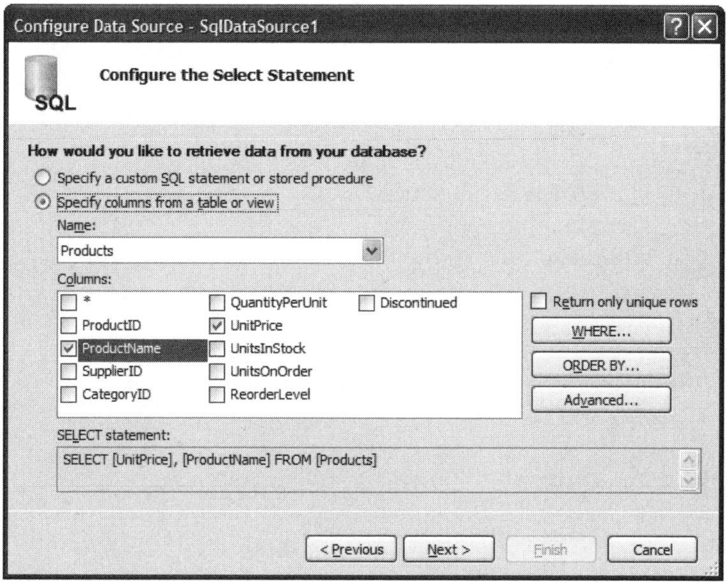

Figure 6-9. *The SELECT statement*

7. You can now test your configured SELECT statement by clicking the Test Query button (Figure 6-10). You will see the information that is going to be returned.

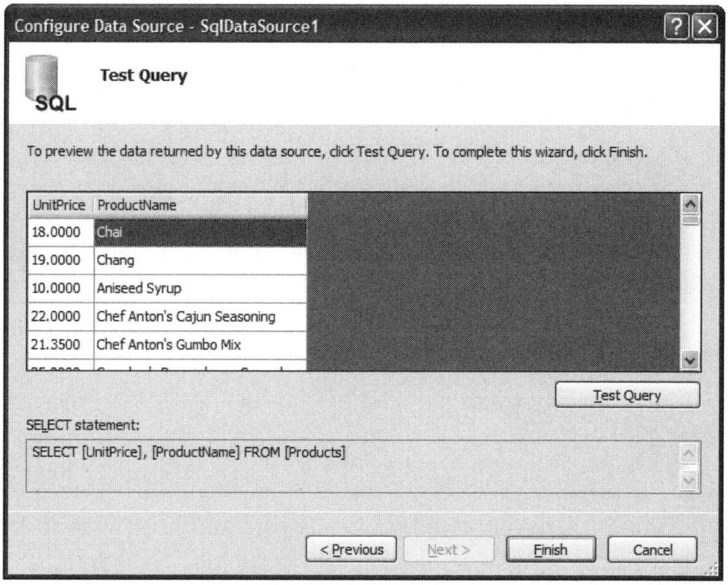

Figure 6-10. *Testing the SELECT statement*

You are now finished setting up and configuring the connection to the data source by means of the SqlDataSource. Click on the Finish button.

8. Before moving forward, let's look at the HTML that was created by the wizard:

```
<%@ Page Language="VB" AutoEventWireup="false"
CodeFile="Default.aspx.vb" Inherits="_Default" %>


<!DOCTYPE html PUBLIC "-//W3C//DTD XHTML 1.1//EN"
"http://www.w3.org/TR/xhtml11/DTD/xhtml11.dtd">


<html xmlns="http://www.w3.org/1999/xhtml" >
<head runat="server">
    <title>Untitled Page</title>
</head>
<body>
    <form id="form1" runat="server">
    <div>
        <asp:SqlDataSource ID="SqlDataSource1" runat="server"
        ConnectionString="<%$ ConnectionStrings:NorthwindConnectionString %>"
        SelectCommand="SELECT [UnitPrice], [ProductName] FROM

[Products]"></asp:SqlDataSource>
    </div>
    </form>
</body>
</html>
```

You can see that the SELECT statement you configured is built into the SqlDataSource element. But you are not finished! You have successfully created a connection to the data you want to use, but you have no mechanism that will display that data. Therefore, let's move on to configuring the GridView to use the SqlDataSource so the information will be displayed.

9. Drag and drop a GridView control over the Web Form. When you place the control on the page, you will see a small window appear that will ask you what to connect to. Select the previously created data source as shown in Figure 6-11. After selecting the data source, click somewhere on an open space within the web page. You now have the GridView configured to use the SqlDataSource to display the information from the database.

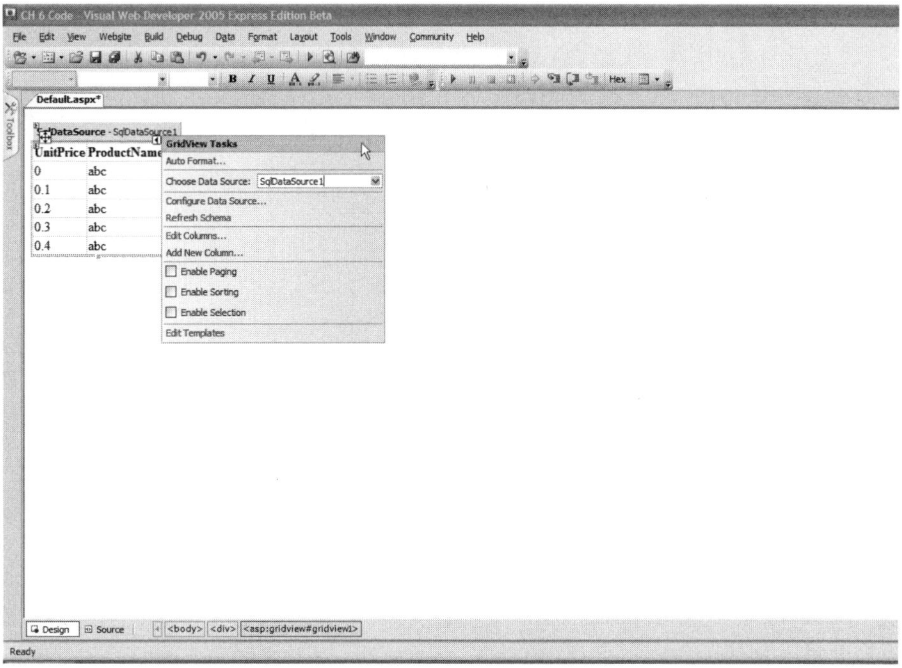

Figure 6-11. *Configuring the GridView*

10. Finally you can build and run the web project and test all of your code and configurations (Figure 6-12).

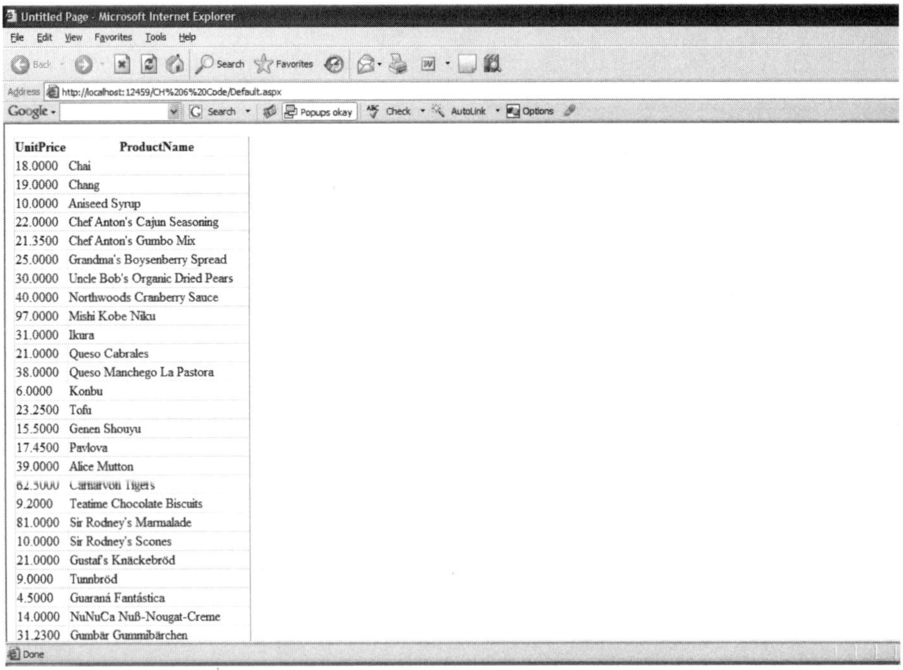

Figure 6-12. *The GridView at runtime*

In Exercise 6-1, you saw how the data source and data controls can work together to display information from the database to the end user on the web page. You used the code generated from the wizard to display this data. However, undoubtedly there will be occasions when you need to have more control over what is displayed from the data source. This brings us to the next topic: data binding.

Data Binding

Data binding is the act of linking the controls placed within a Web Form to the data source. Many of the properties of the controls can have their value data bound to that of the data source. When data binding, typically the values you are seeking are an individual column from a database table. Using data binding to retrieve your values from the data source gives you some additional flexibility over the data itself. Many times the data being returned from the data source needs to have some type of formatting or customized display. Using the specialized syntax of data binding, you can achieve this task quite easily.

You will explore the benefits of data binding soon within an exercise; however, let's first examine exactly how the data binding syntax works and is used. The expression used for data binding is quite simple. Here's an example:

```
<%# Eval("expression") %>
```

In the example you can see that a method is used by the name of `Eval()`. This is the method that will ultimately create the link from the control to the data source by specifying the column name from the database table. The "expression" part of the method, or what can be called the parameter of the `Eval()` method, is where the name of the column from the database table will be specified. Let's assume that the name of the table column is Title. Therefore, to data-bind a control to this value, you would specify the data binding statement in the following manner:

```
<%# Eval( "Title" ) %>
```

Without further ado, let's walk through Exercise 6-2, which demonstrates data binding controls to display data.

Exercise 6-2. Data Binding Controls

In this exercise, you will revisit Exercise 6-1 where you used data controls and data sources; however, you will alter them by using data binding and also format the data that will be displayed on the web page.

1. Proceed to the HTML source view of the GridView control. Locate the code for the GridView, and replace the code for the UnitPrice column with the following:

```
<asp:TemplateField HeaderText="UnitPrice">
      <ItemTemplate>
         <asp:Label ID="labelPrice" runat="server"
               Text='<%# Eval( "UnitPrice" ) %>'></asp:Label>
      </ItemTemplate>
</asp:TemplateField>
<asp:TemplateField HeaderText="Product Name">
      <ItemTemplate>
        <asp:Label ID="labelProductName" runat="server"
            Text='<%# Eval( "ProductName" )   %>'>
        </asp:Label>
      </ItemTemplate>
</asp:TemplateField>
```

This code uses a Label control that is data bound to the UnitPrice of the data source as shown here:

```
<asp:Label ID="labelPrice" runat="server"
                Text='<%# Eval( "UnitPrice" ) %>'></asp:Label>
```

2. Build and run the web project to view the output (Figure 6-13).

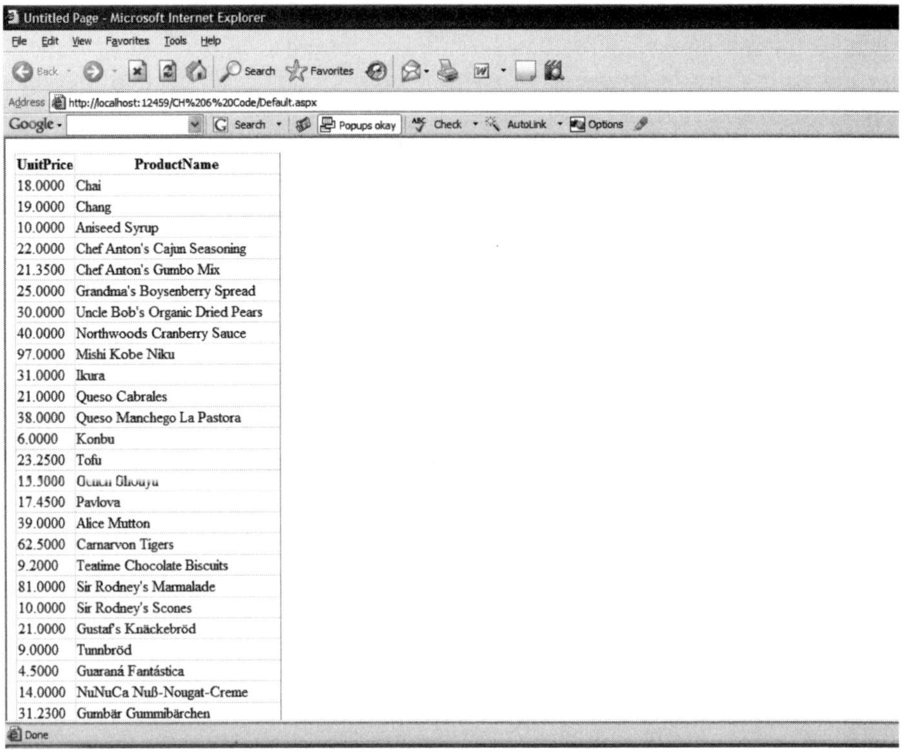

Figure 6-13. *The GridView using data binding*

There is no difference from the original method that displayed the UnitPrice. However, let's add some formatting.

3. Add the following formatting to the data binding expression for the Label control:

```
<asp:Label ID="labelPrice" runat="server"
Text='<%# Eval( "UnitPrice" , "{0:C}" ) %>'>
</asp:Label>
```

4. Notice that we added a currency formatting parameter, "{0:C}", to the data binding expression. This will format the UnitPrice of the product as currency, which includes the currency symbol, as shown in Figure 6-14, when the project is built and run. Note that the currency symbol is capitalized in this example, but it is not case sensitive.

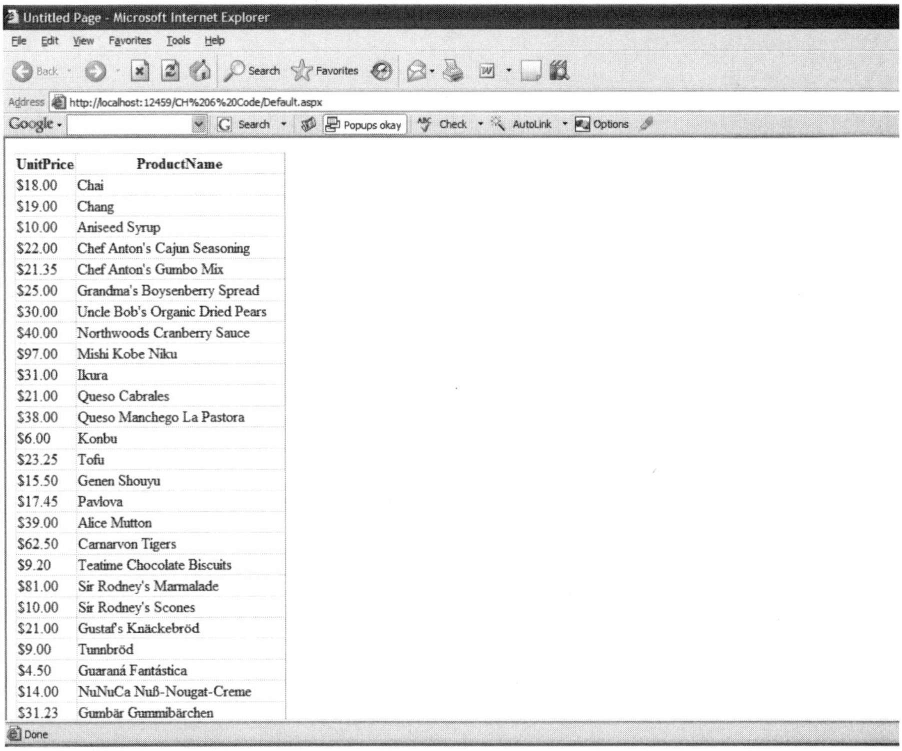

Figure 6-14. *The GridView with currency formatting*

Summary

This chapter explained the importance of the concept of data access to developing web applications. You had the opportunity to configure a data source and connection as well as display the data to the end user.

CHAPTER 7

■ ■ ■

Managing Site Navigation

All well-designed websites and applications need to clearly demonstrate the contents that the site offers. If your visitors cannot find the content on your site, there is a high probability they will move on to another site.

As part of the upgrades and enhancements of ASP.NET 2.0, some techniques and controls are provided for developers to make creating and managing site navigation much easier. In the past, no built-in options were available to manage the navigation. Any navigation had to be implemented manually or developers had to devise their own methodology for the navigation.

At the completion of this chapter, you will have a clear understanding of the following topics:

- Incorporating clear and concise navigation and display throughout the website

- Utilizing the provided controls for navigation

- Understanding the web.sitemap file

- Dynamically loading content to the controls

- Programming with the Site Navigation API

- Implementing security within navigation

- Changing the site navigation on the fly

Building the Site Map

One of the features added to the .NET Framework 2.0 is the web.sitemap. This file is similar to the web.config, but unlike the web.config, it provides a hierarchical allocation of the pages or content within the website or application.

Prior to using any of the controls, many of the controls need to have data for display. The navigation controls are one of these types of controls. This information or data is stored within the web.sitemap file for the navigation controls.

In Exercise 7-1, you will walk through adding the web.sitemap to the web project and configuring it. Think of the web.sitemap as a blueprint for the navigation of the site in which the controls will access the information provided.

Before we move on to the exercise, let's examine the inner workings of the web.sitemap file. The foremost item contained within the file is the `<siteMap>` element. This element must always be present and at the topmost level within the file. Nested beneath the `<siteMap>`

element is at minimum one <siteMapNode> element within the site map. Additional <siteMapNode> elements are located below the root element and can be extended to any quantity. Let's examine the following sample to see how these elements are assembled together.

```
<siteMap>
    <siteMapNode>
        <siteMapNode />
        <siteMapNode />
    </siteMapNode>
</siteMap>
```

Any individual <siteMapNode> element has a Url, title, and description attribute. These attributes are defined as follows:

- Url: The Url attribute may contain a number of items. It can be a virtual path to another page within the web application, a page from another web application, or even a link to another website altogether. Having a Url attribute is important because each of the links needs to have a specified destination in which to redirect the user.

- title: The title attribute contains the text that will be displayed for the Url or link. For example, within the SiteMapPath control, the title is rendered as the visual text that will provide the user a link to click on and then navigate to the respective URL and page. Without specifying a title, there will not be any text for the hyperlink to display.

- description: The description attribute provides some background information about the page associated with the URL. This text or verbiage can be used for such items as a ToolTip or even ALT text. Later in the chapter we will discuss programming with the Site Navigation API in which the description attribute and its uses will become more evident. Including a description is helpful rather than absolutely necessary. If a description is omitted, the navigation will continue to function as specified; however, there will not be any ToolTips or ALT text displayed when the user's mouse hovers over the hyperlink.

■Note It is possible to add additional attributes other than the Url, title, and description. A more detailed discussion of this is outside the scope of this book but always good for any developer to explore.

Now that we have made a thorough examination of the site map and web.sitemap file, let's move on to a hands-on example in Exercise 7-1.

Exercise 7-1. Adding and Configuring the web.sitemap

This exercise demonstrates how to add the web.sitemap file to the web project. Before providing the map, let's add the actual contents or web pages to the project.

1. Navigate to the Solution Explorer window, right-click on the web project, and select Add New Item (Figure 7-1).

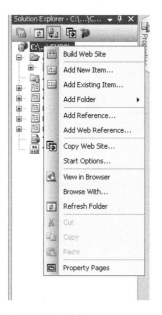

Figure 7-1. *Adding a new item*

2. The Add New Item dialog will appear. Select the upper-left item, Web Form (Figure 7-2). Notice the pre-populated value in the Name field: Default.aspx. This is where you can enter a value for the name of your choice; however, for this example you will leave the name Default.aspx. Be sure to also check the "Place code in separate file" option and verify that the Language is set to Visual Basic.

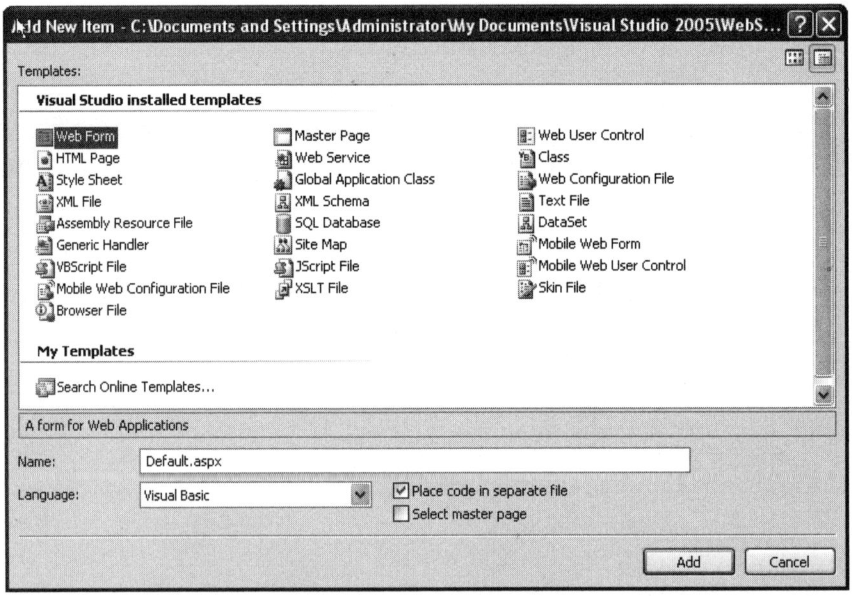

Figure 7-2. *Add New Item window*

3. Now you are going to repeat step 2 for the other web pages in your project that will provide the contents of your site map. The names of these pages are going to be AboutUs.aspx, ContactUs.aspx, and Products.aspx.

4. You now have the contents of your site map, so let's move on and actually build it. Right-click again on the web project and choose Add New Item. This time you will select the Site Map item, which will add the web.sitemap file to your project (Figure 7-3).

■**Note**   When adding the site map file to the web project, you *must* name the file web.sitemap for it to work correctly.

---

5. The web.sitemap file looks like this:

```
<?xml version="1.0" encoding="utf-8" ?>
<siteMap xmlns="http://schemas.microsoft.com/AspNet/SiteMap-File-1.0" >
    <siteMapNode url="" title=""  description="">
        <siteMapNode url="" title=""  description="" />
        <siteMapNode url="" title=""  description="" />
    </siteMapNode>
</siteMap>
```

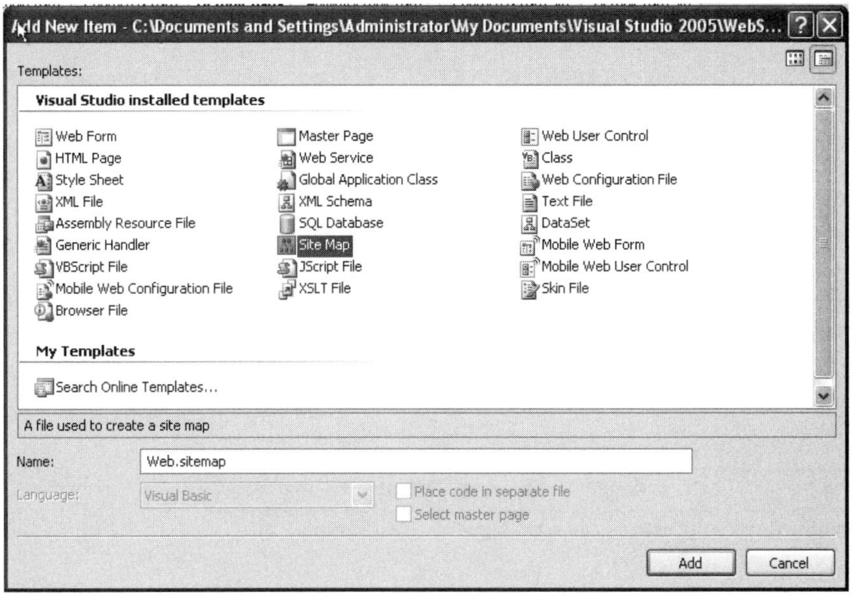

Figure 7-3. *Add New Item window with Site Map selected*

6. Here you will notice that the XML structure has already been provided along with the `<sitemap>` and `<siteMapNode>` elements. All you need to do is complete the attributes.

7. You have to populate the sitemap with the pages you added in step 3. Therefore, add the following values for `Url`, `title`, and `description` attributes to the web.sitemap file:

```xml
<?xml version="1.0" encoding="utf-8" ?>
<siteMap xmlns="http://schemas.microsoft.com/AspNet/SiteMap-File-1.0" >
    <siteMapNode url="Default.aspx" title="Home"
                description="Home Page">
<siteMapNode url="AboutUs.aspx" title="About Our Company"
                description="Our Company History" />
<siteMapNode url="Products.aspx" title="Products"
                description="Products From Our Company" />
<siteMapNode url="ContactUs.aspx" title="Contact Us"
                description="Contact Information" />
    </siteMapNode>
</siteMap>
```

8. The URLs match the Web Forms that are included in the chapter code samples. The site map is now added and configured for use in your web project.

You are all set, now that you have added the site map to your project and the site map contents as demonstrated in step 5. With that foundation in place, let's get ready to explore the individual controls that will utilize the site map and provide navigation for your website.

The Web Controls

Included within the new release of ASP.NET 2.0 are several web controls that are available out of the box to easily create site navigation. Because all websites should provide a professional layout of navigation, each of the three controls—the SiteMapPath, Treeview, and Menu—will be able to accomplish that goal. However, with that said, in different scenarios one control will have a better fit than another. For instance, if the information or data within your web application has many nested values, you might consider using the Treeview control because of how it can collapse and uncollapse those nested values. If your application needs to leave a trail to indicate where the user has been, the Menu control would probably be the best fit. To break down the similarities and differences further and help you decide which control offers the best fit for your scenario according to the examples just described, examine Table 7-1.

Table 7-1. *Navigation Control Details*

Feature	SiteMapPath	Treeview	Menu
Expansion/display	Cascade	Collapse	"Breadcrumb"
Check boxes	No	Yes	No
Layout	Horizontal	Vertical	Horizontal and vertical
Apply styles	Yes	Yes	Yes

   Before you take a hands-on approach to these controls, here's a thorough explanation that identifies the similarities and differences among all three controls:

- *SiteMapPath*: The SiteMapPath control provides users with not only the current page they are viewing but also a history of where they have been or what page they visited prior to the current page. This type of functionality and display is referred to as a *breadcrumb trail*. The SiteMapPath control works exclusively with the SiteMapProvider, which can be set from a property of the control.

- *Treeview*: The Treeview control provides a vertical user interface that is capable of expanding and collapsing with the available nodes.

- *Menu*: The Menu control can have a display that is horizontal or vertical. It pops out with additional submenu items when the end user hovers over the main menu item.

   Now that you have an understanding of each control, let's move on to some examples in the exercises that follow. Exercise 7-2 demonstrates using the SiteMapPath control.

Exercise 7-2. Using the SiteMapPath Control

This exercise will take you step by step through adding and configuring the SiteMapPath control within your web application.

1. Click on the Toolbox window and locate the Navigation panel. Within the Navigation panel, drag and drop a SiteMapPath control to the Default.aspx page (Figure 7-4).

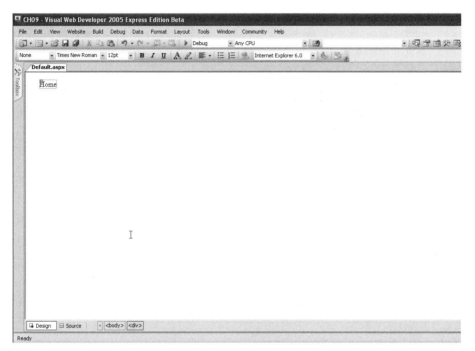

Figure 7-4. *Default.aspx Web Form*

2. Now that the SiteMapPath control is included with the Default.aspx page, you need to perform one remaining step. Drag and drop a SiteMapDataSource control to the page as well. This control will take the default name SiteMapDataSource1, and the SiteMapPath control will automatically bind to the SiteMapDataSource control.

3. Repeat step 2 for each of the additional web pages in the project.

At this point you could build and run the project; however, the only display for the SiteMapPath control would be text showing the current page.

Let's move on to Exercise 7-3 to see how the Treeview control will provide you with links to navigate to the other pages within the project.

Exercise 7-3. Using the Treeview Control

This exercise will demonstrate how to add the Treeview control to the web project. You will also see the SiteMapPath control working in conjunction with it.

1. Drag a Treeview control over from the Toolbox pane located under the Navigation grouping panel to the Default.aspx page. You will notice that the Treeview control already populates the hierarchy based on the web.sitemap you built in the previous section (Figure 7-5).

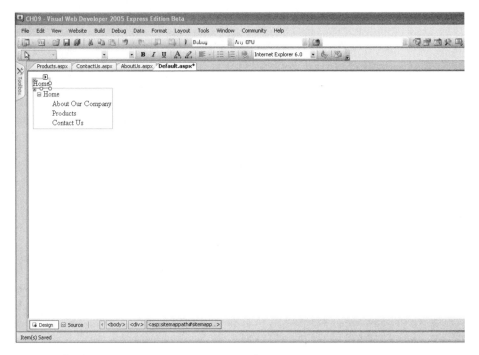

Figure 7-5. *Default.aspx with a Treeview control*

2. Drag a SiteMapDataSource control over from the Toolbox pane located under the Data grouping panel to the Default.aspx page. This will have a default name of SiteMapDataSource1 (Figure 7-6).

3. Right-click on the Treeview control you just added, and choose the Properties option from the menu. From the Properties window, click on the DataSourceID property and choose SiteMapDataSource1, which is the control you just added (Figure 7-7).

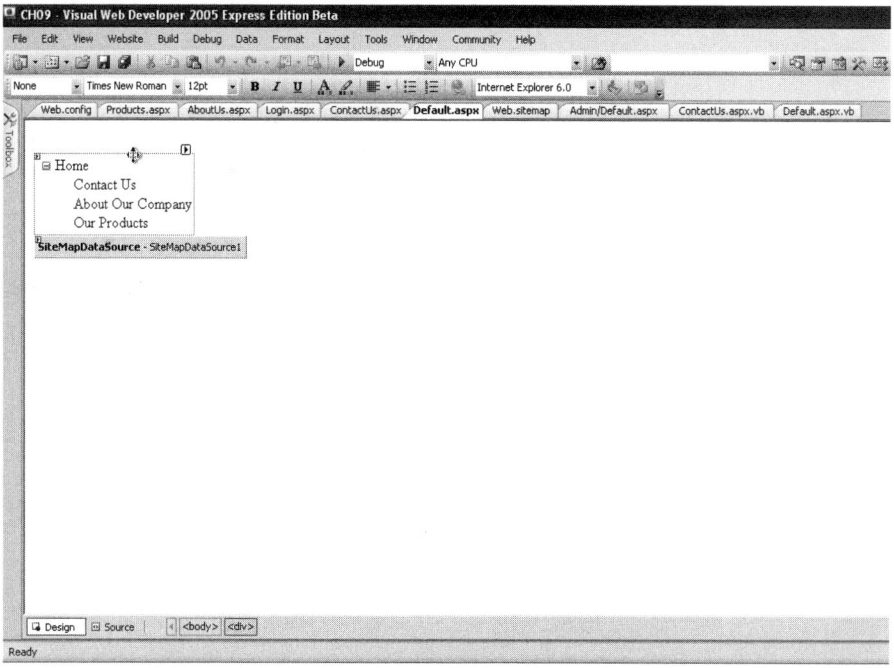

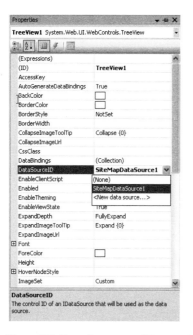

Figure 7-6. *Default.aspx with a Treeview control and SiteMapDataSource*

Figure 7-7. *Treeview control Properties window*

4. You have the Default.aspx page set up; repeat steps 1 through 3 for the remaining Web Forms AboutUs.aspx, ContactUs.aspx, and Products.aspx.

5. You are now ready to build and run the web project and see the Treeview control in action (Figures 7-8 and 7-9). To do so, press the F5 function key or click the green start arrow from the menu. Notice how the SiteMapPath control only displays the current page. When navigating to another page via the Tree-view control, the SiteMapPath control will display the breadcrumb trail of where you have been within the site.

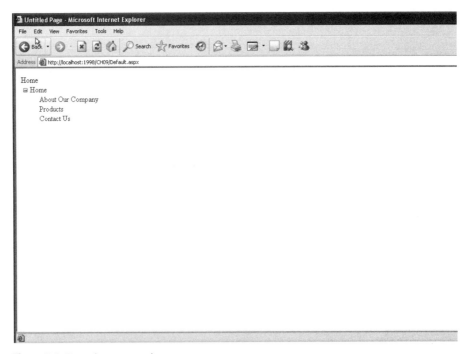

Figure 7-8. *Treeview at runtime*

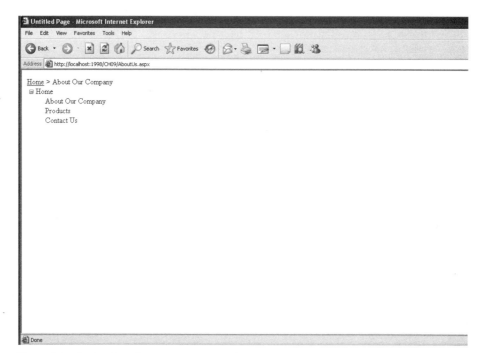

Figure 7-9. *Navigating the Treeview control*

Congratulations! You have now added simple site navigation to your Web project.

Let's move on to demonstrating the last control, Menu, in Exercise 7-4.

Exercise 7-4. Using the Menu Control

The last navigation control is the Menu control. For your code examples, you are simply going to add the Menu control to the web pages. Feel free to use the Menu control in place of the Treeview control. It might make sense to have both of these controls in some web projects and it might not be a good idea in others. The beauty of it is that you are the developer, and it is totally your decision.

1. Drag and drop a Menu control from the Toolbox under the Navigation panel to each of the Web Forms: Default.aspx, AboutUs.aspx, ContactUs.aspx, and Products.aspx. As soon as you place the Menu control on each of the Web Forms, you will notice a small dialog box that gives you some options. The option you are concerned with at this point is the data source. Because you already have a SiteMapDataSource control on each of the pages from the prior examples, simply choose SiteMapDataSource1. After making the data source selection, just click away from the dialog box to apply the setting (Figure 7-10).

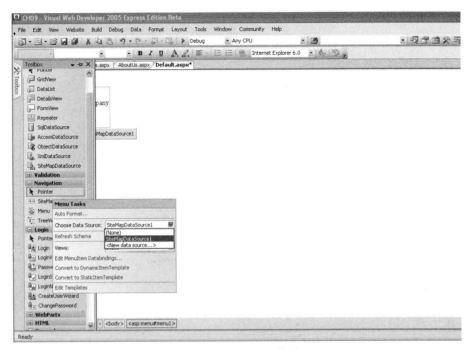

Figure 7-10. *Selecting the SiteMapDataSource control's data source*

2. Now that you have the Menu control on each of your Web Forms, you can build and run the web project to see the Menu control in action. Press the F5 key or click the Start Debugging green arrow. After your new code compiles, you will see the screen shown in Figure 7-11.

   Notice how the unique functionality of the Menu control displays a pop-out region of the other web pages within your web project.

3. Click on the other links in the Menu control to see how it is displayed.

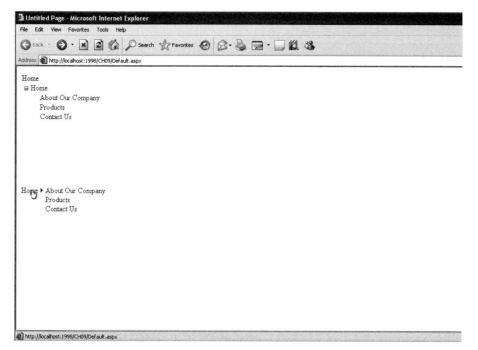

Figure 7-11. *Treeview control during runtime*

This section showed you how to add simple site navigation to your web project with very little code. The next section will show you how to manipulate the site navigation from within the actual code. Let's not waste any time and see how that is achieved.

Programming with the Site Navigation API

Given that .NET Framework 2.0 provides three fully functional controls, there are times when you will have to programmatically access not only the site navigation, but also where the end users last visited and what they are able to navigate to next. This type of functionality is important. Often in web applications, you as the developer want to perform certain actions based on where the end user currently is. Because these actions will be implemented in code, you will have to retrieve this information from the Site Navigation API. This can be implemented by starting with the SiteMap class from the .NET Framework.

This class has a variety of static methods and properties, and the most prominent one is the CurrentNode property, which gives you the ability to retrieve the settings from the web.sitemap file and then return the values from within the code by using built-in features from .NET Framework 2.0. If you are a novice developer or hobbyist unfamiliar with the concept of static classes, refer to the accompanying note.

■**Note**   When referring to a static class and its methods and properties, the class does not need to be instantiated to access the given functionality.

By using this code at any time throughout your web application, SiteMap.CurrentNode will return the name of the current executing page. This is all made possible by the functionality that the .NET Framework provides and being able to read the web.sitemap file that you created earlier.

Along with being able to determine the current page, the Site Navigation API also allows you to determine if there is a previous page or following page. It is useful to determine what the current page is because it gives you—and, of course, the end user—a point of reference on where the code is executing. The pages before and after the current page are referred to as *siblings* to the current page. This can easily be determined by using the SiteMap.CurrentNode. PreviousSibling for any prior pages and SiteMap.CurrentNode.NextSibling for any succeeding pages.

Utilizing this type of feature can be very useful if your application needs to display certain items or text depending on where the end user is within the website. Exercise 7-5 gives you an example with actual code to demonstrate this functionality.

Exercise 7-5. Using Site Navigation Classes

This example displays labels on each web page that will give the end user information on the Url, title, description, and any previous or next siblings. The Url will be the link to which page the user will be directed, the title will provide the text of the hyperlink, and finally the description will provide the user with some additional explanation.

1. Drag and drop a Label web control from the Toolbox to each of the Default.aspx, AboutUs.aspx, Products.aspx, and ContactUs.aspx pages. Right-click on the label of each page, and choose the Properties menu item. Name each of the labels labelNavInfo (Figure 7-12).

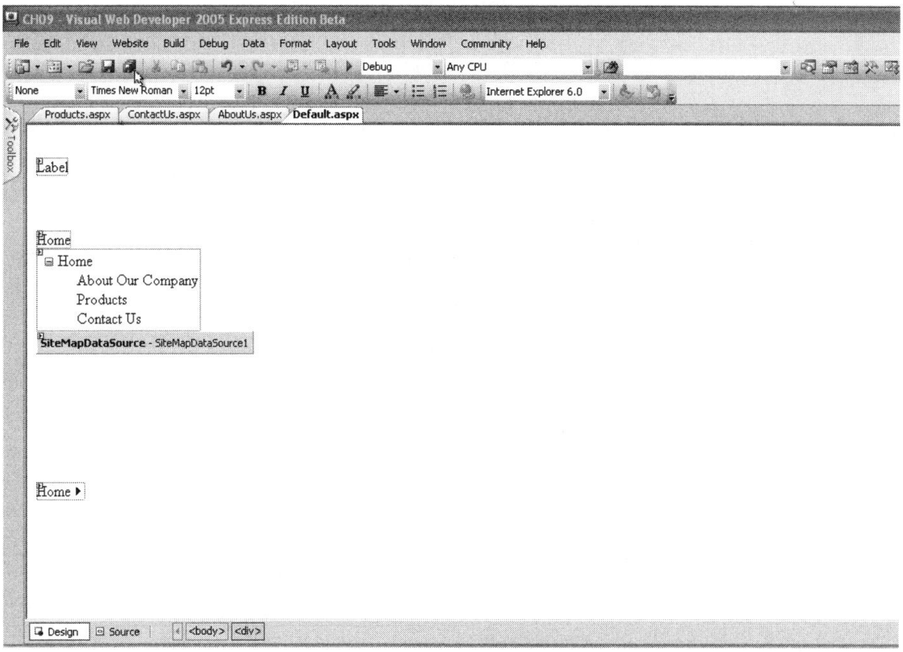

Figure 7-12. *Treeview with SiteMapDataSource control*

2. Double-click on each of the pages to proceed to the code beside the file. The code that will be added is going to first check if the request is a post back, and then if it is not, it will add text to the label to identify the current page. It will then check if there are previous and next siblings, and if they exist, it will determine what they are and add them to the display. Therefore, within the page load event, enter the following code:

```
Protected Sub Page_Load(ByVal sender As Object, ByVal e As System.EventArgs)
    Handles Me.Load
      If (Not Page.IsPostBack) Then
          Dim displaytext As String

          displaytext = "Current Page: " & _
             SiteMap.CurrentNode.ToString & "<br>"

          If Not SiteMap.CurrentNode.NextSibling Is Nothing Then
              displaytext += "Next Page: " & _
                  SiteMap.CurrentNode.NextSibling.ToString & "<br>"
          End If

          If Not SiteMap.CurrentNode.PreviousSibling Is Nothing Then
              displaytext += "Previous Page: " & _
                  SiteMap.CurrentNode.PreviousSibling.ToString & "<br>"
          End If
```

```
                    displaytext += "Url: " & SiteMap.CurrentNode.Url & "<br>"
                    displaytext += "Title: " & SiteMap.CurrentNode.Title & "<br>"
                    displaytext += "Description: " & SiteMap.CurrentNode.Description

                    labelNavInfo.Text = displaytext
            End If
        End Sub
```

To examine the code in further detail, the first method is to determine if the request is a post back event. This is done by the following line:

```
If (Not Page.IsPostBack) Then
```

If the current request is not a post back, the execution of the code will continue on within the page load event. Next a string variable is declared and set to display the current node:

```
Dim displaytext As String
displaytext = "Current Page: " & SiteMap.CurrentNode.ToString & "<br>"
```

Notice that an HTML tag, <br>, is placed in the code. This simply creates a break or skip to the subsequent line after the text is displayed in the browser. The next two statements are conditional statements. They will check if the SiteMap.CurrentNode.NextSibling and SiteMap.CurrentNode.PreviousSibling values are null. If either the NextSibling or PreviousSibling value is in fact null, there will be no additional text added to the string variable for these properties. Also notice the += notation. This will take the string variable and its value and then append the text or values that proceed to the right of the notation.

```
If Not SiteMap.CurrentNode.NextSibling Is Nothing Then
    displaytext += "Next Page: " & _
        SiteMap.CurrentNode.NextSibling.ToString & "<br>"
End If
 If Not SiteMap.CurrentNode.PreviousSibling Is Nothing Then
    displaytext += "Previous Page: " & _
        SiteMap.CurrentNode.PreviousSibling.ToString &  "<br>"
 End If
```

Last, the string variable will append the Url, title, and description values to the display and then set the label, labelNavInfo.Text property, to the string variable.

```
displaytext += "Url: " & SiteMap.CurrentNode.Url & "<br>"
displaytext += "Title: " & SiteMap.CurrentNode.Title & "<br>"
displaytext += "Description: " & SiteMap.CurrentNode.Description
labelNavInfo.Text = displaytext
```

3. After the code is in place on each of the Web Forms—Default.aspx, AboutUs.aspx, Products.aspx, and ContactUs.aspx—you can build and run the web project. Once the project is running, navigate through the different pages to see how you can retrieve the navigation information from code (Figures 7-13 and 7-14).

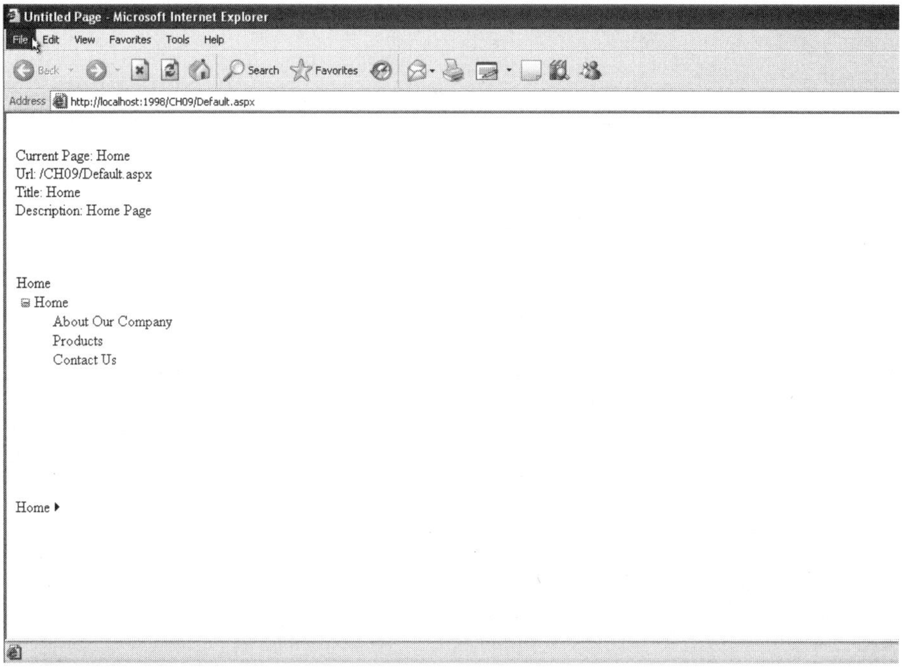

Figure 7-13. *Treeview Control with Node properties displayed*

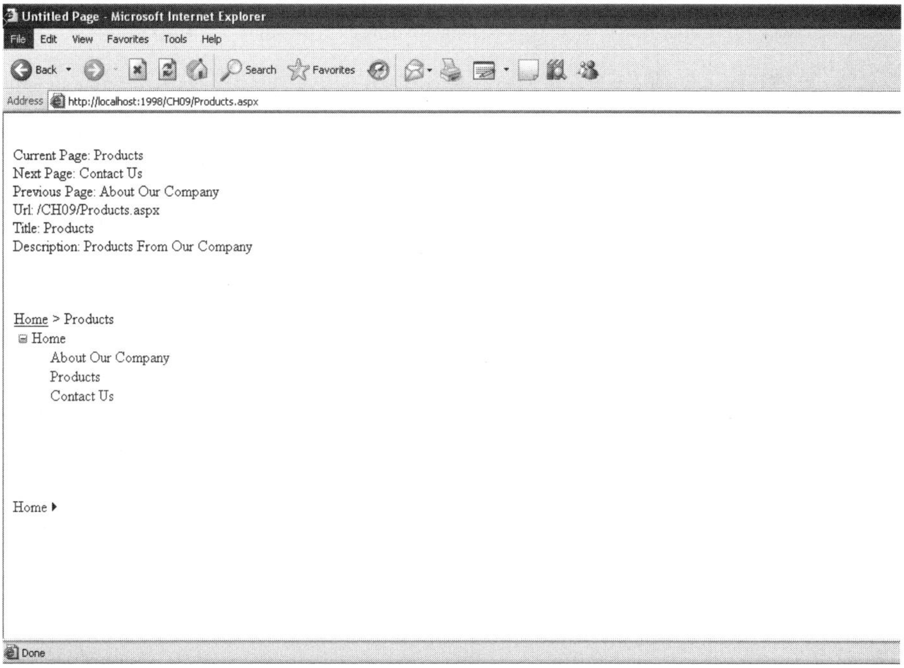

Figure 7-14. *Treeview Control with Extended Node properties displayed*

Once this code is in place on all of the pages, you will be able to see that each web page in your example will give a great deal of information, not only on the current page but on all of the pages within your web project along with the Url, title, and description attributes.

Site Navigation Security

Now that you have programmed with the site navigation class, let's take it one step further. The next step is dealing with navigation security. Many web applications have sections or pages that need to be nonaccessible or invisible to specific users. Typically, these users are classified into roles. Some common roles are "user" and "administrator." The administrator, in this case, will have the ability to view and access certain pages that a standard user will not be able to view or access. The SiteMap class is able to provide this security by filtering out any SiteMapNode instances that are based on authorization rules contained in the web.config. In Exercise 7-6 you will add some additional functionality to your existing code samples.

Exercise 7-6. Implementing Site Navigation Security

This exercise will show how you can optionally show specific pages with the navigation. Because there is a great deal of functionality and controls on your current project, let's create a new web project for the site navigation security.

1. The first order of business is to add the Web Forms to the root of your project. Right-click on the web project and choose Add New Item, and then add a Web Form named Products.aspx.

2. Repeat step 1 to add the following Web Forms: AboutUs.aspx and Login.aspx.

3. You now have all of the main Web Forms in the root of your Web project. These pages will be accessible to all users regardless of their role. Therefore, let's add the restricted Administrators page that only administrators will be able to access. Right-click on the web project, choose Add Folder, and then select Regular Folder. Name this folder Admin. The last step is to add a Web Form to the Admin folder named Management.aspx.

4. Next you need to add a siteMap element to your web.config file. If you have not already added a web.config file to the project, you can do so by right-clicking on the web project, selecting Add New Item, and then selecting the Web Configuration File. Adding this siteMap element will provide the groundwork and blueprint for the navigation being used within your web application. After you add the web.config file, add the following siteMap element:

```
<siteMap defaultProvider="XmlSiteMapProvider" enabled="true">
    <providers>
      <add name="XmlSiteMapProvider"
            description="Demonstrates site navigation security."
            type="System.Web.XmlSiteMapProvider"
            securityTrimmingEnabled="true"
            siteMapFile="web.sitemap"/>
    </providers>
</siteMap>
```

You will notice several attributes within the `siteMap` element. The first attribute being used is the name, `XmlSiteMapProvider`, which is the name of the provider being used—also the default. Next, the description is a quick explanation. The type is the full namespace of the provider being used. The `securityTrimmingEnabled` specifies whether different roles will be able to access specific navigation links. Last, the `siteMapFile` is the name of the web.sitemap file or the blueprint it has been referred to.

5. You need to place a few remaining items within the web.config file to complete your example of security trimming. Place the following code in the web.config for authentication:

```
<authentication mode="Forms">
<forms name=".ASPXAUTH"
            loginUrl="Login.aspx"
            protection="Validation"
            timeout="300"/>
</authentication>
<authorization>
<allow users="*"/>
</authorization>
```

The `<authentication>` element enables the web project with Forms Authentication specifying that the `LoginUrl` is Login.aspx, along with the timeout for the session. The `<authorization>` element has an accompanying `<allow>` element with a user's attribute. The value for the user's attribute is `"*"`, which specifies that all users are allowed to view the root web pages within the web project.

6. We also have to specify that only users in the administrator's role can access the Admin directory. This is accomplished by placing the following in the web.config file:

```
<location path="Admin/Management.aspx">
<system.web>
<authorization>
<allow roles="Administrators"/>
<deny users="*"/>
</authorization>
</system.web>
</location>
```

These elements within the web.config instruct the web application to only allow users who are in the administrator's role to access the Management.aspx page. This is made possible by specifying the following code:

```
<authorization>
        <allow roles="Administrators"/>
        <deny users="*"/>
</authorization>
```

Here you can see that the directory Administrators Only allows those users within the administrator role and prohibits access from all other users as noted with the asterisk, *, within the `deny` attribute.

7. You have addressed all of the individual elements within the web.config. Let's examine the entire file:

```
<?xml version="1.0"?>
<configuration xmlns="http://schemas.microsoft.com/.NetConfiguration/v2.0">
<location path="Admin/Management.aspx">
<system.web>
<authorization>
<allow roles="Administrators"/>
<deny users="*"/>
</authorization>
</system.web>
</location>
<system.web>
<compilation defaultLanguage="C#" debug="true"/>
<authentication mode="Forms">
<forms name=".ASPXAUTH"
              loginUrl="Login.aspx"
              protection="Validation"
              timeout="300"/>
</authentication>
<authorization>
<allow users="*"/>
</authorization>
<roleManager enabled="true">
</roleManager>
<siteMap defaultProvider="XmlSiteMapProvider" enabled="true">
<providers>
<add name="XmlSiteMapProvider"
description="SiteMap provider which reads in .sitemap XML files."
        type="System.Web.XmlSiteMapProvider"
siteMapFile="web.sitemap"
securityTrimmingEnabled="true"/>
</providers>
</siteMap>
</system.web>
</configuration>
```

8. The web.config is complete. You now need to add the web.sitemap file. Right-click on the web project and select Add New Item, and choose the Site Map file from the dialog box. Add the following values to the web.sitemap file:

```
<?xml version="1.0" encoding="utf-8" ?>
<siteMap xmlns="http://schemas.microsoft.com/AspNet/SiteMap-File-1.0" >
<siteMapNode title="Home"
                    url="Default.aspx"
                    description="Home Page">
```

```
<siteMapNode title="Products"
                        url="Products.aspx"
                        description="Products for Sale" />
<siteMapNode title="About Us"
                        url="AboutUs.aspx"
                        description="About the Company"/>
<siteMapNode title="Manage"
                        url="Admin/Management.aspx"
                        description="Management Only" >
</siteMapNode>
</siteMapNode>
</siteMap>
```

Your sitemap is now complete.

Note Steps 9 through 12 cover the Web Site Administration Tool. This topic is discussed in greater detail in Chapter 10.

9. You now need to add users and user roles to the system by using the Web Site Administration Tool. To access this tool, click on the Website menu and choose ASP.NET Configuration. You will see the home page of the Web Site Administration Tool (Figure 7-15).

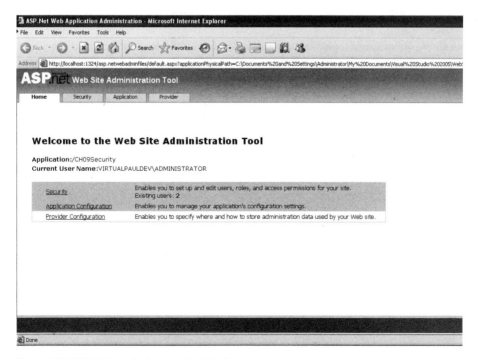

Figure 7-15. *Web Site Administration Tool*

At the home page, click on the Security tab at the top (Figure 7-16). On the Security page you will create your users along with the user roles. Let's first add the user roles. Click on Create or Manage Roles.

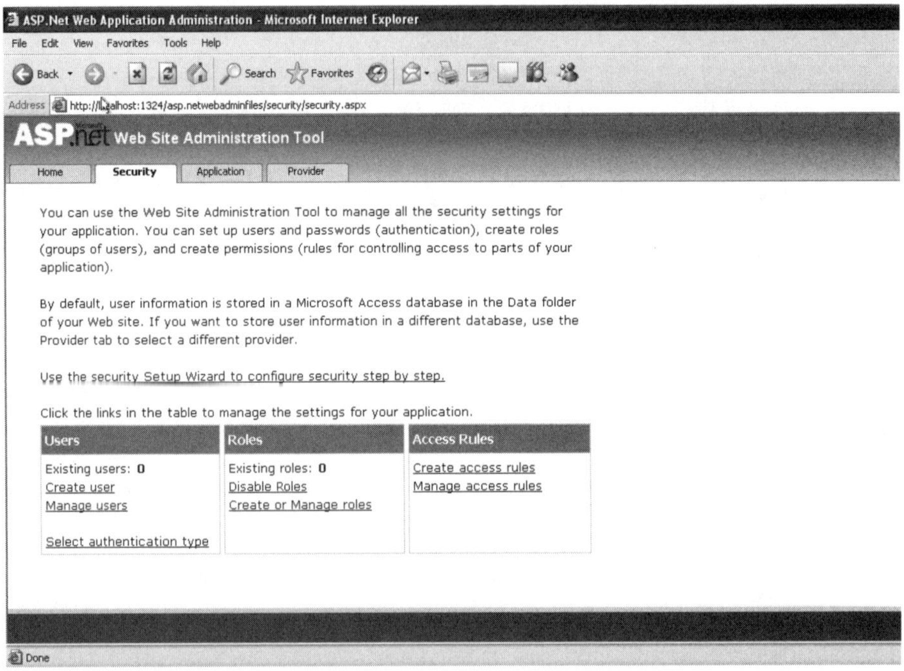

Figure 7-16. *Web Site Administration Tool: Security*

10. We are going to add two roles to our application: Administrators and Guests. Enter these values in the textbox and then click Add Role (Figure 7-17). The two roles have been included within your web application. Click on the Back button located at the lower-right corner to return to the Security page.

11. At the Security page, click on the Create User link located under the Users column. You are going to add a user to the Guests user role. Enter **guestuser** for the username, **Guest!123** for the password, and enter whatever you would like for the email address and security question and answer (Figure 7-18). Be sure to check the Active User option along with the Guests role option. Click Create User and then confirm.

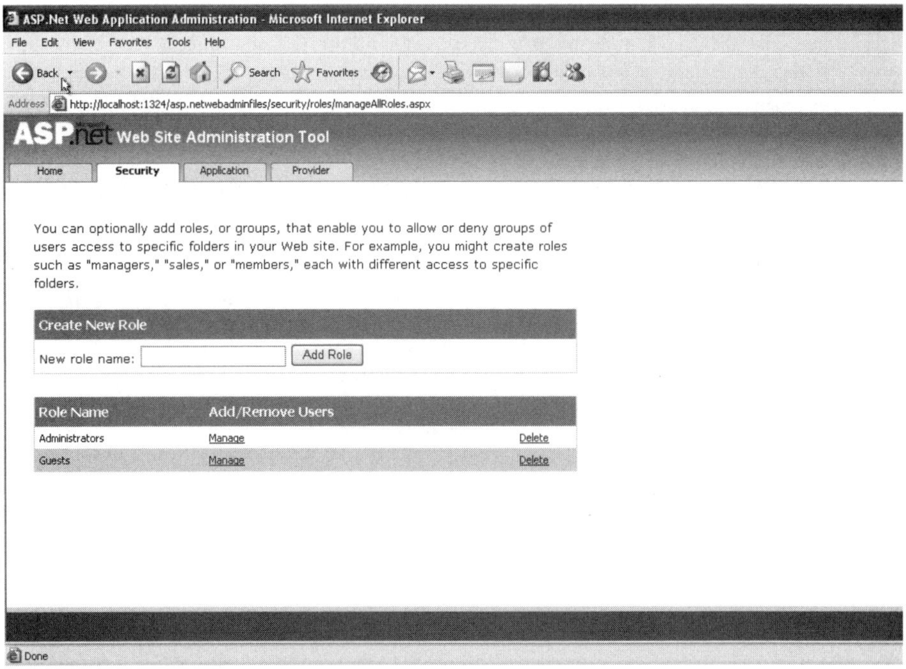

Figure 7-17. *Web Site Administration Tool: User Roles*

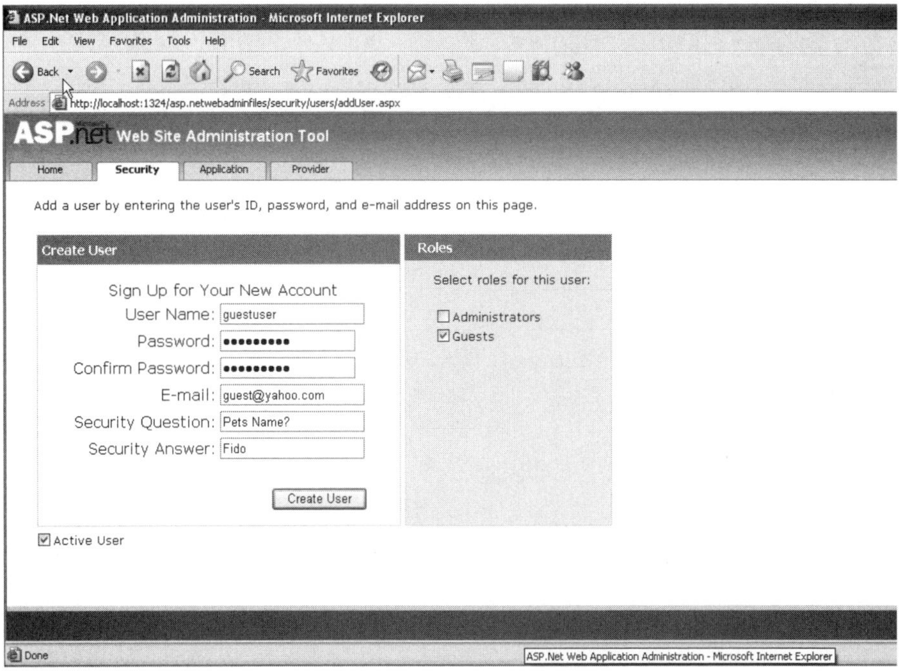

Figure 7-18. *Web Site Administration Tool: Creating a User*

12. Now let's add a user with administrator's privileges. You will repeat step 11 with the following information. Enter the username, **adminuser**, the password **Admin!123**, and whatever you would like for the E-mail and Security Question. Check Active User and Administrators from the Roles. Click Create User and then confirm (Figure 7-19).

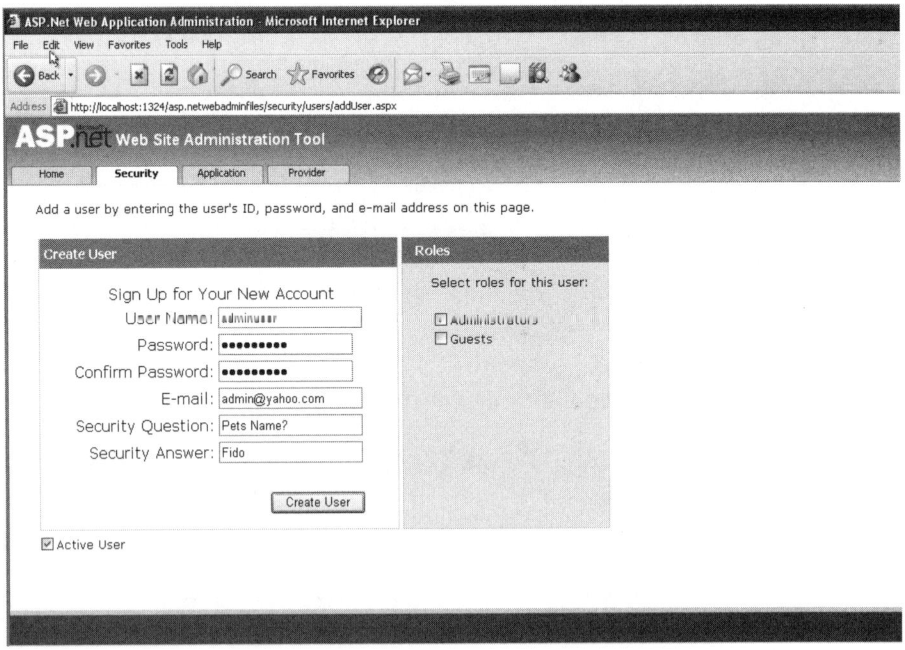

Figure 7-19. *Web Site Administration Tool: Creating a User and Role*

You now have two separate users within your web project with two different roles that will provide different access for each. Close out of the Web Site Administration Tool.

13. Let's move on to the last items to add. Back to the web project, open the Login.aspx page and switch to Design view. From the Toolbox window, drag a Login control to the page. To add some color, you can select the Auto Format menu item by right-clicking on the Login control (Figure 7-20). After the control is on the page, right-click on the Login control and choose Properties. Within the Properties, enter **~/Default.aspx** for the `DestinationPageUrl`. This will redirect users to the Default.aspx page after logging in successfully.

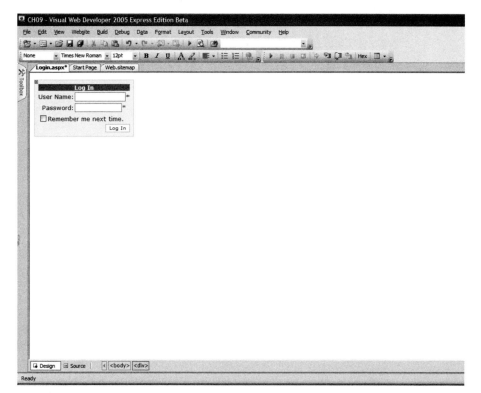

Figure 7-20. *User Login control*

14. You are almost ready to see the security features in action, after just a few more additions. Now for each of the following, drag a Menu, SiteMapDataSource, and Login Status control from the Toolbox. Set the DataSourceIDs for each of the Menu controls to SiteMapDataSource1 (Figure 7-21).

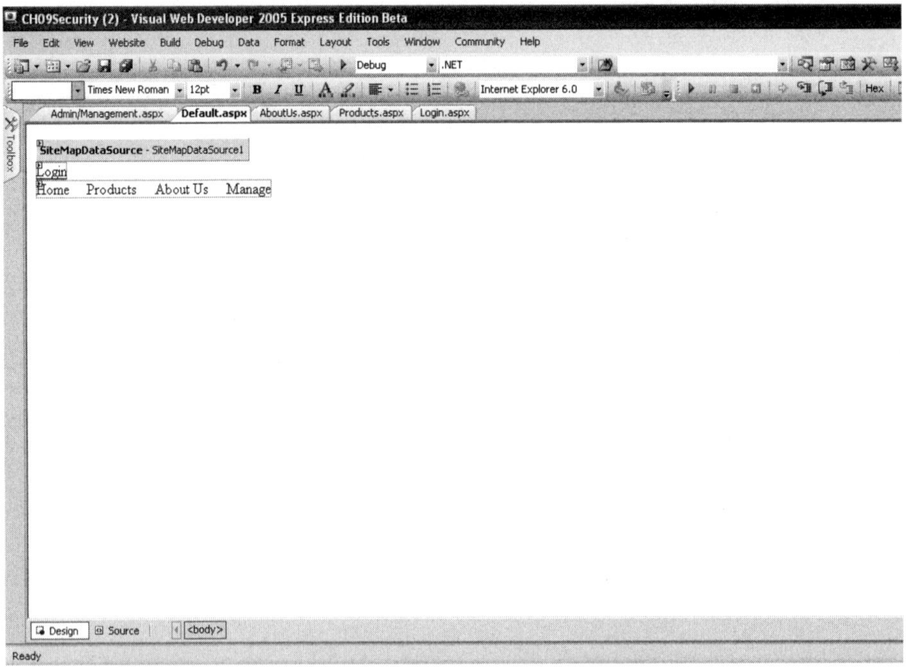

Figure 7-21. *Menu Control*

15. Click on the Login.aspx page and run the project. You will arrive at the Login.aspx page. Let's first see the Guests user access. Log in with the guestuser username with the password **Guest!123**. The Admin directory is not accessible because the Guests user role does not have sufficient permissions to view it. Remember, the attributes set in the web.config file will ensure this, as shown in Figure 7-22.

```
<authorization>
        <allow roles="Administrators"/>
        <deny users="*"/>
</authorization>
```

16. Now let's test the administrator's access. Click on the Logout link to log in under the Administrator account. Remember, the Administrator account's username is adminuser and the password is Admin!123. After logging in as the administrator, notice that you are now able to view the Admin directory with the Manage link (Figure 7-23).

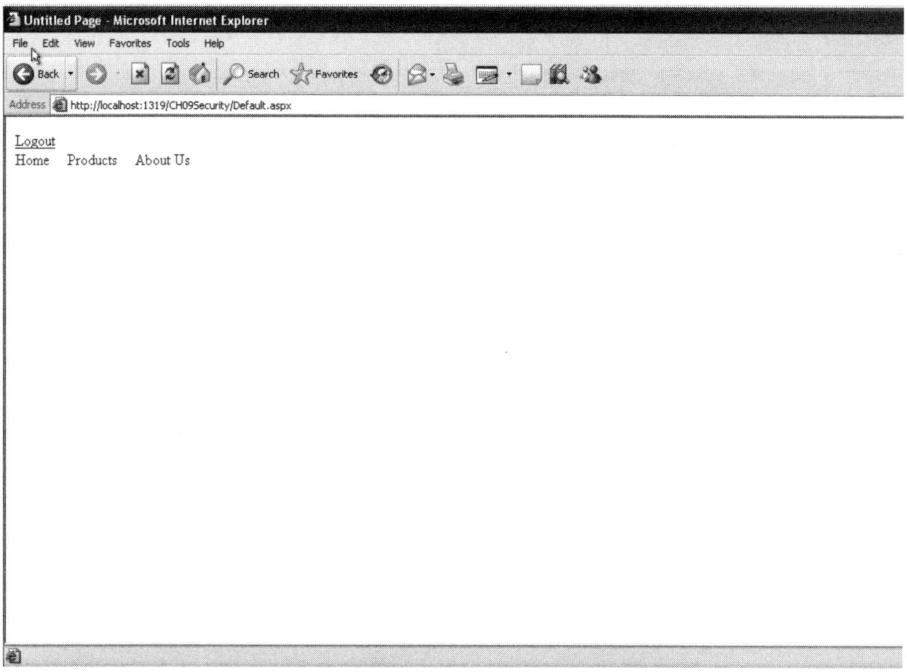

Figure 7-22. *Viewing a guest's navigation*

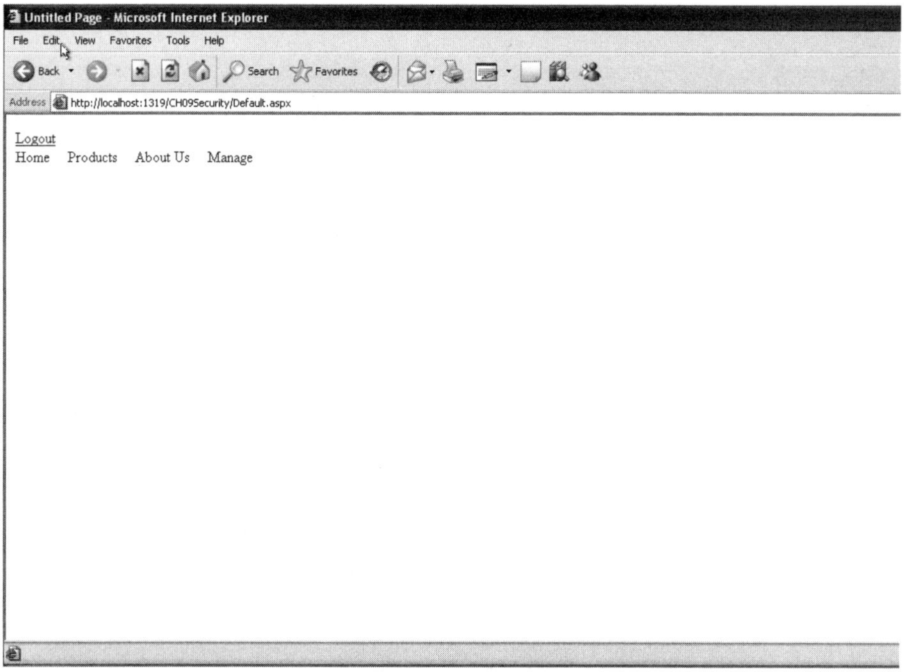

Figure 7-23. *Viewing the administrator's navigation*

17. Click on the Manage link to test the access to the restricted page (Figure 7-24).

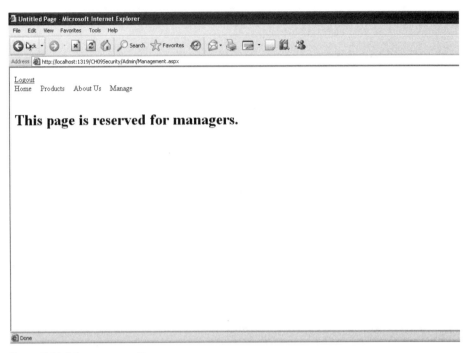

Figure 7-24. *Management Page*

With the completion of this exercise, you have combined some previous exercises using the navigation controls and added security to the navigation.

Modifying Provider Data Returned

This chapter has examined many different displays of website hierarchies. However, all the ones to this point have been static content. In other words, each of the pages has had a unique name and has not dealt with any query string parameters. Many professional web applications typically have a single page to display information, but that information will depend on what query string is passed to it. For example, it might be an ID number for a customer. To demonstrate, an example of a query string is similar to the following:

```
Invoices.aspx?InvoiceID=100
```

The preceding query string is InvoiceID, which is set to 100. Query strings are separated by a question mark: ?. When the Invoices.aspx Web Form is processed, the code within that page can retrieve the value of the query string by using the next code segment, which will return a string value of what the query string is:

```
Request.Querystring("InvoiceID")
```

The current setup of the web.sitemap specifies that each URL needs to be unique. So, looking ahead, this will often present a problem for developers dealing with a more complex web application. We are in luck! The SiteMap.SiteMapResolve event is provided especially for this type of scenario. This event tackles the problem in that it allows nodes to be added to the site map during runtime. This can be useful when your application has dynamic links that are generated from the query strings mentioned earlier.

Because nodes from the XmlSiteMapProvider are read-only, the SiteMapNode needs to be cloned by calling the Clone method and passing true. This will result in a writable copy of the SiteMapNode, which you can then manipulate according to the query strings in question. Let's move on and look at some code.

Within your code, you are going to need to implement a function that will clone a SiteMapNode to alter it and return it. Having this functionality encapsulated within a function will be a wise choice, so that it is contained in one area and the code can simply call this function to make a copy and return it. Next try Exercise 7-7.

Exercise 7-7. Using the SiteMap.SiteMapResolve Event

This exercise simulates an invoice tracking system. The simulation will have site navigation in the form of a SiteMapPath control. Because all the invoices are going to be similar in what they display except for the company name, items, and the price of the invoice, there will be only one page to display all invoices: Invoices.aspx.

1. Start by adding two Web Forms to your web project: Default.aspx and Invoices.aspx. The Default.aspx page will automatically be added when creating the new project.

2. For the Default.aspx page, add a SiteMapDataSource control and a SiteMapPath control. In addition to these controls, you are going to add five hyperlinks that will simulate five different invoices in your system. The HTML code appears next, where a series of hyperlinks will be set in which each link has a query string with a different value.

■**Note** For the purpose of the example in Exercise 7-7, you are going to hard-code the invoice links with their respective query strings attached. In a production or real-world application, these links would be rendered from a database because the quantity of invoices will always be dynamic along with their unique ID number.

```
<asp:HyperLink ID="HyperLink1" runat="server"
                    NavigateUrl="~/Invoices.aspx?InvoiceID=100">
                    Invoice ID: 100</asp:HyperLink><br />
    <br />
    <asp:HyperLink ID="HyperLink2" runat="server"
                    NavigateUrl="~/Invoices.aspx?InvoiceID=101">
                    Invoice ID: 101</asp:HyperLink><br />
    <br />
    <asp:HyperLink ID="HyperLink3" runat="server"
                    NavigateUrl="~/Invoices.aspx?InvoiceID=102">
                    Invoice ID: 102</asp:HyperLink><br />
    <br />
    <asp:HyperLink ID="HyperLink4" runat="server"
                    NavigateUrl="~/Invoices.aspx?InvoiceID=103">
                    Invoice ID: 103</asp:HyperLink><br />
    <br />
    <asp:HyperLink ID="HyperLink5" runat="server"
                    NavigateUrl="~/Invoices.aspx?InvoiceID=104">
                    Invoice ID: 104</asp:HyperLink>
```

3. Now let's address the Invoices.aspx Web Form. Again, as in step 2, add a SiteMapDataSource control and a SiteMapPath control to the Web Form. This is going to be the page that displays every invoice in the tracking system. Based on the invoice ID, different information will be displayed in the invoice fields (Figure 7-25).

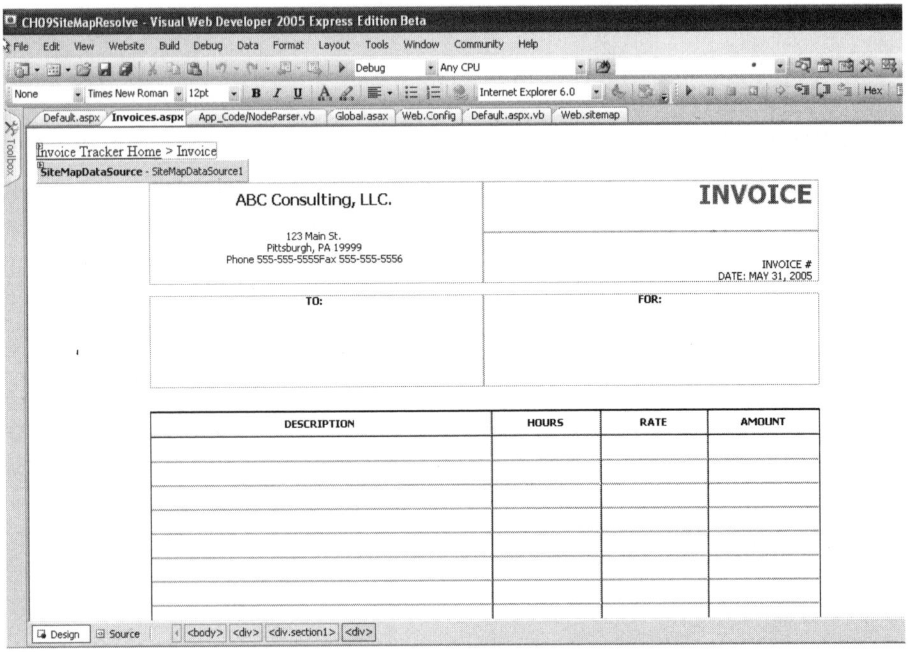

Figure 7-25. *Invoice*

■**Note** Again for the purposes of this demonstration, an invoice style template has been added for display only. Feel free to make your own style and format for an invoice. You can use Microsoft Word or another application that provides the basic HTML in which tables are arranged to resemble a common invoice.

4. Only a few more steps are needed until you are ready to test. Next, add a web.sitemap file to the web project and add the following nodes:

```
<?xml version="1.0" encoding="utf-8" ?>
<siteMap>
<siteMapNode title="Invoice Tracker Home"
                    description="Home Page"
                    url="default.aspx">
<siteMapNode title="Invoice" description="Invoice"
url="Invoices.aspx">
</siteMapNode>
</siteMapNode>
</siteMap>
```

5. Now let's proceed to the actual code that will perform the altering of the nodes. Right-click on the web project and choose Add Folder and then the App_Code folder. Right-click on the App_Code folder and choose Add New Item. Add a class file to the folder and name it NodeParser.vb. Last, add the following code to the class file, which will parse the query string and its value:

```
Imports System
Imports System.Web
Public Class NodeParser
    Public Shared Function ParseQuerystrings
            (ByVal sender As Object, ByVal e As SiteMapResolveEventArgs)
                As SiteMapNode
        'Make a copy of the current SiteMapNode so that
        'we can alter it in memory.
        Dim nodeClone As SiteMapNode = SiteMap.CurrentNode.Clone(True)
        Dim tempNode As SiteMapNode = nodeClone
        'Check if there is an invoiceID value in the
        'query string and that it is not null.
        Dim invoiceID As String = Nothing
        Dim invoiceIDUrlEncoded As String = Nothing
        If Not String.IsNullOrEmpty &_
           (e.Context.Request.QueryString("InvoiceID")) Then
            invoiceID = e.Context.Server.HtmlEncode & _
                (e.Context.Request.QueryString("InvoiceID"))
            invoiceIDUrlEncoded = e.Context.Server.UrlEncode & _
                (e.Context.Request.QueryString("InvoiceID"))
        End If
```

```
            If Not String.IsNullOrEmpty & _
                (e.Context.Request.QueryString("InvoiceID")) Then
                Dim ID As String = _
                    e.Context.Server.HtmlEncode & _
                        (e.Context.Request.QueryString("InvoiceID"))
                Dim IDUrlEncoded As String = _
                    e.Context.Server.UrlEncode & _
                        (e.Context.Request.QueryString("InvoiceID"))
                Dim NewUrl As String = tempNode.Url + "?InvoiceID=" + IDUrlEncoded
                Dim NewTitle As String = tempNode.Title + ": " + ID
                tempNode.Url = NewUrl
                tempNode.Title = NewTitle
        tempNode = tempNode.ParentNode
            End If
            'Return the node that has been cloned and altered.
            Return nodeClone
    End Function
    End Class
```

6. The code just added needs to be called from another web page, most likely within the web project. Therefore, add a Global.asax file to the web project. Within the Global.asax, you are going to add a handler to the preceding code in the Application_Start subroutine. Add the following code to that routine:

```
Sub Application_Start(ByVal sender As Object, ByVal e As EventArgs)
        ' Code that runs on application startup
        AddHandler SiteMap.Provider.SiteMapResolve, & _
            AddressOf NodeParser.ParseQuerystrings
End Sub
```

7. You are finally able to test the functionality (Figure 7-26). Press the F5 key to build and run the web application. After the application builds, the Default.aspx page will be displayed.

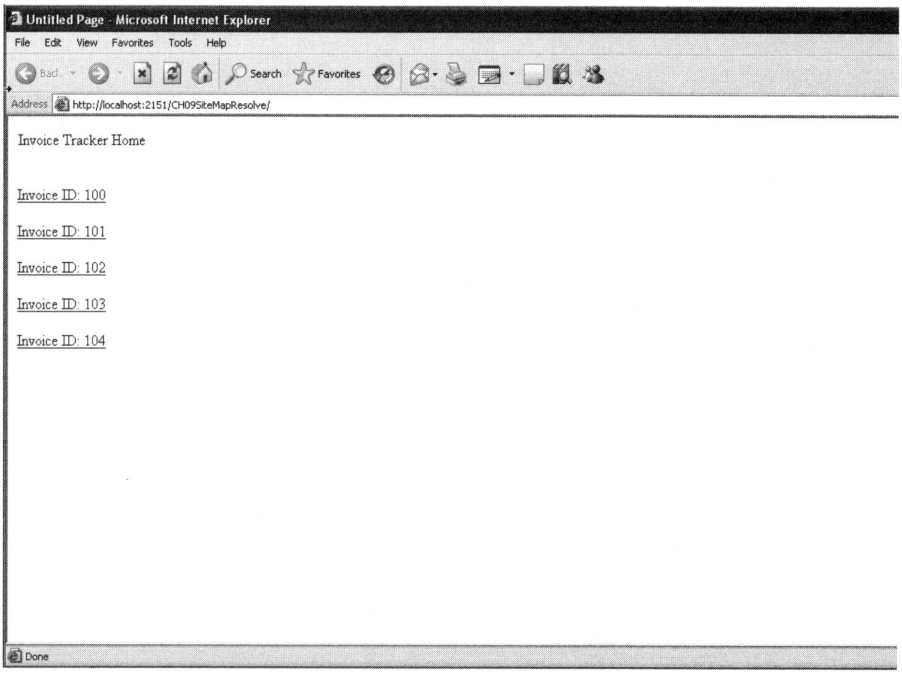

Figure 7-26. *List of invoices*

Click on the different Invoice ID links, and notice on the Invoices.aspx pages that the SiteMapPath control displays the dynamic Invoice ID number (Figure 7-27).

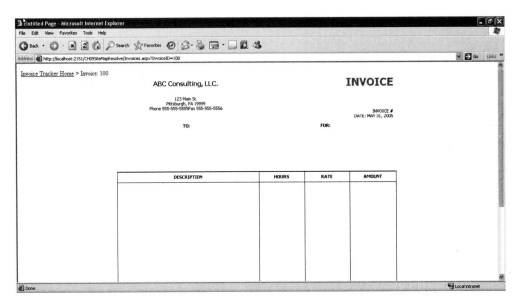

Figure 7-27. *Viewing Invoice 100*

You are finished now with the navigation exercises. This was a simple example in which the framework allowed you to handle dynamic web pages dealing with query strings.

Summary

This chapter on website navigation covered mostly static content sites with static pages, but you also learned how to handle situations where pages will accept query strings providing dynamic content. Implementing this functionality was possible using very little code. The .NET Framework provides these tools for navigation, helping you supply professional and concise navigation in all of your web applications.

CHAPTER 8

■ ■ ■

Localization

With the nature and intent of websites to be reachable all around the world, it is inevitable that many users will not speak the same language and/or come from the same culture as the person or team developing the website. Consequently, all developers have an additional challenge when designing websites.

To start our discussion, you first should be familiar with some specific terminology. When the term *globalization* is used within the context of websites and web design, it is referring to the overall planning and design, including all resources available so that modifications can easily be made to a website to accommodate different cultures and languages. The term *localization* is the actual translation and transformation of content to the user's local language and culture.

What exactly changes in your website when you need to localize the information? The following list highlights these tasks:

- *Date formatting*: Date formats vary extensively across cultures and languages. In the United States, for example, 6/5/2005 means June 6, 2005. However, the same date abbreviation, 6/5/2005, in the United Kingdom means May 6, 2005.

- *Text display*: Most web pages contain a great deal of text, static or dynamic. In either case, the translation of this text needs to be addressed for targeting different languages and cultures.

- *Currency*: Different cultures and countries have different currencies. So you need to account for different currency symbols. For instance, the symbol for the American dollar is $ and for the British pound is £.

- *Text/page direction*: Most languages read left to right. However, some languages, Arabic for instance, read right to left. You will need to address this type of situation.

We know how important it is to have web applications globalized, and we must accept the extra challenge of localizing the content for our users. Luckily, the .NET Framework provides an extensive toolset to minimize the effort of this additional challenge.

We will cover the following topics in this chapter:

- How to set the preferred language

- How to use auto browser detection

- How to change the language programmatically

Your Preferred Language

The first order of business is to gain an understanding of the current language setting for your browser. This setting will determine how the content you view on websites will be handled with regard to language and cultural differences.

■**Note** We focus here on the Internet Explorer browser. However, if you prefer using another browser, consult the browser's Help files and documentation on setting the preferred language.

To gain the fullest understanding, let's examine how Windows enables you to have content on your computer that is within your own culture and language, and also provides the ability for computers to have worldwide access.

Within Internet Explorer, when you first purchase your computer or when you install Windows for the first time, the specific language version of your copy of Windows automatically sets this language as your browser's default and preferred language. With this said, Windows offers a number of different languages to which you can switch or make the default language.

Refer to Table 8-1 to see a list of the languages used in various cultures that you can choose from.

Table 8-1. *Languages and Cultures*

Language/Culture	Description
en-us	The English language used in the United States
en-gb	The English language used in Great Britain or the United Kingdom
de-ch	The German language used in Switzerland
fr-ca	The French language used in Canada
de	The German language used in Germany

The descriptions in Table 8-1 also apply to different formatting that is used within the listed language and culture. With this background information in mind, let's look at how you can modify these settings in Exercise 8-1.

Exercise 8-1. Modifying Your Preferred Browser Language

1. Click on the Windows Start button, then Control Panel, and select Internet Options. You see the dialog box window in Figure 8-1.

Figure 8-1. *Internet Properties window*

2. From this dialog box, click on the Languages button located near the bottom. You can see in Figure 8-2 that our preferred language is set to English (United States), or en-us.

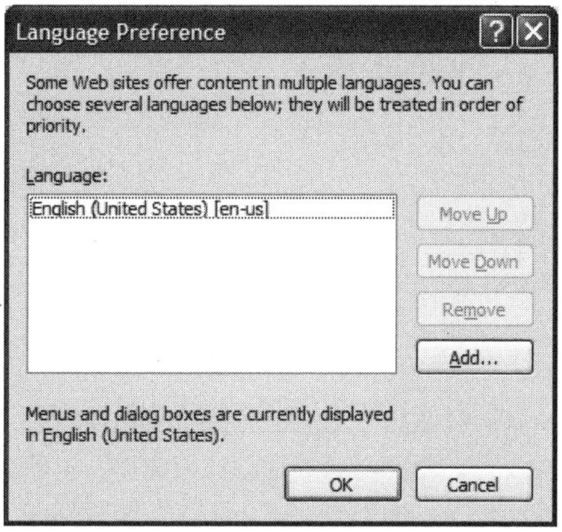

Figure 8-2. *Language Preference window*

3. For the purposes of this chapter, we are going to add a few other languages to our preference so you can change them in the examples later in the chapter. It's very easy to do. Click on the Add button and you are presented with the Add Language dialog box window shown in Figure 8-3.

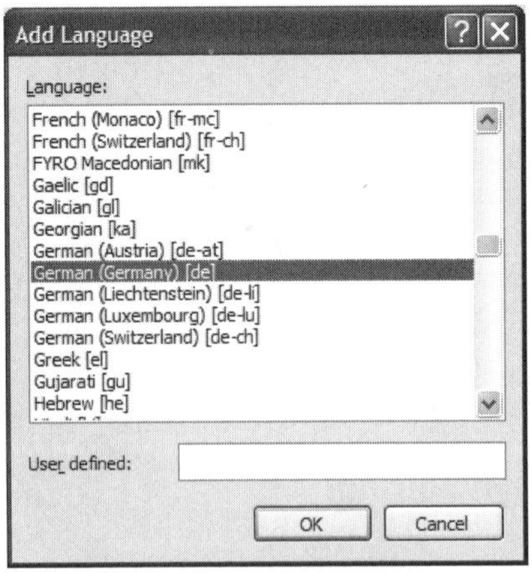

Figure 8-3. *Add Language window*

4. From the extensive list of different languages shown in Figure 8-3, we are going to select German (Germany) [de] and French (France) [fr] for our example. Feel free to choose whichever language you like or as many as you like. When you are finished, click the OK button as shown in Figure 8-4.

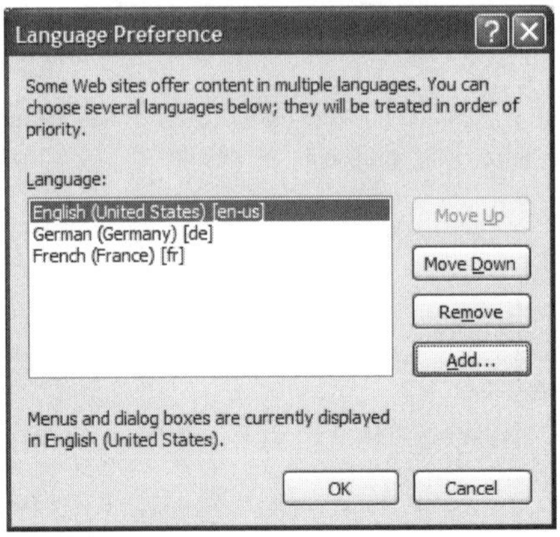

Figure 8-4. *Language Preference window showing multiple languages and cultures*

5. Back at the Language Preference dialog box, English is still set to our preferred language. If we want to change this, we can do this easily by simply selecting another language from the list and clicking the Move Up or Move Down buttons until the language we want to select is in the topmost position. The language at the very top of the list is the browser's primary language preference. When you are finished with your selection, click OK on the Language Preference window and also on the Internet Properties window.

Now that you know how to change your browser's preferred language setting as described in step 5, later in the chapter when you want to test your examples, you can refer back to this exercise to change the preferred language. Just remember to refresh your browser after making any language setting changes to see the updated language localized.

Using Automatic Browser Detection

One of the tools provided by the .NET Framework for localization is a simple method in which you can instruct the browser to auto-detect the preferred language set in the user's browser. You can implement this very easily by adding essentially one word to your code in each page or in one location if you want the project to have this behavior projectwide. Let's move on to enabling your Web Forms and web pages to auto-detect the language.

For each Web Form or .aspx page where you want to auto-detect the language setting of the user, you must specify a page declarative. Look at the following piece of code:

```
<%@ Page Culture="auto" %>
```

Here within the Page Declaration tags, we have enabled the page to auto-detect the language by specifying `Culture="auto"`.

With this included in the web page, the page automatically checks the preferred language in the user's browser, and if the language specified is a match, the ASP.NET running thread sets the CurrentCulture to that specified culture. This means that all formatting, text, and currency, if set up properly, will be localized to that language and culture. This functionality occurs very early in the ASP.NET page life cycle.

If your entire web application calls for auto detection, instead of placing this page directive in each page of the application, you can specify it within the web.config, and it will be applied throughout. The following element is placed in the web.config:

```
<system.web>
<globalization culture="auto" uiCulture="auto">
</system.web>
```

To give you some practice, let's move on to Exercise 8-2, where you will test the auto-detection of the preferred language within your web project.

Exercise 8-2. Language Auto-Detection

In this exercise, you are going to format a date string. Without changing any code, the format of the date will reflect whatever the preferred language is set to for the browser.

1. Create a new web project, and after the project loads, click on the Source tab of the Default.aspx page that was included in the project. At the top of the page will be the following page declaratives:

```
<%@ Page Language="VB" AutoEventWireup="false" CodeFile="Default.aspx.vb"
        Inherits="_Default" %>
```

You are going to add the following page declarative:

```
Culture="auto"
```

The complete page declarative will look like this:

```
<%@ Page Culture="auto" Language="VB" AutoEventWireup="false"
        CodeFile="Default.aspx.vb" Inherits="_Default" %>
```

The Default.aspx page is all set up for the page to auto-detect the preferred language of the user's browser.

2. Now let's add the actual code. Double-click on the Design view of the Default.aspx page. Add the following code to the Page_Load method:

```
Response.Write("Today is: " & DateTime.Now.ToLongDateString())
```

This code will write the current date to the browser in a long date string format.

3. First let's make sure the default language is set to English, or en-US. Refer to the earlier example on how to change the default language. You might not have to change your setting at all. Once the language is set, you are ready to test your example.

4. Build and run the web project. Figure 8-5 shows the localization of the current date on the web page.

Figure 8-5. *English localization of current date*

You will notice that a caption is written to the browser displaying the current date with an English format that is used in the United States. Let's test another language.

5. Click on the Tools menu in the Internet Explorer browser of your running web application. Choose Internet Options and you will be presented with the Internet Options dialog box window. From there click on the Language button, and if you don't have another language in the list, add one from the language list. For this example; we are going to choose German (Germany) [de]. The last step is to ensure that the German selection is at the top of the list. Upon doing so, click OK on the language window and OK on the Internet Options window. Finally, click the Refresh button on the browser. In Figure 8-6 you will see the same code for displaying the date in a German format.

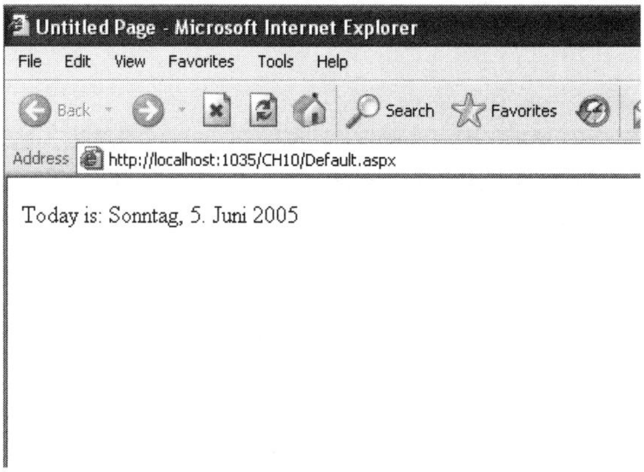

Figure 8-6. *German localization of current date*

6. Practice and experiment changing your preferred languages for your browser. This will simulate what other users will see in other countries and other cultures.

This exercise showed you how without changing any code and by using the auto page declarative, the format of the date will change according to the language preference set in the browser.

Resource Expressions

Many times you will need to have more control over what your web pages display for different languages and cultures that the auto detect does not provide. More control will come in the form of using resource files, which are XML-based files usually with an extension of .resx when used with ASP.NET 2.0 that contain objects and strings within the XML tags. In regard to our focus on localization and globalization in this chapter, they contain the different language information. The two main types of resource files are explicit and implicit. Let's look at their similarities and differences.

- *Explicit*: Provides more control on how the properties are set for controls within Web Forms. The expression is evaluated by pointing to a specific resource file. Once the expression is located in the resource file, it is evaluated and the value is set to the property. The ability to have more control over how the properties will be set for controls is helpful, in that you need to specify the properties and the scenario is not an all-or-nothing proposition, thus allowing you to pick and choose what needs to be set. This type of localization is best used for large bodies of text or for implementing custom messages.

- *Implicit*: Implicit localization is a more general type of formatting. It is used for controls, but not all properties need to be identified to be localized. This differs from the explicit type because the properties specified are read automatically from the resource file.

We'll demonstrate implicit localization in Exercise 8-3 and explicit localization in Exercise 8-4.

Exercise 8-3. Implicit Localization

This implicit example is simple and to the point so it just demonstrates implicit localization for a control. Again, all controls with the specified properties on the page will be automatically translated by reading the resource file.

1. Create a new web project. After the project loads within the Integrated Development Environment (IDE), right-click the web project and choose Add Folder and select the App_LocalResources folder.

2. Right-click on the web project again, select Add New Item from the menu, and select Assembly Resource File. Change the name to Default.aspx.resx. Click OK.

3. Proceed to double-click on the Default.aspx.resx file in the Solution Explorer, and you will see the Resource Editor as shown in Figure 8-7.

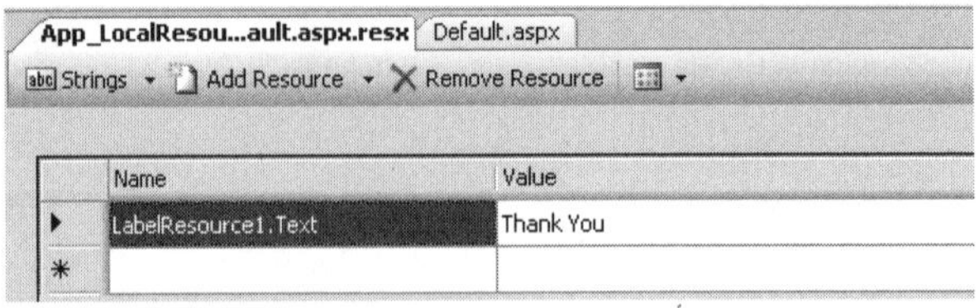

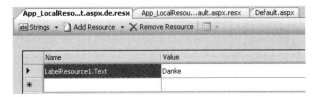

Figure 8-7. *Resource Editor*

Enter **LabelResource1.Text** under the Name column and **Thank You** under the Value column. When finished, save the file.

4. Right-click on the Default.aspx.resx file and choose Copy. Right-click on the App_LocalResources folder and choose Paste. Rename the pasted file to Default.aspx.de.resx. We chose to use German for this file, which is why it is named Default.aspx.de.resx. The naming convention is *filename.aspx.culturecode.resx*.

5. Double-click on the newly created file, Default.aspx.de.resx, so you can see the Resource Editor. When the Resource Editor is opened, change the text **Thank You** to the German translation **Danke** under the Value column as shown in Figure 8-8. When you are finished, save and close the file.

Figure 8-8. *Using the Resource Editor*

■Tip Google provides a great tool that can translate words and phrases, which you can find at
`http://www.google.com/language_tools`.

6. Now it's time to address the actual web page itself. Double-click on the Default.aspx page in the Solution Explorer. Click on the Design view and drag a Label control to the page from the Toolbox.

7. Switch back to the Source view of the Default.aspx page and you will now see the label in HTML format.

```
<asp:Label ID="Label1" runat="server" Text="Label"></asp:Label>
```

8. You're not finished with the Label control, however. You need to add an additional property. Add the following property to the Label control:

```
meta:resourcekey="LabelResource1"
```

Here's the complete code for the Label control:

```
<asp:Label ID="Label1" runat="server" Text="Label"
        meta:resourcekey="LabelResource1"></asp:Label>
```

The Label control is now complete for our example. Let's finish the final step.

9. The final step is to add the page declaratives to the Default.aspx. Click on the Source tab on the Default.aspx and add `Culture="auto"` and `UICulture="auto"` so the entire page declaration resembles the following:

```
<%@ Page Culture="auto" UICulture="auto" Language="VB"
        AutoEventWireup="false" CodeFile="Default.aspx.vb"
        Inherits="_Default" %>
```

10. You can now build and run the web project. When the page is displayed, and assuming that you set the preferred language in your browser back to English; the page will simply display the words "Thank You" (Figure 8-9).

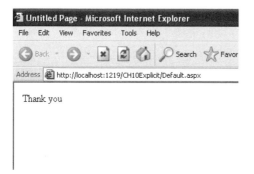

Figure 8-9. *Implicit localization: English*

11. Change the default preferred language for the browser to German (Germany) [de]. Click OK on the Language Preference window and then again on the Internet Properties window. Click the Refresh button on the browser and you will see the German equivalent: "Danke" (Figure 8-10).

Figure 8-10. *Implicit localization: German*

Exercise 8-4. Explicit Localization

We will keep our example using explicit localization simple yet very descriptive and to the point. Let's begin. Our goal for this exercise is to demonstrate how the Label control on the page will have its text property set to read from the resource file, hence the term *explicit*.

1. Create a new web project. After the project loads within the IDE, right-click the web project, choose Add New Item, and select Assembly Resource File. Keep the default name: Resource.resx. You will then be prompted with the message box shown in Figure 8-11.

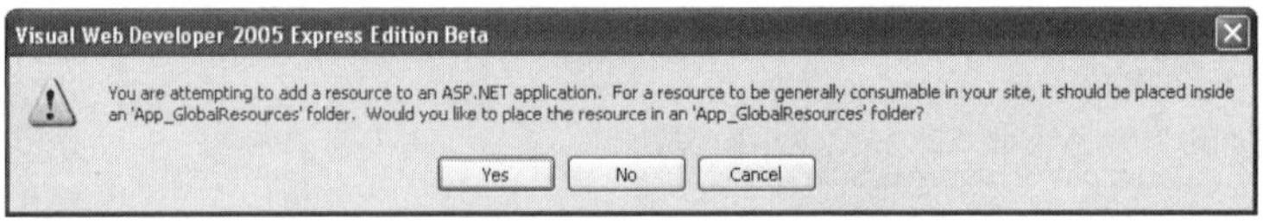

Figure 8-11. *Message box prompt*

This message simply is informing you that for resource files to be accessible within the web project, they should be placed in the App_GlobalResources folder and is asking you if the folder should be created. Click Yes, which will create the App_GlobalResources folder and place the newly created Resource.resx file in it.

2. Double-click on the Resource.resx file and you will see the Resource Editor. Under the Name column, type **Message**, and for the Value column type **Thank You** (as shown in Figure 8-12). Save the file.

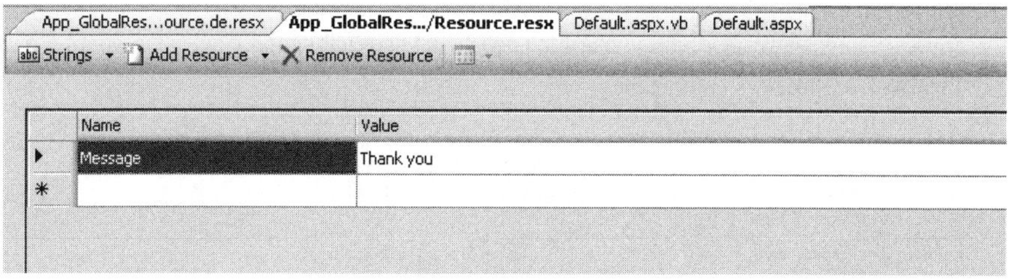

Figure 8-12. *Thank You in the Resource Editor*

3. Right-click on the Resource.resx file and choose Copy, and then right-click the App_GlobalResources folder and choose Paste. This will copy the Resource.resx file under the App_GlobalResources folder named Copy of Resource.resx. Right-click on this file, choose Rename, and rename the file Resource.de.resx. This is going to be the German-based language resource file.

4. Double-click on the Resource.de.resx file, and change the text "Thank you" under the Value column to "Danke," the German translation (Figure 8-13).

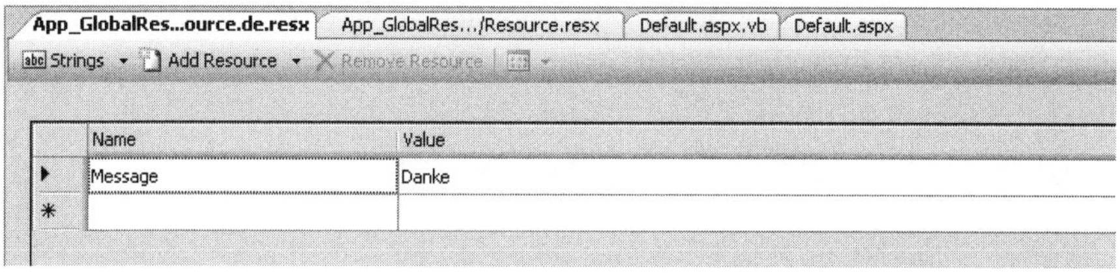

Figure 8-13. *Danke in the Resource Editor*

Save the file.

5. You now have the resource files all set for your example. Let's look at the `Default.aspx` page. Drag a Label control to the `Default.aspx` page. Click on the Source tab and add the following to the `Text` property:

```
Text="<%$ Resources:Resource, Message %>"
```

Therefore, the entire label tag will look like this:

```
<asp:Label ID="Label1" Runat="server" Text="
<%$ Resources:Resource, Message %>">
        </asp:Label>
```

6. The last step is to add the page declaratives to the Default.aspx. Click on the Source tab on the Default.aspx and add `Culture="auto"` and `UICulture="auto"` so that the entire page declaration resembles the following:

```
<%@ Page Culture="auto" UICulture="auto" Language="VB"
        AutoEventWireup="false" CodeFile="Default.aspx.vb"
        Inherits="_Default" %>
```

7. You can now build and run the web project. When the page is displayed, and assuming that you set the preferred language in your browser back to English; the page will simply display the words "Thank you" as shown in Figure 8-14.

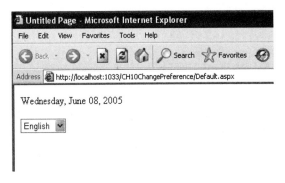

Figure 8-14. *Explicit localization: English*

8. Change the default preferred language for the browser to German (Germany) [de]. Click OK on the Language Preference window and then again on the Internet Properties window. Click the Refresh button on the browser and you will see "Danke," the German equivalent (Figure 8-15).

Figure 8-15. *Explicit localization: German*

After walking through two examples, you might be wondering how this can help you globalize your website. Here's the answer. By using implicit and explicit localization, you can target a number of different languages and cultures. You can translate the text within the resource files and not have to change a line of code. It is even scalable because additional languages and cultures can be added after the initial release of a web application. Again, all is made possible via the resource files.

Changing the Language Programmatically

Up to this point you have utilized the auto-detecting feature to display the preferred language and accomplish localization. But what if a person is traveling in a foreign country and wants to view a website in his or her own language? Simply using the auto-detect feature does not address such an issue because most likely any browsers used there would be set to the language of that region. Therefore, the web content will be displayed in that language, which is foreign to the end user at the time. By providing a mechanism in which end users can select their own language, they can make their own choice.

With that said, you now are faced with a situation that your web application at times will have to provide users the choice of language and culture in which they would like to view the website content. Again, the .NET Framework provides specific class libraries, starting with the Globalization and Threading namespaces, to accomplish this.

To gain the best understanding of how to accomplish this will take a bit of code in your application. Some popular websites ask users the first time they visit in what language they would like to view the website. Perhaps it would take the form of a drop-down list or different links. Maybe they even write a cookie to remember the user after his or her initial visit. Regardless, many sites must have the ability to change the language and culture dynamically; therefore, the localization will occur on the fly.

Let's move on to an example. Exercise 8-5 will utilize a drop-down list to change the content of your site or localize the content. For simplicity's sake, we include only three separate languages and cultures. Most enterprise applications will provide a great deal more.

■**Note** *Overriding* is a term used in object-oriented programming to describe a situation where another method can be executed from the parent class instead of the base class.

Exercise 8-5. Storing Language Preferences

In this exercise, you will need to address a couple of issues before diving into the code. Because you are going to change the language setting programmatically, you will need to intercept or override the code that works with setting the browser to auto-detect the setting. The reason for this is that the preferred language setting will remain unchanged within the browser; however, the content displayed on the website will be shown according to the setting the end user chooses. The method needed to be overridden is the InitializeCulture() subprocedure. This is the method that is used in conjunction with the auto detection of the preferred browser language. Because you will allow users to change to the preference they want, you need to have other code executed instead of what is in the base class.

The next issue is adding a profile property to the web.config. We will examine this in more detail in Chapter 9 dealing with personalization.

1. Create a new web project and add a web.config file to the project.

2. Open the web.config file and within the <system.web> element tags, add the following profile element:

```
<profile>
    <properties>
        <add name="Culture" type="System.String" />
    </properties>
</profile>
```

3. Let's focus on the Default.aspx page, which is where most of the code will need to be implemented. Double-click on Default.aspx from the Solution Explorer. Click on the Design tab and add a DropDown-List control to the web page from the Toolbox window. Right-click on the DropDownList control, choose Properties from the menu, name the control **dropdownlistLanguages**, and set the AutoPostBack property to true. This will be the drop-down list that contains the different languages you can select.

4. Double-click on Default.aspx to proceed to the code-beside file, Default.aspx.vb. Add the following libraries to the top of the page:

```
Imports System.Globalization
Imports System.Threading
```

Here the two namespaces, Globalization and Threading, need to be declared at the top of the code because of the functionality that will be needed. The culture classes are located within the Globalization namespace, and setting the current culture during runtime will be found within the Threading namespace.

5. We are now going to add an override the InitializeCulture() method. To do so, add the following method to the code:

```
Protected Overrides Sub InitializeCulture()

End Sub
```

6. Now that you have the method to override the InitializeCulture() method, let's add the new code that will set the language preference.

```
Dim currentUserCulture As String =
Profile.GetPropertyValue("Culture").ToString()

If currentUserCulture <> "" Then
    Thread.CurrentThread.CurrentUICulture = New
CultureInfo(currentUserCulture)
    Thread.CurrentThread.CurrentCulture = CultureInfo.CreateSpecificCulture
      (currentUserCulture)
End If
```

Here you see that the code will check the Profile setting in the web.config file with regard to the "Culture" string, and if its value is not set, the current culture thread is set to that stored within the Profile. With regard to the current thread, in this instance, it is referred to as the currently running execution of the selected culture. If the culture string's value is not set, the current execution of the code will use the browser's preferred setting. Otherwise, by using the thread classes, you can change the culture to that selected by the end user.

7. Next, let's address the dynamic loading of the DropDownList control with the three languages you are going to provide. This functionality will be focused within the Page_Load method of the Default.aspx page. Locate the Page_Load method, and let's examine the code in which to add. The first order of business is to add the code to check if the page request is a post back event.

```
If Not IsPostBack Then

End If
```

Next you are going to load the DropDownList control with the available languages in which the user can localize the content. Remember, for our example we are going to provide three languages and cultures, but if you wanted to add more, you would add them in the same way. Here the languages are loaded into a String array:

```
Dim languagearray As String() = {"de", "fr", "en"}
Dim language As String
```

Now you are going to loop through the String array of the listed languages and determine the culture and language name from the CultureInfo() class to populate the DropDownList control. Each of the specified languages in the string array will be added to a new ListItem, and the newly created ListItem will then be added to the DropDownList, hence populating it. Let's take a look.

```
For Each language In languagearray
            Dim temporaryCultureInfo As New CultureInfo(language)
Dim LanguageList As New ListItem
        (temporaryCultureInfo.NativeName, temporaryCultureInfo.Name)

            If temporaryCultureInfo.Equals(CultureInfo.CurrentUICulture) Then
                LanguageList.Selected = True
            End If

dropdownlistLanguages.Items.Add(LanguageList)
    Next language
```

Lastly, you will write the current date to the browser window with the Response.Write() method.

```
Response.Write(DateTime.Now.ToLongDateString())
```

For clarity, let's look at the entire Page_Load method now that you have added the additional code.

```
Protected Sub Page_Load(ByVal sender As Object, ByVal e As System.EventArgs)
    Handles Me.Load
        If Not IsPostBack Then
            'List of languages.
            Dim languagearray As String() = {"de", "fr", "en"}
            Dim language As String

            For Each language In languagearray
                Dim temporaryCultureInfo As New CultureInfo(language)
        Dim LanguageList As New ListItem
            (temporaryCultureInfo.NativeName, temporaryCultureInfo.Name)
              If temporaryCultureInfo.Equals(CultureInfo.CurrentUICulture)
            Then
                LanguageList.Selected = True
              End If
```

```
                    dropdownlistLanguages.Items.Add(LanguageList)
                Next language
            End If

            'Write the date to the browser.
            Response.Write(DateTime.Now.ToLongDateString())
        End Sub
```

8. You are now on to the last step of coding. You have to add code for when a value is selected in the DropDownList control. Remember, you set the `AutoPostBack` property of the DropDownList control to true, which will fire the `SelectedIndexChanged` method of the DropDownList when a value is selected. With that said, you will have to set the Culture profile to the selected value from the list.

Here you use the `SetPropertyValue` method of the Profile class to populate the Culture string to the value of the DropDownList.

```
Profile.SetPropertyValue
        ("Culture", dropdownlistLanguages.SelectedValue.ToString())
```

The last step to perform is to reload the page and force the `InitializeCulture()` method to fire again because you just updated the Culture profile. This can be achieved easily by the following code:

```
Response.Redirect(Request.Url.LocalPath)
```

Now let's look at the entire `SelectedIndexChanged` method of the DropDownList:

```
Protected Sub dropdownlistLanguages_SelectedIndexChanged
        (ByVal sender As Object, ByVal e As System.EventArgs)
    Handles          dropdownlistLanguages.SelectedIndexChanged
        'Save selected user language in profile
        Profile.SetPropertyValue("Culture",
.......dropdownlistLanguages.SelectedValue.ToString())

        'Force the page to fire the InitializeCulture() method again to set
        'the newly selected language.
        Response.Redirect(Request.Url.LocalPath)
    End Sub
```

You are finally ready to test your code.

9. Build and run the web project. When the Default.aspx page is displayed in the browser, you will see that because your preferred language setting is English, that will be the value preselected from the DropDownList, and the date will also reflect that formatting (Figure 8-16).

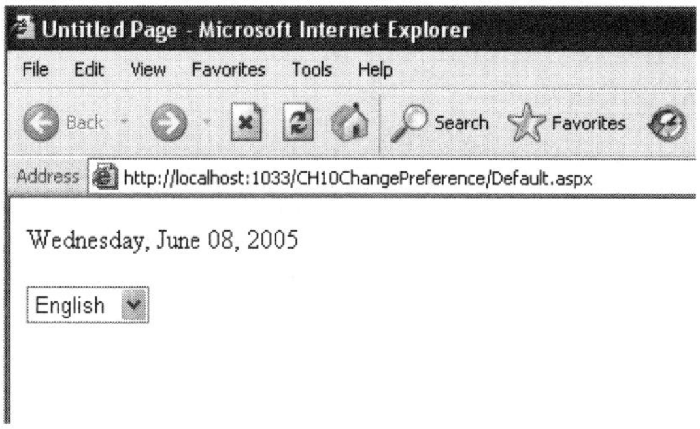

Figure 8-16. *Default.aspx: English*

10. Now for the real testing. From the drop-down list, choose German or Deutsch and when the page is finished loading, you will see the date is localized to German, even though your preferred language setting for the browser is set to English (Figure 8-17).

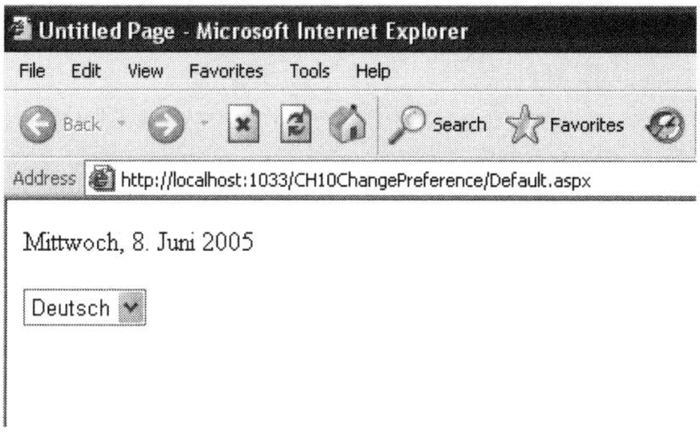

Figure 8-17. *Default.aspx: German*

11. Practice changing the localization to the other provided languages, and watch the date become localized to the chosen culture and language.

Not a bad exercise, right? You were able to demonstrate with the complete code shown here that you can provide end users with a choice of their own localization options in which to view your website.

```
Imports System.Globalization
Imports System.Threading

Partial Class _Default
    Inherits System.Web.UI.Page
    Protected Overrides Sub InitializeCulture()
        ' Override and determine if the profile contains a language setting.
        Dim currentUserCulture As String = _
            Profile.GetPropertyValue("Culture").ToString()
```

```vbnet
            If currentUserCulture <> "" Then
                Thread.CurrentThread.CurrentUICulture = _
                    New CultureInfo(currentUserCulture)
                Thread.CurrentThread.CurrentCulture = _
                    CultureInfo.CreateSpecificCulture(currentUserCulture)
            End If
        End Sub

    Protected Sub Page_Load(ByVal sender As Object,
     ByVal e As System.EventArgs)
        Handles Me.Load
        If Not IsPostBack Then
            'List of languages.
            Dim languagearray As String() = {"de", "fr", "en"}
            Dim language As String

        For Each language In languagearray
            Dim temporaryCultureInfo As New CultureInfo(language)
            Dim LanguageList As New ListItem(temporaryCultureInfo.NativeName,
                temporaryCultureInfo.Name)
            If temporaryCultureInfo.Equals(CultureInfo.CurrentUICulture) Then
                LanguageList.Selected = True
            End If
            dropdownlistLanguages.Items.Add(LanguageList)
        Next language
        End If
        'Write the date to the browser.
        Response.Write(DateTime.Now.ToLongDateString())
    End Sub

    Protected Sub dropdownlistLanguages_SelectedIndexChanged
     (ByVal sender As Object, ByVal e As System.EventArgs) Handles
dropdownlistLanguages.SelectedIndexChanged
        'Save selected user language in profile
        Profile.SetPropertyValue
            ("Culture", dropdownlistLanguages.SelectedValue.ToString())

        'Force the page to fire the InitializeCulture() method again to set
        'the newly selected language.
        Response.Redirect(Request.Url.LocalPath)
    End Sub
End Class
```

Localizing Static Content

Most of the content with ASP.NET happens to be dynamic. However, there are still many instances where websites have sections that have static content. If you want to make such sections localizable, again the .NET Framework provides the tools to perform such tasks. You learned in an earlier section that you can localize the content implicitly or explicitly.

There is also one other tool you can use, the `<asp:Localize></asp:Localize>` tags. These tags look similar to that of the Label or Textbox controls; however, you will not be able to find them in the Toolbox.

The main advantage of this tool is apparent when you need to provide some static content, for instance, a copyright message or disclaimer that is often found at the bottom of web pages. Here you would not have to use a Label control; instead, you use the Localize control, and the content itself has the ability to be altered not only in the Resource Editor but within the design view of the .aspx page as well.

Summary

This chapter discussed how important it is to enable websites with global capabilities and showed how easily this can be achieved with the tools provided in the .NET Framework.

CHAPTER 9

■■■

Personalization

Throughout this book, we have talked at great length about providing a rich experience for the end users visiting your website. An important additional skill is offering end users the ability to customize or personalize the way in which they view their content.

In the context of websites and web applications, *personalization* gives end users the choice and ability to alter both the content displayed and how it will be displayed. Users might be able to choose having local weather information or their favorite local sports team's scores on their home page. Or maybe they want this content but in a different color or style. These are all capabilities of personalization. This chapter will teach you how to achieve such tasks in your web applications.

We focus on three main tools that provide personalization to your end users: Web Parts, user profiles, and themes. We examine each topic in detail and provide some hands-on examples of each. At the conclusion of this chapter, you will have a thorough understanding of the following topics:

- Using the Web Part Framework

- Creating and managing Web Parts

- Creating user profiles

- Applying themes

Web Parts

The first major tool in providing websites with personalization is called a *Web Part*, a unit of content that resembles a small window on a web page. These windows or units can be interchanged with other units and can be repositioned on the web page as well as expanded or collapsed.

Before we get into our own examples, let's look at a popular and well-known site with similar functionality. My MSN allows users essentially to build their own web page from existing content. Let's examine the sample in Figure 9-1 as we show one author's `http://my.msn.com` page.

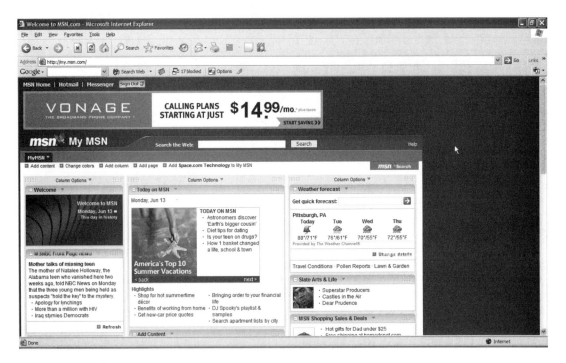

Figure 9-1. *My MSN*

You can see that this instance of an MSN home page has local weather information in Pittsburgh, Pennsylvania (a lot of rain in the forecast, unfortunately). There also is a section that has the most up-to-date news headlines. The type of content displayed is strictly up to the user, and the displayed content along with the location of the content on the web page can be changed at any time.

My MSN is a prime example of a public site that utilizes Web Parts. Users can arrange the columns of information to whatever location that they desire, thus customizing or personalizing the web page.

With Web Part technology, you can emulate this exact functionality within your own websites. Before we move on and explore Web Parts in further detail, we need to take a step back and look at the entire Web Part Framework.

The Web Part Framework

An actual Web Part is only one piece of the overall picture. It is, however, the central element. The Web Part Framework consists of several components, including the WebPartManager, WebPartZone, CatalogPart, CatalogZone, ConnectionsZone, EditorPart, and EditorZone. Each of these components has an individual role to play during the process of personalizing your web application with Web Parts.

When planning out the design of your web application to utilize Web Parts, a thorough understanding of each of the Web Part Framework components is essential. To begin the process, a Web Part manager component is the first item to use or add to the web page. A Web Part manager does not have a visual interface; however, it acts as the glue for all the individual Web Parts that you will add later.

Next is the Web Part zone, which will act as the container for one or more individual Web Parts. These zones are usually organized into columns or rows and segregate the entire page from which to add and change the content. Refer back to the My MSN example in Figure 9-1, where three columns are displayed on the page: a welcome message, the latest news headlines, and the current weather. All three of these sections can be thought of as Web Part zones.

Last, as mentioned previously, the central element, the actual Web Part component, is used to provide the functionality or information the end user can use or build to achieve personalization. The Web Parts are placed into the individual WebPartZones, and then the customization of the Web Part is applied. As shown in the My MSN example, this customization can be a feed from a weather service or just some information displayed that is specific to the application, perhaps a listing of information queried from the database. We will get into more detail about this in Exercise 9-1.

For reference and descriptions of all the components within the Web Part Framework, let's examine Table 9-1.

Table 9-1. *Web Parts Framework Components*

Component	Description
Web Part	Contains the actual content an end user views.
WebPartManager	Manages all Web Parts on a single page. Has no interface and cannot be seen during runtime.
WebPartZone	Contains one or more Web Part controls and provides the overall layout for the Web Parts it contains.
CatalogPart	Contains a list of the available Web Parts to use.
CatalogZone	Contains the CatalogPart.
ConnectionsZone	Contains the connections that are defined between Web Parts on a web page.
EditorPart	Allows modifications to Web Parts.
EditorZone	Contains the EditorPart.

Now that we have discussed the components and their associated roles and functionality, let's move on to Exercise 9-1, which demonstrates Web Parts and the Web Part Framework in action and permits the end user to personalize your web application.

Exercise 9-1. Creating Web Parts

This exercise is quite lengthy, but it will show you some great ways to create Web Parts on your pages and change the layout. You will be placing the different controls from the Web Part Framework to gain a full understanding of how they all interact together. The functionality will be similar to that of the My MSN example but on a much smaller scale.

1. Create a new web project.

2. Within the Design view on the Default.aspx page, add a DropDownList control—check the Auto Post-back option—and under the Web Parts panel, add a WebPartManager. You can keep the default names of the controls.

3. Click on the Layout menu item, and select Insert Table from the choices. You will then be presented with the dialog box shown in Figure 9-2.

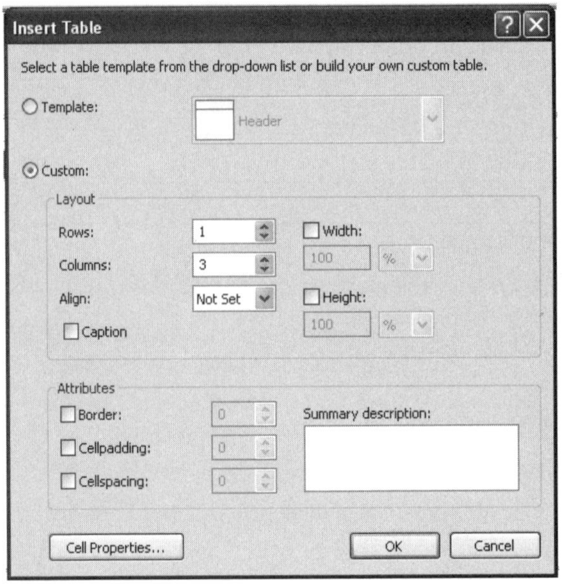

Figure 9-2. *Inserting an HTML table*

Choose the custom radio button option so you can specify more details regarding the rows, columns, and alignment. Enter one row and three columns in the respective areas. Click OK. You now have an HTML table on your web page.

4. Add a WebPartZone in each of the columns of the table. Remember that a WebPartZone provides the container in which the Web Parts will be placed. When adding the WebPartZones, you will notice a menu option that appears with a link saying Auto Format. You can click on this link to choose a more pleasing style. For our example, we chose the Professional format. We now have three separate WebPartZones in each of the table columns.

5. Now let's add some content to the WebPartZones. Add a Label control to the WebPartZone in the first column on the left, add a Calendar control to the WebPartZone in the middle column, and leave WebPartZone in the column on the right empty. When complete, your web page will resemble Figure 9-3.

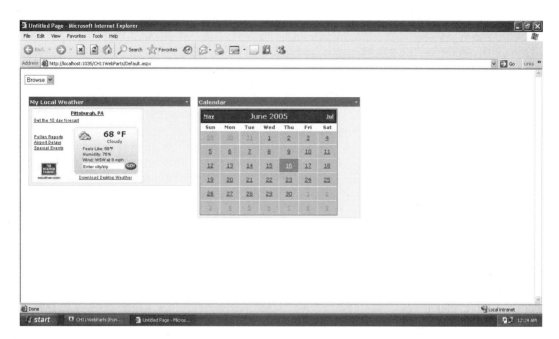

Figure 9-3. *WebPartZones in Design view*

Next, click on the Source tab and examine the HTML code:

```
<html>
<head runat="server">
    <title>Untitled Page</title>
</head>
<body>
    <form id="form1" runat="server">
    <div>
<asp:DropDownList ID="DropDownList1" runat="server" AutoPostBack="True">
    </asp:DropDownList><br />
    <asp:WebPartManager ID="WebPartManager1" runat="server">
    </asp:WebPartManager>
    <br />
    <div style="text-align: center">
        <table width="100%">
            <tr>
                <td width="33%" valign="top">
                    <asp:WebPartZone ID="WebPartZone1" runat="server"
BorderColor="#CCCCCC" Font-Names="Verdana"
                        Padding="6" Width="100%">
```

```
                                            <PartChromeStyle BackColor="#F7F6F3"
                                                 BorderColor="#E2DED6"
Font-Names="Verdana" ForeColor="White" />
                                            <MenuLabelHoverStyle ForeColor="#E2DED6" />
                                            <EmptyZoneTextStyle Font-Size="0.8em" />
                                            <MenuLabelStyle ForeColor="White" />
                                            <MenuVerbHoverStyle BackColor="#F7F6F3"
BorderColor="#CCCCCC" BorderStyle="Solid"
                                                 BorderWidth="1px" ForeColor="#333333" />
                                            <HeaderStyle Font-Size="0.7em"
ForeColor="#CCCCCC" HorizontalAlign="Center" />
                                            <ZoneTemplate>
                                                <asp:Label ID="Label1" runat="server"
                                                        title="My Local Weather"
Text="&lt;scriptsrc='http://voap.weather.com/weather/oap/15205
?template=GENXH&amp;par=null&amp;unit=0&amp;
key=df211ac3bd5c06bae8989210bd3ca8ec'&gt;&lt;/script&gt;
" Height="53px"></asp:Label>
                                            </ZoneTemplate>
                                            <MenuVerbStyle BorderColor="#5D7B9D"
BorderStyle="Solid" BorderWidth="1px" ForeColor="White" />
                                            <PartStyle Font-Size="0.8em"
ForeColor="#333333" />
                                            <TitleBarVerbStyle Font-Size="0.6em" Font-
Underline="False"
ForeColor="White" />

                                            <MenuPopupStyle BackColor="#5D7B9D"
BorderColor="#CCCCCC" BorderWidth="1px" Font-Names="Verdana"
                                                 Font-Size="0.6em" />
                                            <PartTitleStyle BackColor="#5D7B9D"
Font-Bold="True" Font-Size="0.8em" ForeColor="White" />
                                        </asp:WebPartZone>
                                         
                                    </td>
                                    <td width="33%">
                                        <asp:WebPartZone ID="WebPartZone2" runat="server"
BorderColor="#CCCCCC" Font-Names="Verdana"
                                            Padding="6" Width="100%">
                                            <PartChromeStyle BackColor="#F7F6F3"
BorderColor="#E2DED6" Font-Names="Verdana" ForeColor="White" />
                                            <MenuLabelHoverStyle ForeColor="#E2DED6" />
                                            <EmptyZoneTextStyle Font-Size="0.8em" />
                                            <MenuLabelStyle ForeColor="White" />
                                            <MenuVerbHoverStyle BackColor="#F7F6F3"
BorderColor="#CCCCCC" BorderStyle="Solid"
                                                 BorderWidth="1px" ForeColor="#333333" />
```

```
                                    <HeaderStyle Font-Size="0.7em" ForeColor="#CCCCCC"
HorizontalAlign="Center" />
                                <ZoneTemplate>
                                    <asp:Calendar ID="Calendar1" runat="server"
BackColor="White" BorderColor="Black"
                                            BorderStyle="Solid" CellSpacing="1" Font-
Names="Verdana" Font-Size="9pt" ForeColor="Black"
                                            Height="250px" NextPrevFormat="ShortMonth"
Width="330px" Title="Calendar">
                                        <SelectedDayStyle BackColor="#333399"
ForeColor="White" />
                                        <OtherMonthDayStyle ForeColor="#999999" />
                                        <DayStyle BackColor="#CCCCCC" />
                                        <TodayDayStyle BackColor="#999999"
ForeColor="White" />
                                        <NextPrevStyle Font-Bold="True" Font-
Size="8pt" ForeColor="White" />
                                        <DayHeaderStyle Font-Bold="True" Font-
Size="8pt" ForeColor="#333333" Height="8pt" />
                                        <TitleStyle BackColor="#333399"
BorderStyle="Solid" Font-Bold="True" Font-Size="12pt"
                                            ForeColor="White" Height="12pt" />
                                    </asp:Calendar>
                                </ZoneTemplate>
                                <MenuVerbStyle BorderColor="#5D7B9D"
BorderStyle="Solid" BorderWidth="1px" ForeColor="White" />
                                    <PartStyle Font-Size="0.8em" ForeColor="#333333" />
                                    <TitleBarVerbStyle Font-Size="0.6em" Font-
Underline="False" ForeColor="White" />
                                    <MenuPopupStyle BackColor="#5D7B9D"
BorderColor="#CCCCCC" BorderWidth="1px" Font-Names="Verdana"
                                        Font-Size="0.6em" />
                                    <PartTitleStyle BackColor="#5D7B9D"
Font-Bold="True" Font-Size="0.8em" ForeColor="White" />
                                </asp:WebPartZone>
                            </td>
                            <td width="33%" valign="top">
                                <asp:WebPartZone ID="WebPartZone3" runat="server"
BorderColor="#CCCCCC" Font-Names="Verdana"
                                    Padding="6" Width="100%">
                                    <PartChromeStyle BackColor="#F7F6F3"
BorderColor="#E2DED6" Font-Names="Verdana" ForeColor="White" />
                                    <MenuLabelHoverStyle ForeColor="#E2DED6" />
                                    <EmptyZoneTextStyle Font-Size="0.8em" />
                                    <MenuLabelStyle ForeColor="White" />
```

```
                                        <MenuVerbHoverStyle BackColor="#F7F6F3"
        BorderColor="#CCCCCC" BorderStyle="Solid"
                                        BorderWidth="1px" ForeColor="#333333" />
                                        <HeaderStyle Font-Size="0.7em" Fore-
        Color="#CCCCCC" HorizontalAlign="Center" />
                                        <MenuVerbStyle BorderColor="#5D7B9D"
        BorderStyle="Solid" BorderWidth="1px" ForeColor="White" />
                                        <PartStyle Font-Size="0.8em" ForeColor="#333333" />
                                        <TitleBarVerbStyle Font-Size="0.6em" Font-
        Underline="False" ForeColor="White" />
                                        <MenuPopupStyle BackColor="#5D7B9D"
        BorderColor="#CCCCCC" BorderWidth="1px" Font-Names="Verdana"
                                        Font-Size="0.6em" />
                                        <PartTitleStyle BackColor="#5D7B9D" Font-
        Bold="True"
        Font-Size="0.8em" ForeColor="White" />
                                    </asp:WebPartZone>
                                </td>
                        </tr>
                    </table>
            </div>
        </div>
        </form>
    </body>
</html>
```

Here you can see the HTML that was generated from the controls being placed on the web page. Let's look specifically at the first column in the table where you placed a Label control.

6. The Label control you placed in the first column in the WebPartZone is going to display the local weather information. Note that to ensure that the weather information is displayed, a live Internet connection is needed. This information will be provided from The Weather Channel. Let's look at the label more closely.

```
<ZoneTemplate>
<asp:Label ID="Label1" runat="server" title="My Local Weather"
Text="<script src='http://voap.weather.com/weather/oap
/15205?template=GENXH&par=1009624279&unit=0&
key=bce0ccdcde3556afd178545e369e6038'></script>"
Height="53px">
</asp:Label>
</ZoneTemplate>
```

You now have all the content necessary within the WebPartZones.

■**Note** The example that shows the local weather information can be obtained by registering for a free account with The Weather Channel at `http://www.weather.com/services/oap.html?from=footer`. When signing up for this account, The Weather Channel asks for some basic information, along with the postal code of where you would like the weather report. The preceding code resembles the local information for Pittsburgh, Pennsylvania. Enter your own local postal code, and the script will be generated automatically for you.

7. The next step is to implement code with the DropDownList you added so that at runtime you can edit the layout of the Web Parts. Therefore, click on the Design view of the Default.aspx page, and double-click on the page to switch over to the code view. Here you will add the following code to the `_Default` class:

```
Partial Class _Default
    Inherits System.Web.UI.Page
                Dim _wpmmngr As WebPartManager
                Protected Sub Page_Init(ByVal sender As Object,
ByVal e As EventArgs)
Handles Me.Init
        _wpmmngr = WebPartManager.GetCurrentWebPartManager(Page)
        Dim browseModeName As String = _WebPartManager.BrowseDisplayMode.Name
' Populate the drop-down list with the names of supported display modes.
Dim displaymode As WebPartDisplayMode
        For Each displaymode In _wpmmngr.SupportedDisplayModes
            Dim modeName As String = displaymode.Name
            ' Ensure a mode is enabled before adding it.
            If displaymode.IsEnabled(_wpmmngr) Then
        Dim item As New ListItem(modeName, modeName)
DropDownList1.Items.Add(item)
            End If
        Next displaymode
    End Sub
    Protected Sub DropDownList1_SelectedIndexChanged(ByVal sender As Object,
ByVal e As System.EventArgs) Handles DropDownList1.SelectedIndexChanged
        Dim dropdownSelectedMode As String = DropDownList1.SelectedValue
        Dim md As WebPartDisplayMode = _
_wpmmngr.SupportedDisplayModes(dropdownSelectedMode)
        If Not (md Is Nothing) Then
    _wpmmngr.DisplayMode = md
        End If
    End Sub
End Class
```

Let's look at each section of the code. First, you need to populate the drop-down list, which is handled in the Page_Init method of Default.aspx.

```
Protected Sub Page_Init(ByVal sender As Object, ByVal e As EventArgs)
Handles Me.Init
      _wpmmngr = WebPartManager.GetCurrentWebPartManager(Page)
      Dim browseModeName As String = _
        WebPartManager.BrowseDisplayMode.Name
      ' Populate the drop-down list with the names of
      'supported display modes.
      Dim displaymode As WebPartDisplayMode
      For Each displaymode In _wpmmngr.SupportedDisplayModes
          Dim modeName As String = displaymode.Name
          ' Ensure a mode is enabled before adding it.
          If displaymode.IsEnabled(_wpmmngr) Then
              Dim item As New ListItem(modeName, modeName)
              DropDownList1.Items.Add(item)
          End If
      Next displaymode
    End Sub
```

This code essentially populates the DropDownList control with the different display modes available for the Web Parts you placed on your page. You will see that the values placed in the drop-down list are Browse and Design. When users want to alter the layout of the Web Parts, they can select the Design option from the drop-down list. This changes the mode and allows the Web Parts to be moved to and from different zones. Let's take a look at that code.

Note Those readers who used the Beta 1 version of ASP.NET 2.0 might have noticed that the WebPartPageMenu control was removed from the Beta 2 versions and possibly the final release version as well. Therefore, you need to implement your own mechanism for changing the mode.

```
Protected Sub DropDownList1_SelectedIndexChanged
(ByVal sender As Object, ByVal e As System.EventArgs)
Handles DropDownList1.SelectedIndexChanged
      Dim dropdownSelectedMode As String = DropDownList1.SelectedValue
      Dim md As WebPartDisplayMode = _
        _wpmmngr.SupportedDisplayModes(dropdownSelectedMode)
      If Not (md Is Nothing) Then
          _wpmmngr.DisplayMode = md
      End If
    End Sub
```

This code will automatically change the display mode of the Web Parts when the different values are selected from the drop-down list.

8. Finally, you can test your code. Build and run the web project as shown in Figure 9-4.

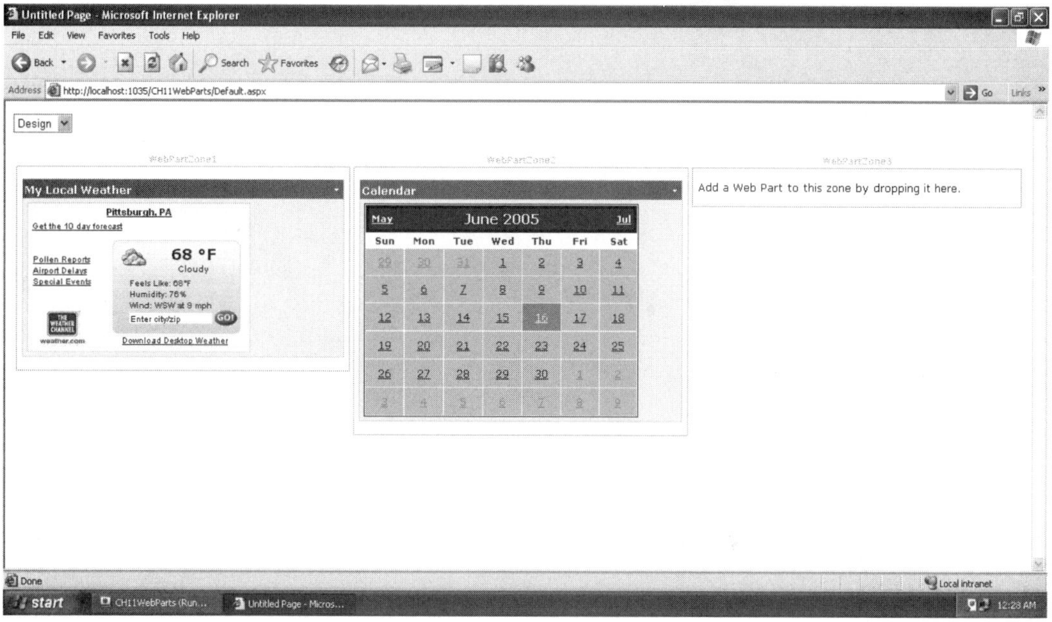

Figure 9-4. *Web Parts and WebPartZones during runtime in browse mode*

The page displays the Web Parts you have built. You can see the local weather information along with a simple calendar.

9. Click on the drop-down list, and chose the Design option. This will put the page in edit mode and allow you to change the layout of the Web Parts (Figure 9-5).

Figure 9-5. *Web Parts and WebpartZones during runtime in design mode*

Notice that you can now see the third WebPartZone that was placed in the right column of the table. Because you purposely did not include any content, it displays a message saying "Add a Web Part to this zone by dropping it here." Click on the headers of the Web Parts and move each of them to different zones (Figure 9-6).

Figure 9-6. *Moving Web Parts during runtime in design mode*

Here we changed the layout of the Web Parts to have the weather information on the right side of the page and the calendar on the left, leaving the middle of the page blank. Feel free to experiment and try moving your Web Parts to the different zones on the page. When finished, click on the DropDownList to choose Browse, which will end the edit mode session.

That was a long exercise, but it was definitely worth seeing the functionality of using Web Parts. Now let's move on to user profiles.

User Profiles

The second feature to provide personalization is setting up and managing user profiles. Essentially every website needs the ability in some degree to have specific data about each individual user that is able to be stored. For example, let's take the local weather example. It needs the local postal code to retrieve the information; therefore storing the postal code in the user profile would be helpful in that it could be extracted quite easily. User profiles are typically applied in two different instances: when a user must first authenticate and then the profile is stored for that specific user and then for anonymous users who do not have to authenticate. Whether the user authenticates or not, the profile settings are dynamically created within the profile application programming interface (API).

The Profile Schema

To utilize the profile features in ASP.NET 2.0, first you need to implement some specific configurations to the web.config file. These configurations will consist of properties and a specific type. After these properties are added to the web.config, from the profile class within the source code, you as the developer will have the ability to access these properties to set the value and also retrieve the values as well. Let's look at the individual elements in Tables 9-2 and 9-3 that need to be implemented in the web.config.

Table 9-2. *User Profile Elements in the web.config*

Element	Description
profile	The main element for user profiles
properties	The object that will be set or retrieved
add	The element that adds the property

Table 9-3. *User Profile Attributes in the web.config*

Attribute	Description
name	The name of the property and the only attribute that is required.
allowAnonymous	This allows the storing of data for anonymous users. Default value is false.
defaultValue	The default value of the property.
provider	Name of the provider or the mechanism in which the profile information will be stored.
readOnly	Indicates whether the property value is read-only. False by default.
serializeAs	Specifies how to serialize the value of the property. Available choices are XML Binary, String, and ProviderSpecific.
type	The data type of the property. If not specified, the data type will default to a string.

The first step is to add a `profile` element and add an `enabled` attribute that is set to true within the web project's web.config file. The easiest way include this is to enter the elements and attributes to the web.config file manually. Here is a sample:

```
<configuration>
  <system.web>
    <profile enabled="true" >
    </profile>
    </system.web>
</configuration>
```

The next step is to add your profile properties by adding individual `add` elements. Notice that you have only added the `name` and `type` attribute to the `add` element. As referenced in Table 9-3, the only mandatory attribute is the `name` attribute; the remaining are optional. However, be aware of what the default values will be if you exclude attributes.

```
<add name="FavoriteBackgroundColor" type="System.Drawing.Color"  />
```

The `name` element is what the property of the profile can be identified from, and the `type` element is the data type of the specified property and can be any of the Common Language Runtime (CLR) data types. We can continue adding additional profile properties in the same manner. For clarity, let's look at the entire schema now:

```
<configuration>
  <system.web>
    <profile enabled="true" >
      <properties>
        <add name="FavoriteBackgroundColor" type="System.Drawing.Color" />
      </properties>
    </profile>
    </system.web>
</configuration>
```

After adding all of the properties for the profile, they are accessible from the code and even included in the IntelliSense. However, save and build the website project prior to doing so within the code base.

Grouping Properties

You also have the ability to add a `<group>` element within your profile schema. The `<group>` element enables you to categorize related properties. Grouping properties are helpful in that you have the ability to arrange related properties to one customized grouping. This will allow for easier use with the code. Here is an actual code example:

```
<configuration>
  <system.web>
    <profile enabled="true" >
      <properties>
        <add name="FavoriteBackgroundColor" type="System.Drawing.Color" />
        <group name="Font">
```

```
            <add name="Bold" type="bool"/>
            <add name="Underline" type="bool"/>
        </group>
      </properties>
    </profile>
    </system.web>
</configuration>
```

More specifically, let's look at the group element:

```
<group name="Font">
            <add name="Bold" type="bool"/>
            <add name="Underline" type="bool"/>
  </group>
```

Here you have a group named Font that has defined properties of Bold and Underline. This adds some additional functionality to categorize your properties within the user profile.

Providers

The information that is specified in the user profiles needs to be stored somewhere in your application. Luckily, the .NET Framework handles a great deal of this for you in that if your application allows the default provider to handle the storage, you do not have to implement any additional code or configurations for user profiles.

A provider is where the profile information will be stored and later retrieved. This is commonly a database that is already supplied, and you will not have to be concerned about constructing or implementing this to your own database structure. The default provider is called AspNetAccessProvider in which an Access database is added to the App_Data folder in your web project and automatically configured for use.

If Access proves not to be sufficient for your project, there are alternatives you can use. The first alternative is to use SQL Server instead of Access for profile storage, or for advanced developers, you can customize your own provider. For the examples and purposes in this book, we use the default provider.

Accessing User Profiles in Code

Now that you have defined the profiles for use, the last step is to show how you can access these profiles and set values for them. For example, let's take a look at the following section of code that will extract the value of the user's favorite background color and set that for an object placed on the web page.

```
Protected Sub Page_Load(ByVal sender As Object, ByVal e As System.EventArgs)
Handles Me.Load
        Panel1.BackColor = Profile.FavoriteBackgroundColor
End Sub
```

In this example, you have a panel control placed on the web page and you set the BackColor property to that color stored within the user profile. Perhaps the user can select from a drop-down list of colors. Upon making a selection, the value selected is stored within the user profile. This particular profile has a type of System.Drawing.Color, which is the same type as the BackColor property of the panel.

All profiles can be accessed in the same manner. The profile class within the .NET Framework will access what was set within the web.config and allow you easily to extract that value from the provider that was specified with little coding required.

Themes

Themes provide a visual experience and layout for the end user. Usually they refer to different colors or styles being applied to the web page. Within the web page, it could be changing the overall color or layout of the controls on the page. This is accomplished by providing different style sheets and possibly even skin files.

To begin our discussion, first let's examine an example that many of you have probably come across, the very popular MSN website (http://www.msn.com). At the top of this site are two choices presented to users for setting the color or theme of the entire site. The choices are Simple White and Classic Blue. Take a look at Figures 9-7 and 9-8 to see each choice applied.

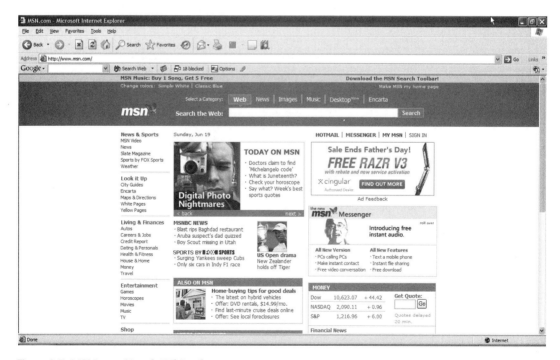

Figure 9-7. *MSN.com Simple White theme*

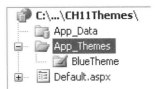

Figure 9-8. *MSN.com Classic Blue theme*

Theme Structure

Themes are composed of .css (Cascading Style Sheet) files, images, and even skin files. When all of these elements are combined, they create a theme that provides the customization of the visual layout by changing the visual appearance of the website. The advantage of this is when a change needs to be made, the change can be performed in one location and all changes will propagate throughout all the associated sections within the web project.

There are included themes within ASP.NET 2.0 that can be readily used within your web applications. These themes can be located at the following directory on your computer after installing the .NET Framework 2.0:

```
%WINDIR%\Microsoft.NET\Framework\<version>\ASP.NETClientFiles\Themes
```

The beginning of the path, %WINDIR%, refers to the default installation of the Windows operating system. Typically this will be C:\WINDOWS, depending if your version of Windows was installed in the default location and if your hard drive was partitioned. The <version> notation refers to the version of the .NET Framework.

On the other hand, if you do not want to use the provided themes for your web application, you can certainly add your own. These themes will be defined at the application or project level instead of at the machine level in which the included themes are accessible. Regardless of using an included theme or one of your own customized themes, it is still consistent with how you need to implement the instructions for telling the websites what theme to use. You can instruct the website to use a theme at the page level or at the project or application level if you want a theme to propagate throughout your entire website.

Let's first examine having a single web page in your application using the selected theme. This will be set at the top of the page in the HTML portion in the page declarations. Here is the entire page declaration code:

```
<%@ Page Theme="BlueTheme" Language="VB" AutoEventWireup="false"
CodeFile="Default.aspx.vb" Inherits="_Default" %>
```

For this particular page, Default.aspx, the theme named BlueTheme is being used and will only affect the Default.aspx page. This theme is located within your application and placed in the App_Themes folder within the web project. More detail is provided on this in the following exercises.

Your other option is to have a theme defined in one place that will propagate to all web pages within the project or website. To do so, the web.config file needs to have additional elements placed within it. Let's look at the sample here:

```
<system.web>
    <pages theme="BlueTheme"/>
</system.web>
```

When this is defined in the web.config, the specified theme will be applied throughout every web page in the site. Now that we have the basics laid out, let's work through a hands-on example in Exercise 9-2.

Exercise 9-2. Creating and Implementing a Theme

This exercise will show you how to create a theme of your own and apply it to the entire web project.

1. Right-click on the web project in the Solution Explorer and choose the Add Folder option and then Theme Folder from the submenu. A subdirectory will be created under the App_Theme folder displaying a default name of Theme1. Change this directory name to BlueTheme. The web project tree will now look like Figure 9-9.

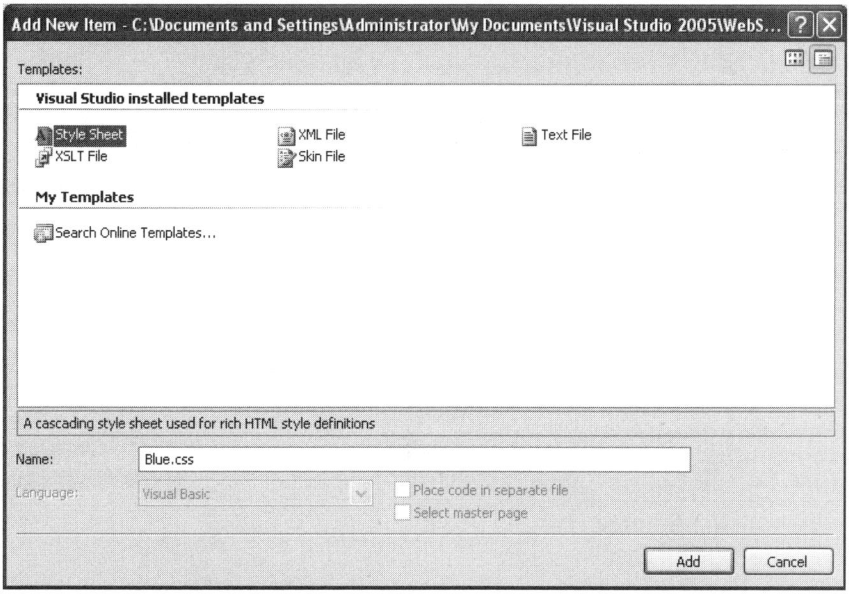

Figure 9-9. *App_Themes folder*

2. Right-click on the newly created folder BlueTheme and choose Add New Item. From the Add New Item dialog window, select Style Sheet, and name the style sheet **Blue.css** (Figure 9-10).

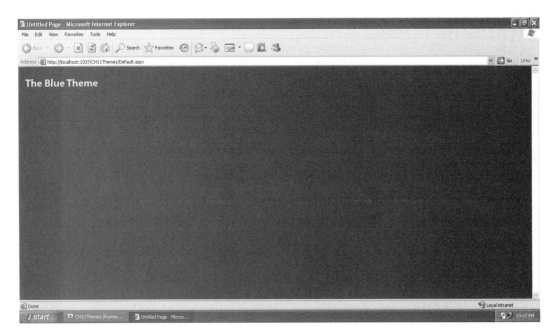

Figure 9-10. *Adding a style sheet to the web project*

3. This will create a Cascading Style Sheet within your web project where you can set the properties for your theme. For this example, you are going to address the body attribute in the css file. Add the following code to the newly created .css file:

```
body {  background: blue;
        color: navy;
        font-family: "arial";
        font-size: 14pt;
        }
```

4. Now on to the final step. You need to inform the site to use your new theme. Add a web.config file to the web project. Within the web.config file, add the following element within the system.web elements:

```
<configuration>
   <system.web>
        <pages theme="BlueTheme"/>
   </system.web>
</configuration>
```

All the settings are in place now except for some simple text to view on your web page. For simplicity, we added the text The Blue Theme on the Default.aspx page. Feel free to add whatever you like.

5. Let's test your work. Build and run the web project, and you will see the web page reflect the theme you created (Figure 9-11).

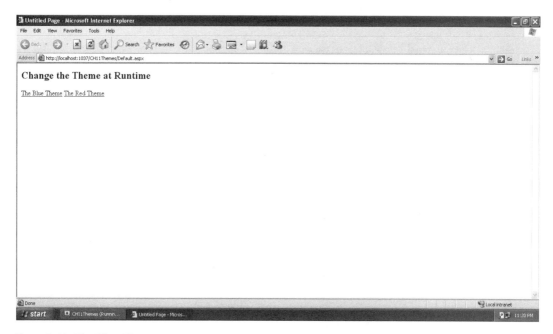

Figure 9-11. *The Blue Theme*

You see that the Default.aspx page has been loaded and reflects the attributes you defined in the .css file within the BlueTheme.

Changing the Theme at Runtime

We have examined adding a theme to your web project at design time; however, to take the extra step and provide your users with the ability to change to the theme of their own preference, you need to be able to change the theme during runtime. To achieve this, you will build on what you have already learned and add it to some code.

Exercise 9-3. Change Theme Programmatically

1. Take the web project you created in Exercise 9-2, and add another theme folder to the web project. Name the folder **RedTheme**. As you did in the previous exercise, add a .css file to the RedTheme folder and name it **Red.css**. Within your new css file, change the background color of the body attribute to red as shown in the following code:

```
body {  background: red;
        color: navy;
        font-family: "arial";
        font-size: 14pt;
         }
```

2. You now have two different themes your users can pick from. Let's move on to adding the code that will allow your users to change the theme. Within the web.config, delete the element you added in the previous exercise. By doing so, no theme will be applied until the user selects a theme.

3. Click on the Default.aspx page and then on the Source tab to view the HTML section of the page. You are going to add two hyperlinks with query strings that will enable the user to change from one theme to another. The HTML code will look like this:

```
<html>
<head runat="server">
    <title>Untitled Page</title>
</head>
<body>
    <form id="form1" runat="server">
    <div>
        <h2>Change the Theme at Runtime</h2>
      <a href="Default.aspx?Theme=BlueTheme">The Blue Theme</a>
      <a href="Default.aspx?Theme=RedTheme">The Red Theme</a>
</div>
    </form>
</body>
</html>
```

Here you see the two hyperlinks and a quick message for the user.

4. The last piece of code that needs to be added is to set the `Page.Theme` property for the selected theme. Click on the Design tab of the Default.aspx page and double-click on the page to view the code in the Default.aspx.vb file. Within the code, you need to detect what the user selected and set the theme very early in the page cycle. Setting this in the `Page_Load` method will be too late; therefore you need to add this functionality in the `Page_PreInit` method as follows:

```
Protected Sub Page_PreInit(ByVal sender As Object,
ByVal e As System.EventArgs)
Handles Me.PreInit
                Page.Theme = Request.QueryString("Theme")
End Sub
```

Here in this code, you added the `Page_PreInit` method along with the handler `Handles Me.PreInit`. Within this method, you get the `Page.Theme` property, which is a string, and set it to the selected theme requested from the user. You determine what the user selected by using the `Request.QueryString("Theme")` method. Looking back on the hyperlinks you added, they each had a query string of either `Theme=BlueTheme` or `Theme=RedTheme` that will be passed along when the user clicks one of the hyperlinks. The `Request.QueryString("Theme")` method will be able to determine which theme was selected and set the Page.Theme property, respectively.

5. You can now test the code, build and run the web project, and try to change the themes (Figure 9-12). When the page first loads, there will be no theme associated because you deleted the element from the web.config file.

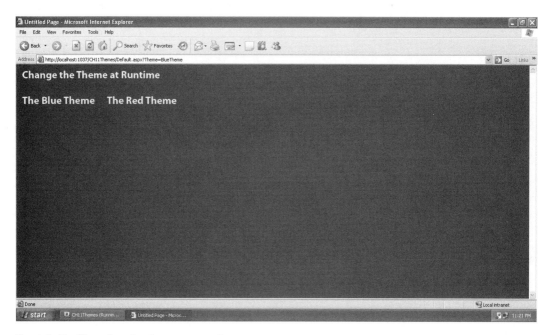

Figure 9-12. *Changing the theme at runtime*

6. Here you see the two links to change the theme. Click on the link The Blue Theme, and you will see the page as shown in Figure 9-13.

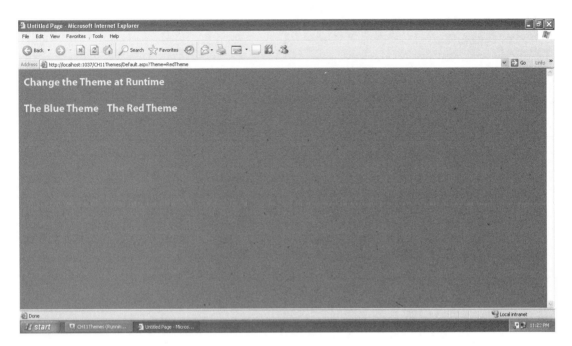

Figure 9-13. *The Blue Theme changed at runtime*

Now click on the link The Red Theme and view the page as shown in Figure 9-14.

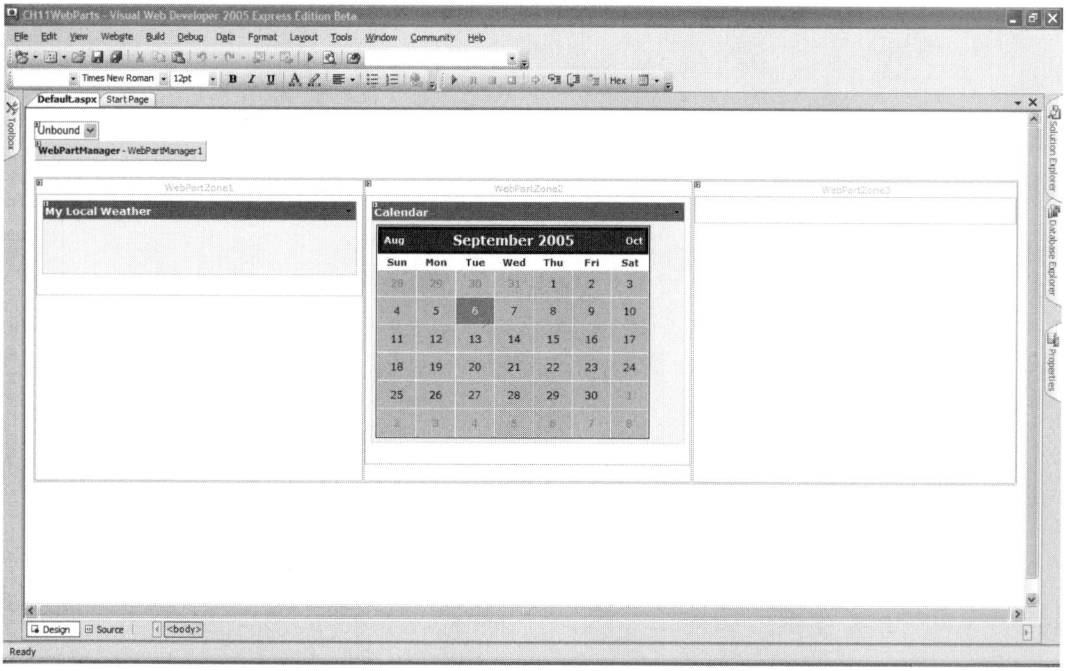

Figure 9-14. *The Red Theme changed at runtime*

Congratulations! With just a little code and effort, you allowed your users to personalize their experience of your website even more.

Summary

In this chapter you learned how to add customization to your web application to give it a more personal and intimate feel. With the advancement and complexity of web applications, many end users and customers want to be able to have a certain degree of control or customization over their content. By using the tools discussed in this chapter, you will be able to deliver this type of rich user experience.

CHAPTER 10

■■■

Administration
and Configuration

All websites need to store configuration settings along with addressing administration needs. Configurations can consist of application-specific settings or end-user settings. For instance, a web application has to address the needs of storing information, such as the email server or SMTP server that the application will use to send email messages. End users may be able to choose the theme or default language they prefer, as we discussed earlier. All of these choices are different settings that need to be defined. Administration settings typically come in the form of where and how these settings are going to be stored.

This chapter focuses on these issues and demonstrates the different techniques you can use to store and retrieve settings and configurations, along with how to administer the different options. These are the main topics covered:

- Examination of the machine.config and web.config files and their structure

- The Configuration Management API

- Administration tools

Configuration Files

At the heart of the settings and configurations in ASP.NET web applications are the configuration files. Each of these files is XML based, so all rules regarding XML apply.

■**Tip** Because the configuration files are all XML based, a good resource to review prior to getting into the details is `http://www.w3.org/XML`, which offers a thorough introduction and/or refresher of XML and its intricacies.

These files can be placed in any directory or subdirectory in the website project. Subdirectories automatically inherit any settings from the parent directory and also give you the ability to override functionality if you so desire.

When web.config file are in use, they are only read from or accessed from within the web application itself. ASP.NET automatically instructs the Internet Information Server (IIS) or the web server not to allow direct access to this file from the browser. For instance, if you attempt to view the web.config file from the browser by typing in the URL for the web.config, it would resemble the following:

```
http://localhost/mywebsite/web.config
```

Such an attempt returns a "This type of page not served" browser error, as shown in Figure 10-1.

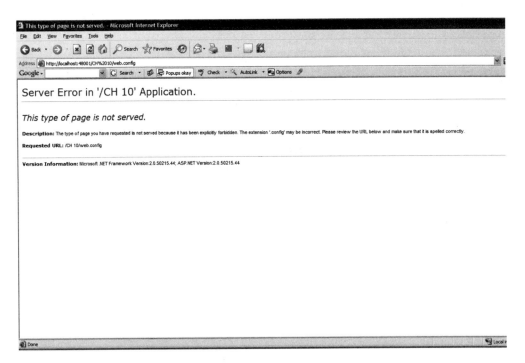

Figure 10-1. *Page not served browser error*

How Does It Work?

When the .NET Framework compiles the ASP.NET application, at runtime the web.config is read for each incoming URL request only once and then cached across any subsequent requests. The framework looks for the configuration file in a specific order and in specific locations and computes the settings that are subsequently cached. Table 10-1 outlines the sequence.

Table 10-1. *Order of Configuration Settings Executed and Location of Configuration File*

Purpose	Path or Location
Base configuration settings for machine	C:\Windows\Microsoft.NET\Framework\v2.0.*xxxxx*\config\machine.config
Root web configuration settings for machine	C:\Windows\Microsoft.NET\Framework\v2.0.*xxxxx*\config\web.config
Configuration settings for site (root application)	C:\inetpub\wwwroot\web.config
Override application configuration settings	C:\MyWebsite\web.config
Override subdirectory	C:\MyWebsite\Subdirectory\web.config

■**Note** The file paths specified in Table 10-1 may differ slightly on individual machines depending on the individual and default installation of the operating system.

So when an ASP.NET application is compiled and run, the framework looks for and caches the settings, starting with the machine.config file found at the base of the .NET Framework installation directory. Next it examines the web.config file in the same location, followed by the web.config file in the root directory of the web server, and finally the web.config in the root directory of the web project. For any requests in a subdirectory, those settings take effect from there.

Now that you have a firm grasp on how the settings are retrieved from the Framework in sequential order, let's look at the web.config and its details.

Configuration Sections

As we mentioned earlier, the web.config file is an XML-based file. Therefore, the web.config has all the common items found in XML. The root element of the web.config file is always a <configuration> tag. Nested within the <configuration> tag are the ASP.NET and end-user settings. Let's examine this tag:

```
<configuration>
    <!-- Additional / *ASP.NET and end-user settings
              placed within this region. */ -->
</configuration>
```

Within the <configuration> tag, you can specify ASP.NET settings by nesting the system.web or <system.web> section group tags. These contain all built-in ASP.NET settings.

```
<configuration>
    <system.web>
      <pages enableSessionState="true" />
    </system.web>
</configuration>
```

All settings are defined within the top-level <configuration> tag and applied to the current directory and all subdirectories beneath it. As web applications grow in size and scale, you will find that including web.config files within subdirectories of your project layout will be beneficial. There are times when you will need to apply a specific setting to a child or subdirectory from the parent. You can do this by using the <location> tag and the path element. Let's take a closer look:

```
<configuration>
   <location path="MySubDirectory">
     <system.web>
       <pages enableSessionState="false" />
     </system.web>
   </location>

   <location path="MySubDirectory2">
     <system.web>
       <pages enableSessionState="false" />
     </system.web>
   </location>
</configuration>
```

By adding this to your web.config file, the two subdirectories, MySubDirectory and MySubDirectory2, have settings applied from the parent directory to set the enableSessionState attribute to "false" where the parent or root directory has the same value set to "true."

However, your requirements may call for not allowing a subdirectory to override settings from the parent. You can lock these settings into effect by adding the element allowOverride to "false" within the location element as displayed here. You may want to do this when your web application grows in size and has a number of subdirectories that segregate and classify the Web Forms. These subdirectories typically all have something in common. For instance, the Web Forms found in the respective subdirectory might show detailed information from a main list of data.

```
<configuration>
   <location path="MySubDirectory" allowOverride="false">
     <system.web>
       <pages enableSessionState="false" />
     </system.web>
   </location>

   <location path="MySubDirectory2" allowOverride="false">
     <system.web>
```

```
      <pages enableSessionState="false" />
   </system.web>
  </location>
</configuration>
```

With this setting in place, if the application attempts to override the settings in either the MySubDirectory or MySubDirectory2 subdirectories, an exception is thrown.

The Configuration Management API

Because the web.config file is vital to your web applications, you are probably wondering if there's an easy way to read these settings or even change them. This is where the Configuration Management API comes in quite handy. Having a built-in library within the .NET Framework 2.0 provides numerous advantages for developers. Let's highlight these advantages:

- Settings are exposed as objects that can easily be programmed against.

- Support for inheritance is provided, plus each level of the application hierarchy of the API offers a readable representation of the merged settings for that level.

- Navigation of the hierarchy within the web application and access to settings in application subdirectories is easy.

- Access to remote web applications in addition to local applications is facilitated.

To access these features, you will deal with two namespaces within the .NET Framework 2.0: System.Configuration and System.Web.Configuration. Within these namespaces, you will use the classes ConfigurationManager and the WebConfigurationManager.

From these classes, you will use one of the several available static members to extract and manipulate the settings and configurations located within the various web.config files. These static members each return a System.Configuration object. The Configuration objects are the settings and configurations of the corresponding level. See Table 10-2 for comparison.

Table 10-2. *Configuration Actions and Members*

Action	Static Member of Class
Access machine.config file on the local machine	WebConfigurationManager.OpenMachineConfiguration()
Access root web.config on the local machine	WebConfigurationManager.OpenWebConfiguration(null)
Access web.config within local website	WebConfigurationManager.OpenWebConfiguration ("/MyWebsite")
Access web.config within a subdirectory of the local website	WebConfigurationManager.OpenWebConfiguration("/MyWebsite/Subdirectory")

Again, remember that each member returns a `Configuration` object whose values are obtained from within the `Configuration` object. This is important because when retrieving these values, an object of the same type, configuration, will need to be configured.

Let's look at some code examples that demonstrate how to obtain the configuration settings from the respective web.config files.

Reading and Examining Configurations

When obtaining the `Configuration` object back from the static members just mentioned, you will be presented with a collection that needs to be iterated through to make any sense of the values you're seeking.

Our example highlights accessing a web.config that is in the root directory of your web application project. We are going to focus on the `<appSettings>` section or, more specifically, the `<appSettings>` tags. This section is apart from the `System.web` section where you will define the specific keys for later retrieval from the code. First, within your web project, let's add a web.config to the root and add the `<appSettings>` tags as follows:

```
<appSettings>
    <add key="SearchEngine"
                value="http://www.google.com" />
</appSettings>
```

For additional clarity, let's view the entire web.config file with the newly added `<appSettings>` tags and the other default values added:

```
<configuration>
        <appSettings>
        <add key="SearchEngine"
                        value="http://www.google.com" />
    </appSettings>
    <connectionStrings/>
      <system.web>
        <compilation debug="true"/>
        <authentication mode="Windows"/>
      </system.web>
      </configuration>
```

You're all set with the web.config file now. Within the `<appSettings>` grouping you have added a key, SearchEngine, and the value of the key, `http://www.google.com`. You could use this particular setting within your web application to specify Google as the default search engine or possibly to provide a link to a major search engine for your end users. The purpose of the `appSetting` and the context used is entirely up to you.

The next step is to extract the `appSetting` group values and write them to the browser. Proceed to the Default.aspx page that was included when your web project was created, and open the code view: Default.aspx.vb. Add the following code to the `Page_Load` method:

```
Protected Sub Page_Load(ByVal sender As Object,
        ByVal e As System.EventArgs) Handles Me.Load
    Dim config As System.Configuration.Configuration
```

```
config = System.Web.Configuration.WebConfigurationManager.
          OpenWebConfiguration("/CH10API")

Dim element As KeyValueConfigurationElement =
CType(config.AppSettings.
Settings("SearchEngine"),
KeyValueConfigurationElement)
Response.Write(element.Value)
End Sub
```

Let's examine the preceding code line by line for a thorough understanding. The line

```
Dim config As System.Configuration.Configuration
```

declares a variable, config, with the type System.Configuration.Configuration. This config
variable is then assigned to open the web.config file in the root directory of your web project,
as shown here:

```
config = System.Web.Configuration.WebConfigurationManager.
OpenWebConfiguration("/CH10API")
```

The OpenWebConfiguration static method is used, and the name of the web project,
"/CH10API", is passed as a parameter. When this line of code is executed, the config variable
is populated with the settings from the project root web.config file.

Now that the config variable is populated with the setting information, you can access
the variable to view the information. The next line declares and assigns another variable of a
KeyValueConfigurationElement type, which is then set to the specific key in the <appSettings>, in
this case the SearchEngine key.

```
Dim element As KeyValueConfigurationElement =
CType(config.AppSettings.Settings("SearchEngine"),
KeyValueConfigurationElement)
```

Here you'll see that we use the previous config variable to access the SearchEngine key via
the AppSettings.Settings() method. One last step, however, is that you must cast the type
returned from the AppSettings.Settings() method to a KeyValueConfigurationElement. You
need to cast the types here because you want the object being returned to be the same type.
After doing so, you are now ready to access the element variable to determine the value of the
SearchEngine key.

This takes us to the final line of code that will write the value of the SearchEngine key to
the browser:

```
Response.Write(element.Value)
```

When the entire code in the Page_Load method is compiled and run, you will see that the
value of the SearchEngine key is http://www.google.com, as shown in Figure 10-2.

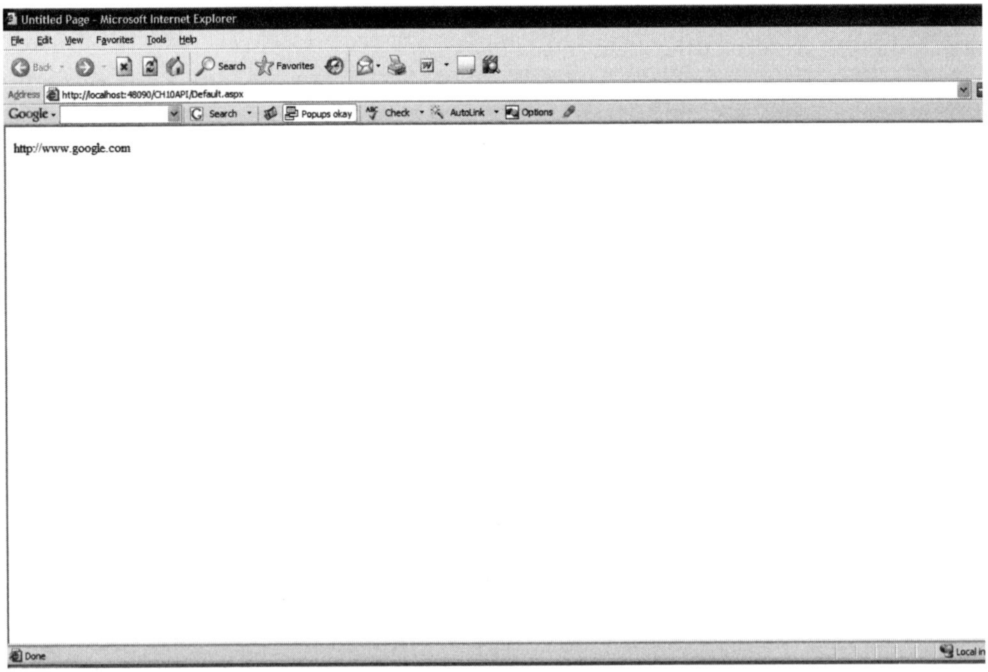

Figure 10-2. *Reading from the web.config file*

Updating Configurations

Now you know how to access and read the configuration settings. The next part is to alter the values and save the changes back to the web.config file. This functionality leverages on the classes and namespaces we mentioned and used earlier. When changing the value of the original key to the newly desired value, the Save() method is called, and then the settings are changed in the web.config value.

For this example, you will add a textbox, label, and a command button to the web page. When the page loads, the SearchEngine value will be displayed in the text of the label. You will then be able to enter a new value into the textbox and click the command button to update the settings. Let's look at the actual code:

```
Protected Sub Page_Load(ByVal sender As Object,
        ByVal e As System.EventArgs) Handles Me.Load
    If Not Page.IsPostBack Then
        Dim config As System.Configuration.Configuration

        config = System.Web.Configuration.WebConfigurationManager.
                    OpenWebConfiguration("/CH10API")
```

```
        Dim element As KeyValueConfigurationElement =
CType(config.AppSettings.
Settings("SearchEngine"),
            KeyValueConfigurationElement)
        labelAppSetting.Text = "Search Engine: " & element.Value
    End If
End Sub
```

Here is the Page_Load method's code. You are simply going to set the text of the label to the value of the SearchEngine key.

```
labelAppSetting.Text = "Search Engine: " & element.Value
```

When the code is compiled and the web page displayed, you will see that the SearchEngine key is displayed (Figure 10-3).

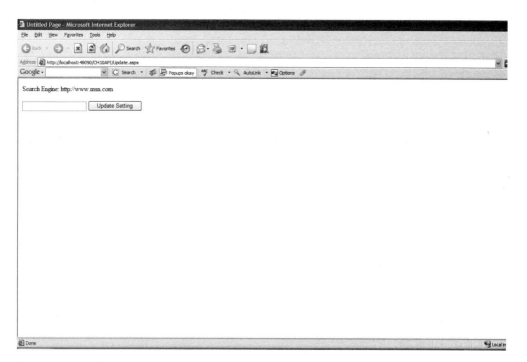

Figure 10-3. *Displaying the current key value*

Now let's move on to the code that will accept the new value from the end user, inputting it into the textbox and saving the new value back to the settings in the web.config. This code is placed in the Click event of the command button.

```
Protected Sub Button1_Click(ByVal sender As Object,
        ByVal e As System.EventArgs) Handles Button1.Click
        Dim config As System.Configuration.Configuration
        config = System.Web.Configuration.WebConfigurationManager.
                            OpenWebConfiguration("/CH10API")

        Dim element As KeyValueConfigurationElement =
CType(config.AppSettings.
Settings("SearchEngine"),
            KeyValueConfigurationElement)
        element.Value = TextBox1.Text

        Try
            config.Save()
            Response.Redirect(Request.CurrentExecutionFilePath)
        Catch ex As Exception
            Response.Write("An error has occurred saving
                    the configuration settings.  Make sure the
                    ASP.NET process account has write permissions
                    enabled.")
        End Try
  End Sub
```

The only new code within this section is the `Value` property of the
`KeyValueConfigurationElement` and the `Save()` method from the `Configuration`
class. Let's examine each line.

```
element.Value = TextBox1.Text
```

Here you set the `Value` property to whatever text the end user enters into the textbox.
This populates the element with the new value to be saved back to the web.config file.

```
            config.Save()
            Response.Redirect(Request.CurrentExecutionFilePath)
      Catch ex As Exception
Response.Write ("An error has occurred saving
the configuration settings.  Make sure the
ASP.NET process account has write permissions enabled.")
      End Try
```

Here the `Save()` method is called, and if executed successfully, you can essentially refresh
the page by calling the `Reponse.Redirect()` method by specifying the current page, which you
obtain programmatically with the `Request.CurrentExecutionFilePath` property.

There is one additional piece of information you need to be aware of here when saving and
updating settings. The directory in which the web.config is located needs to have write permissions enabled for the ASP.NET process. When creating a new web project, the ASP.NET process
typically has this permission enabled automatically. However, you should use a Try Catch
block to catch a possible error writing the new value back to the web.config file.

Finally, let's compile and run the project to see the code in action. As you saw in Figure 10-3, the SearchEngine key still has the same value: `http://www.google.com`. Let's change the SearchEngine key to use MSN instead of Google. Enter `http://www.msn.com` into the textbox, and click the Update command button. The page will refresh and show the new value for the SearchEngine key to be `http://www.msn.com`, as shown in Figure 10-4.

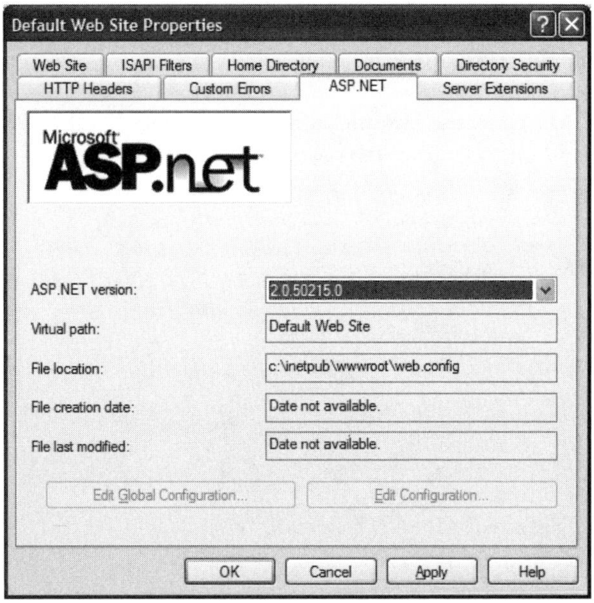

Figure 10-4. *Updated key value*

Proceed back to the web.config file, and you will see the new settings that took effect.

```
<configuration>
  <appSettings>
    <add key="SearchEngine"
                  value="http://www.msn.com" />
  </appSettings>
  <connectionStrings/>
      <system.web>
            <compilation debug="true"/>
            <authentication mode="Windows"/>
      </system.web>
</configuration>
```

Here you see the new value for the SearchEngine key was saved successfully to the web.config.

```
<add key="SearchEngine" value="http://www.msn.com" />
```

Practice entering new values in this example, and you will see that with a small amount of code, you can easily change configuration settings within the web.config file of your web application.

Encrypting Configurations

Many times in your web applications, you will want to take extra precautions in securing the settings we have examined thus far. It may be unlikely that you want to encrypt the SearchEngine key's value, but for purposes of this example we explore encrypting and decrypting this value in the code.

You will take your current web.config file and see how the values are encrypted by the API. Next, you will add a label and a command button to the web page. Proceed to the code, and within the Page_Load event, add the following:

```
Protected Sub Page_Load(ByVal sender As Object,
          ByVal e As System.EventArgs) Handles Me.Load
       If Not Page.IsPostBack Then
           Dim config As System.Configuration.Configuration
config = System.Web.Configuration.WebConfigurationManager.
         OpenWebConfiguration("/CH10API")

           Dim appSettings As ConfigurationSection
                   = config.GetSection("appSettings")
           labelAppSetting.Text = "Search Engine: " &
Server.HtmlEncode(appSettings.SectionInformation.
GetRawXml())
       End If
 End Sub
```

Within this piece of code, you set up a similar situation to the previous sections. The config variable is set to be populated by the OpenWebConfiguration() method.

```
Dim config As System.Configuration.Configuration
config = System.Web.Configuration.WebConfigurationManager.
       OpenWebConfiguration("/CH10API")
```

Then the variable appSettings is declared as a ConfigurationSection object and is populated by the Configuration method GetSection(), passing in the appSettings argument.

```
Dim appSettings As ConfigurationSection
             = config.GetSection("appSettings")
```

The final step is to set the text of the label to the raw XML that is contained in the appSettings object by utilizing the SectionInformation.GetRawXml() method.

```
labelAppSetting.Text = "Search Engine: " &
 Server.HtmlEncode(appSettings.SectionInformation.
GetRawXml())
```

Your web application is now set up to read the <appSettings> XML. Let's look at the code that you will place in the Click event of the command button to encrypt the settings:

```
Protected Sub Button1_Click(ByVal sender As Object,
        ByVal e As System.EventArgs) Handles Button1.Click
    Dim config As System.Configuration.Configuration
    config = System.Web.Configuration.WebConfigurationManager.
        OpenWebConfiguration("/CH10API")

    Dim appSettings As ConfigurationSection
            = config.GetSection("appSettings")
    If (appSettings.SectionInformation.IsProtected) Then
        appSettings.SectionInformation.UnprotectSection()
    Else
        appSettings.SectionInformation.
            ProtectSection("DataProtectionConfigurationProvider")
    End If
    Try
        config.Save()
        Response.Redirect(Request.CurrentExecutionFilePath)
    Catch ex As Exception
        Response.Write("An error has occurred
                    saving the configuration settings.  Make sure the
                    ASP.NET process account has write permissions enabled.")
    End Try
End Sub
```

This code reads the configuration settings and then evaluates whether the settings are encrypted or not.

```
Dim appSettings As ConfigurationSection
        = config.GetSection("appSettings")
    If (appSettings.SectionInformation.IsProtected) Then
        appSettings.SectionInformation.UnprotectSection()
    Else
        appSettings.SectionInformation
            .ProtectSection("DataProtectionConfigurationProvider")
    End If
```

You achieve this evaluation by using the SectionInformation.IsProtected property. This is a Boolean property that returns "true" if the <appSettings> are already encrypted and "false" if they are not. If the property's value is "true," you will call the SectionInformation.UnprotectSection() method in the conditional statement clause, thus decrypting the information.

```
appSettings.SectionInformation.UnprotectSection()
```

However, if it is not encrypted, the code used is the `SectionInformation.ProtectSection()` method, which requires that the protection provider argument be passed with the method.

```
appSettings.SectionInformation
          .ProtectSection("DataProtectionConfigurationProvider")
```

You specify the default provider: `DataProtectionConfigurationProvider`. The last step is to save the new configuration back to the web.config, which will be similar to the previous examples. Try this:

```
          config.Save()
          Response.Redirect(Request.CurrentExecutionFilePath)
Catch ex As Exception
          Response.Write("An error has occurred
                    saving the configuration settings. Make sure
                    the ASP.NET process account has write
                    permissions enabled.")
End Try
```

The identical `Save()` method is called, and if successful, you refresh the page, or if there is an error saving, you write a message to the browser to alert the user.

There is an important issue to be aware of here, however. When the page refreshes, the values in the web.config are actually encrypted; however, when extracting the values from the API, if they are encrypted, the decrypted values are automatically returned. Thus you will see no difference in this particular example. However, let's compare the web.config files before encryption and after the `<appSettings>` are encrypted.

Here is the original and unencrypted web.config:

```
<configuration xmlns
          ="http://schemas.microsoft.com/.NetConfiguration/v2.0">
  <protectedData />
  <appSettings>
    <add key="SearchEngine" value="http://www.msn.com" />
  </appSettings>
  <connectionStrings/>
      <system.web>
            <compilation debug="true"/>
            <authentication mode="Windows"/>
      </system.web>
</configuration>
```

After the successful execution of the encrypting and saving of the configuration settings, the web.config resembles the following:

```
<configuration>
  <protectedData>
    <protectedDataSections>
      <add name="appSettings" provider
                    = "DataProtectionConfigurationProvider"
         inheritedByChildren="false" />
    </protectedDataSections>
  </protectedData>
  <appSettings>
    <EncryptedData>
      <CipherData>
      <CipherValue>AQAAANCMnd8BFdERjHoAwE/Cl+sBAAAAtfdg
          H6wRSEqOtCAxlsp3VAQAAAACAAAAAAADZgAAqAAAABAA
          AADEkVbmJrspolU5Ht6uSOa2AAAAAASAAACgAAAAEAAAAL
          6YpIfIIx+Qk1enSdCYPHe4AAAAaMAI50OPCbfgiwHmRMVhvK
          PzP8g771V9+sWQVcRtk8nYQUW7vpbi9w+fqln7ntHZGSgQfYl
          DmUqVvDh6GC/M/09J9jTYQc4d8aLInaioDQRpoi3XgqQC9wc
          Epwbv82JfIpqpM6fSs8Uk1yYv0gbKuracnqH7DBvhZug+KhxDq
          ShQcmdNn7d/xFWZnCHOGmZOfZLiHnXVZJ6eFF1PfnH9qR
          76lApJdhsyPbwSzPr6f39RfrxKLhQotxQAAAB8h6wKWK6o3
          YhDMEVAONLSYYIUIA==</CipherValue>
      </CipherData>
    </EncryptedData>
  </appSettings>
  <connectionStrings/>
      <system.web>
            <compilation debug="true"/>
            <authentication mode="Windows"/>
      </system.web>
</configuration>
```

The encrypted version of the web.config file is quite different than the original. You can see that a `<protectedData>` section has been added, along with the provider we specified.

```
<protectedData>
    <protectedDataSections>
      <add name="appSettings"
                    provider="DataProtectionConfigurationProvider"
         inheritedByChildren="false" />
    </protectedDataSections>
  </protectedData>
```

Finally, the actual section that holds the encrypted values of the `<appSettings>` looks like this:

```
<appSettings>
    <EncryptedData>
      <CipherData>
      <CipherValue>AQAAANCMnd8BFdERjHoAwE/Cl+sBAA
                AAtfdgH6wRSEqOtCAxlsp3VAQAAAACAAAAAAADZgA
                AqAAAABAAAADEkVbmJrspolU5Ht6uSOa2AAAAAASA
                AACgAAAAEAAAAL6YpIfIIx+Qk1enSdCYPHe4AAAAaMA
                I5OOPCbfgiwHmRMVhvKPzP8g771V9+sWQVcRtk8nYQU
                W7vpbi9w+fqln7ntHZGSgQfYlDmUqVvDh6GC/M/O9J9jTY
                Qc4d8aLInaioDQRpoi3XgqQC9wcEpwbv82JfIpqpM6fSs8
                Uk1yYvOgbKuracnqH7DBvhZug+KhxDqShQcmdNn7d/xF
                WZnCHOGmZOfZLiHnXVZJ6eFF1PfnH9qR76lApJdhsyP
                hwS7Pr6f39RfrxKI hQotxQAAAB8h6wKWK6o3YhDMEV
                AONLSYYIUIA==</CipherValue>
      </CipherData>
    </EncryptedData>
  </appSettings>
```

Because the web.config file potentially can be viewed by those who have unauthorized access, you should encrypt the values of your keys, thus making the values virtually impossible to be read and determined.

Administration Tools

All web applications, and software for that matter, need to be able to implement administration tasks easily. The .NET Framework 2.0 provides several management tools that you can use to perform such administrative tasks. These tools come in the form of the Microsoft Management Console (MMC) Snap-In, the Web Site Administration Tool, and, finally, command-line tools.

In this section, we focus primarily on the Web Site Administration Tool; however, we also supply details about the other tools available.

Web Site Administration Tool

Included within each of the web projects you create is the Web Site Administration Tool. This tool, as the name implies, is web based and allows you to access and configure a variety of settings, including the following:

- Using application security along with authentication and authorization

- Creating and managing users and roles

- Using application settings

- Configuring the SMTP email server and settings

- Taking the application offline

- Debugging and tracing

- Setting a default custom error page

- Selecting and configuring providers

You can access the Web Site Administration Tool in any web project by clicking on the Website menu item and selecting the ASP.NET Configuration item. This launches the Web Site Administration Tool in a new browser.

ASP.NET Microsoft Management Console Snap-In

Integrated with the IIS Snap-In is the ASP.NET Snap-In. It is accessed with an additional tab labeled ASP.NET, which provides settings for specifying the version of the .NET Framework along with the configuration file being used for the particular website showing its file path. It also shows when the configuration file was created and last modified.

To view the ASP.NET Snap-In, launch the IIS Management Console Snap-In, which you will find under the Administrative Tools. Let's take a look at the default website on your machine by right-clicking on the default website in IIS and choosing the Properties menu item. Last, click on the ASP.NET tab, as shown in Figure 10-5.

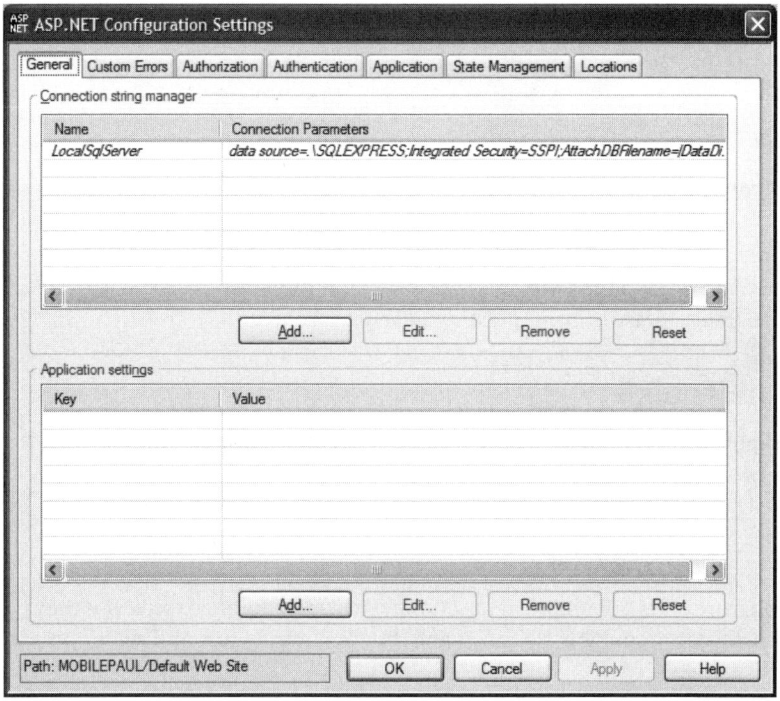

Figure 10-5. *ASP.NET Microsoft Management Console Snap-In*

Here you can choose the version of ASP.NET to use with the website, along with the configuration file currently being used. At this point, you can even change the configuration settings by clicking on the Edit configuration button, which will then give you an interface where you can alter or add to your settings (Figure 10-6).

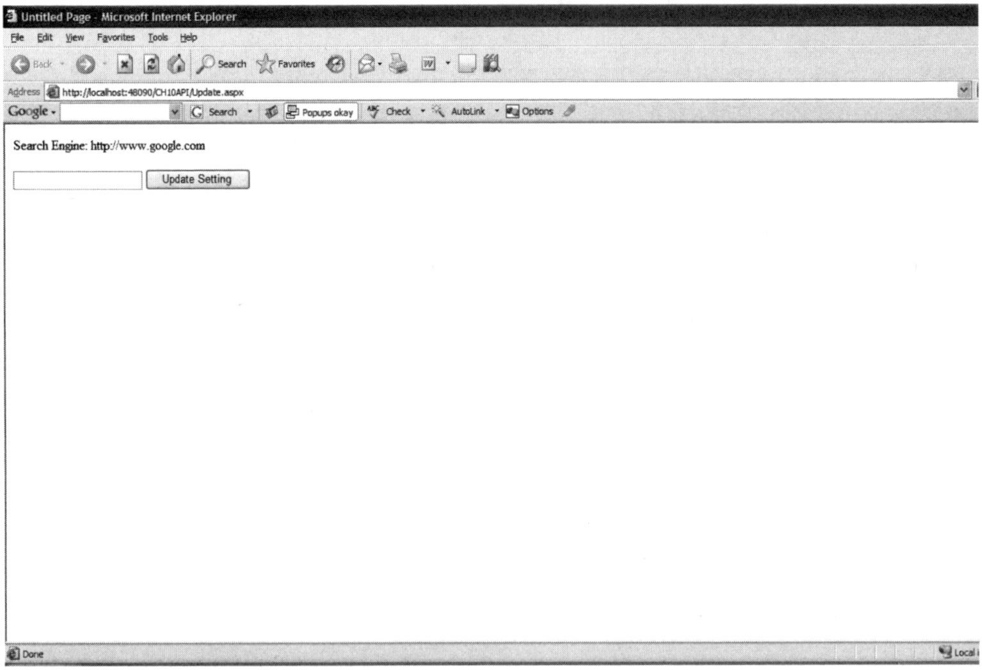

Figure 10-6. *ASP.NET configuration settings*

This dialog window shows several tabs that represent the different sections within the web.config. Therefore, in addition to adding or editing settings directly within the web.config file, you also have the ability to use this interface to make your changes.

Command-Line Tools

In addition to the graphical interface tools, command-line tools are included with the .NET Framework 2.0. The two main command-line tools are ASPNET_REGSQL and ASPNET_REGIIS, which you can locate from the following directory:

```
C:\WINDOWS\Microsoft.NET\Framework\v2.0.xxxx
```

Each of these tools provides the identical functionality as the graphical tools, but they are used strictly from the command line by specifying different arguments and switch-line commands.

Summary

In this chapter, you learned the importance of having configuration settings and administrative functionality to address these settings. All of the settings are confined within the web.config and machine.config files, which are both XML-based files.

You can access and view these settings easily from a variety of methods, including the Configuration Management API, which provides programmatic access, and the Web Site Administration Tool.

CHAPTER 11

■■■

Securing Websites

One of the hottest topics today with regard to technology, and more specifically the Internet, is security. It is a fact that there is a continual threat to networks and web applications because undoubtedly someone is trying to compromise this content. These kinds of threats may come in the form of a hacker scanning for open ports on a server or exploiting a security flaw in an operating system. Given this fact, you must prepare and take the necessary precautions to safeguard your websites and projects.

You can equate this concept or line of thinking to locking the doors to your home or perhaps enabling an advanced security system. Websites and web applications need to have sensitive data locked down or the security system needs to be enabled.

In this chapter, we discuss the following methodologies and techniques that are available within the .NET Framework to safeguard your applications:

- Authentication and authorization

- Memberships and roles

- Security web controls

Having a firm understanding of how to apply these features greatly reduces any chances of unauthorized access to sensitive data in your web content.

Authentication

ASP.NET applications work hand in hand with the Internet Information Server (IIS) in many aspects. This is very much the case with security and authenticating users to view the information in your web projects. Given this information, you can choose three different schemes or methods to help authenticate users who want to gain access to your ASP.NET applications: Windows, Forms, and Passport authentication. Each has its own strengths for different scenarios. After reading this chapter you will have a full understanding of each method so you can decide which method is best for your individual application or project. Before getting into great detail, Table 11-1 compares the authentication methods.

We do not discuss at length any authentication associated with your web content, but we need at least to mention that it is possible and an available option.

Lastly, regardless of the method of authentication, the web.config file holds the name and configuration settings for the method you choose. Next let's look at each individual method in detail.

Table 11-1. *Authentication Methods*

Method Name	Description
None	No ASP.NET authentication is active. IIS can still offer security services, but this is not recommended for use.
Windows	ASP.NET authentication services attach a WindowPrincipal object (`System.Security.Principal.WindowsPrincipal`) to the web request. This authorizes against a domain or NT user group.
Forms	ASP.NET authentication services utilize a cookie and ensure any unauthorized requests to a specific login page or URL where users can supply their credentials.
Passport	A Software Development Kit (SDK) provided by Microsoft in which the author of the web application registers with the Passport service that provides the authentication.

Windows Authentication

Windows authentication is best when your web application is used internally. Internal use means an intranet or some other piece of web software that only known users will attempt to access in a given environment that is only used within the local area network (LAN). In other words, the application is not available to the general public on the Internet where anyone can register for an account. In this type of scenario, you do not have to be concerned about where or how the user credentials are stored or configured. You only need to perform verification against the WindowsPrincipal credential.

Before proceeding, let's define a WindowsPrincipal by breaking the word into its two separate individual words: Windows and principal. The Windows portion refers to a Windows user and the associated role of Windows. A principal in this context relates to the identity of a user and his or her associated role.

This application typically authenticates against an Active Directory or Domain Controller on a LAN. All users and groups are configured and maintained from this one location.

■**Note** The Active Directory is a centralized user directory maintained within one server on a network. A good resource to learn more about Active Directory is `http://www.microsoft.com/activedirectory`.

Let's look at the web.config file and its configuration for Windows authentication:

```
<configuration>
    <appSettings/>
      <connectionStrings/>
    <system.web>
          <authentication mode="Windows"/>
    </system.web>
</configuration>
```

You can see that the configuration is quite simple in that one element, `authentication`, and its attribute, `mode`, is set to "`Windows`". Now that the web.config file is set up, let's move on to the Global Application Class or, more specifically, the Global.asax file.

The Global Application Class has several methods that are executed throughout the lifetime of the web application and the requests. The method we are interested in is the `WindowsAuthentication_OnAuthenticate()`. Within this method, we are going to attach a WindowsPrincipal object to the current user who is requesting the content from your web application. Here is the entire method that needs to be added to the Global.asax file:

```
Public Sub WindowsAuthentication_OnAuthenticate
        (ByVal Source As Object,
             ByVal e As  WindowsAuthenticationEventArgs)
                e.User = New System.Security.Principal.WindowsPrincipal(e.Identity)
End Sub
```

As mentioned, after this method is executed, the current request attaches the WindowsPrincipal object, which can then be accessed and utilized later in your application. This is important because the current request will then carry along the security information with it so it can be accessed throughout the entire web application.

You now have the web.config and Global.asax files all complete with configurations. Next you can move into the main content of your web application where you can use the User object to find out about each user who requests your application. Let's look at the Default.aspx Web Form to examine in more detail how you can use the User and User.Identity objects. The following code is within the `Page_Load` method of the Default.aspx Web Form:

```
Protected Sub Page_Load(ByVal sender As Object,
     ByVal e As System.EventArgs) Handles   Me.Load
        Response.Write("Name: " & User.Identity.Name & "<br>")
        Response.Write("Authentication Type: " &
            User.Identity.AuthenticationType & "<br>")
        Response.Write("Is Authenticated: " &
            User.Identity.IsAuthenticated & "<br>")

        If User.IsInRole("Administrators") Then
            Response.Write("User is an Administrator")
        Else
            Response.Write("User is NOT an Administrator")
        End If
End Sub
```

Here you can see that you will simply be writing some information out to the browser via the `Response.Write()` method. It all starts with the User object. The User object returns the `System.Security.Principal.IPrincipal` interface. From this object, you can access the `User.Identity` along with the `User.IsInRole()` methods. When building and running the web page, you can view the information about the current user, as shown in Figure 11-1.

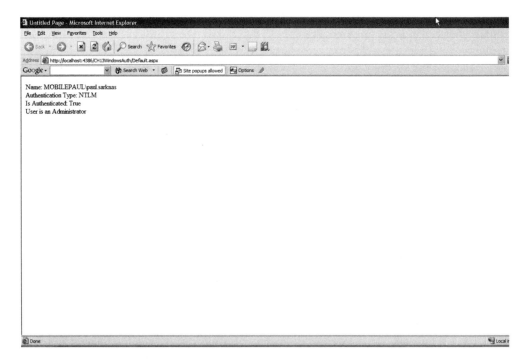

Figure 11-1. *Windows authentication information*

When the information is written to the browser, it displays the name of the current user or the user currently logged into your computer. It displays the computer name along with the login name. The computer name in our example is MOBILEPAUL, and the login name is paul.sarknas; therefore, we get the following for the output in the browser:

```
Name: MOBILEPAUL\paul.sarknas
```

The following output describes the authentication type, whether we are authenticated or not and if our username is within the Administrators group. The following is the output:

```
Authentication Type: NTLM
Is Authenticated: True
User is an Administrator
```

You can see that the authentication is Windows; I am authenticated because I'm logged in to my computer and I am part of the Administrators group. NTLM is an abbreviation for the Windows NT LAN Manager, which is a proprietary protocol developed by Microsoft and displayed in this example because it is used by Internet Explorer.

Forms Authentication

The second and probably most common method of authentication is called Forms authentication. Forms authentication is the way ASP.NET enables web applications to have their own login methodology and perform their own credential validation.

As mentioned with Windows authentication, the web.config file needs to be configured to use Forms authentication. We can do so by adding the following code to the web project's web.config file:

```
<configuration>
    <appSettings/>
    <connectionStrings/>
    <system.web>
        <compilation debug="true"/>
      <authentication mode="Forms"/>
      <authorization>
        <deny users="?" />
      </authorization>
    </system.web>
</configuration>
```

Forms authentication uses a cookie for each user that requests content of the protected web application. The details of the cookie are also specified in the web.config file, as shown here:

```
<configuration>
    <appSettings/>
    <connectionStrings/>
    <system.web>
        <compilation debug="true"/>
      <authentication mode="Forms">
        <forms name=".ASPXFORMSAUTH"
               loginUrl="login.aspx"
               protection="All"
               timeout="30"
               path="/">
        </forms>
      </authentication>
      <authorization>
        <deny users="?" />
      </authorization>
    </system.web>
</configuration>
```

Here you can see that additional attributes were added to the individual `<forms>` element. To help you understand all of the different options and configurations in the web.config, examine Table 11-2 to see the attributes and descriptions of each.

Table 11-2. *Forms Authentication Attributes*

Attribute	Description
loginUrl	Specifies the name of the web page to log in to and provide credentials. All unauthorized requests are redirected to this web page.
name	The name of the cookie created for the user's request.
timeout	The amount of time measured in minutes when the cookie will expire. A default value of 30 is given. The timeout is a sliding value, meaning that it is reset after each request until the final request is made. At that time, when a timeout occurs, the user is redirected to the specified login web page.
path	The path where the cookie is created. The default value is "/" and for our purposes, it's fine to use the default.
protection	Method where the cookie data is protected. There are a number of options you can use to protect the data as opposed to using clear text: All: Utilize both validation and encryption to protect the cookie data. None: Although providing the best performance, information is stored in a clear-text format. This option is not recommended. Encryption: Encrypts the cookie information in either the TripleDES or DES (Data Encryption Standard) encryption formats. Validation: No encryption used, but the information within the cookie is validated to determine if the information was altered between requests.

Upon completing the setup in the web.config, you have to provide a login page that matches the specified loginUrl you entered previously into the web.config configurations.

The login page needs to capture the username, typically an email address because of its uniqueness, a password, and a command button or link to initiate the verification of the entered credentials. You will then have a main page or home page that users need to be authenticated to access. This page is set as the default or startup page. When requested by the browser, the home page or main page is not available until authentication is performed successfully, thus redirecting the user to the login page. The user enters his or her credentials, and after being successfully verified, the application calls the following:

```
FormsAuthentication.RedirectFromLoginPage(textUsername.Text, False)
```

This code automatically directs the user to the originally requested web page, in this case the home or main page. If the credentials are not verified successfully, typically a login error message should be displayed.

After being authenticated, the user is able to browse any pages that allow access for the credentials that were supplied.

Now that you have a general overview of how to implement Forms authentication, let's walk through Exercise 11-1.

Exercise 11-1. Implementing Forms Authentication

This exercise will show you how to completely implement Forms authentication, from the web.config to using the `FormsAuthentication` class.

1. Again, all authentications begin with configuring the web.config file accordingly. For Forms authentication, add the following to the web.config file:

```
<configuration>
<appSettings/>
<connectionStrings/>
<system.web>
        <compilation debug="true"/>
        <authentication mode="Forms">
            <forms name=".ASPXFORMSAUTH"
                        loginUrl="login.aspx"
                        protection="All"
                        timeout="30"
                        path="/">
            </forms>
        </authentication>
        <authorization>
            <deny users="?" />
        </authorization>
</system.web>
</configuration>
```

2. Within your web project, you are going to add the following Web Forms: Login.aspx, Logout.aspx, and Home.aspx. After adding the Web Forms, right-click on the Home.aspx Web Form, and choose Set as Start Page. This sets the Home.aspx page as the default page within the application, and because you are not authenticated for access, you will be redirected to the login page specified within the web.config.

3. Now that you have all the Web Forms set up, let's look specifically at the Login.aspx Web Form. Add two textboxes and a command button to the Web Form. After adding these controls, double-click on the Command button to add an event handler to process the validating of the credentials.

■Note For the purposes of this exercise, assume that two users already have a username and password configured within the web.config file.

```
<configuration>
        <appSettings/>
            <connectionStrings/>
    <system.web>
            <compilation debug="true"/>
            <authentication mode="Forms">
                        <forms name=".ASPXFORMSAUTH"
                                    loginUrl="login.aspx"
                                    protection="All"
                                    timeout="30"
                                    path="/">
                        <credentials passwordFormat="Clear" >
                                    <user name="John.Doe@Yahoo.com"
                                            password="Test"/>
                                    <user name="Jane.Doe@Msn.com"
                                            password="Test"/>
                        </credentials>
                        </forms>
            </authentication>
            <authorization>
                        <deny users="?"/>
            </authorization>
    </system.web>
</configuration>
```

The passwords will also be stored in clear text, which is not recommended for professional or production applications but will suffice for the exercise. You will learn how to add users with an encrypted password in the final section of this chapter. Therefore, you will utilize the `FormsAuthentication.Authenticate()` method to verify the credentials for the exercise.

4. The code to process the credentials will be the following within the `Page_Load` method of the Login.aspx Web Form:

```
Protected Sub Button1_Click(ByVal sender As Object,
        ByVal e As System.EventArgs)  Handles Button1.Click
    If FormsAuthentication.Authenticate
                (textUsername.Text, textPassword.Text) Then
                FormsAuthentication.RedirectFromLoginPage
                    (textUsername.Text, False)
```

```
        Else
            Response.Write("Invalid Login!")
        End If
    End Sub
```

Here the `FormsAuthentication.Authenticate()` method will verify the credentials within the web.config file, and, if successful, the following code will execute; otherwise, an invalid message is written to the browser.

```
FormsAuthentication.RedirectFromLoginPage(textUsername.Text, False)
```

This code, when executed, will assume that the credentials are validated successfully and redirect the user to the originally requested web page. Let's take a look at how it works when running the web application. Because the startup web page is the Home.aspx page, you'll see that the following URL is displayed in the browser when the login page is displayed: `http://localhost:3194/ CH11FormsAuthentication/login.aspx?ReturnUrl=%2fCH11FormsAuthentication% 2fHome.aspx`.

Notice that the querystring refers to the Home.aspx Web Form:
`...?ReturnUrl=%2fCH11FormsAuthentication%2fHome.aspx`.

If authenticated, the browser will redirect to the originally requested page. When looking at the login page, you need to supply the credentials (Figure 11-2).

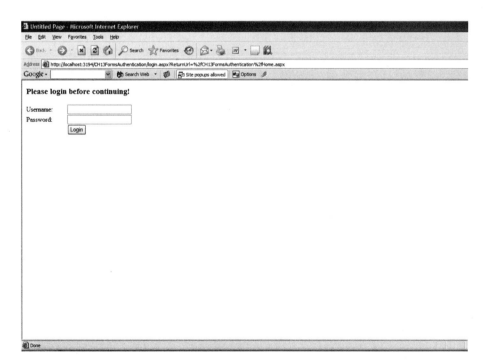

Figure 11-2. *Forms authentication login page*

Let's use the given credentials: username is jane.doe@msn.com with a password of Test. You will be redirected to the home web page. The home web page has a static table for demonstration purposes that represents four different items within an account.

5. Once your credentials are authenticated, you'll see you can access the home page. For demonstration purposes, we have included some static content in the form of an HTML table with fictitious data emulating account details (Figure 11-3).

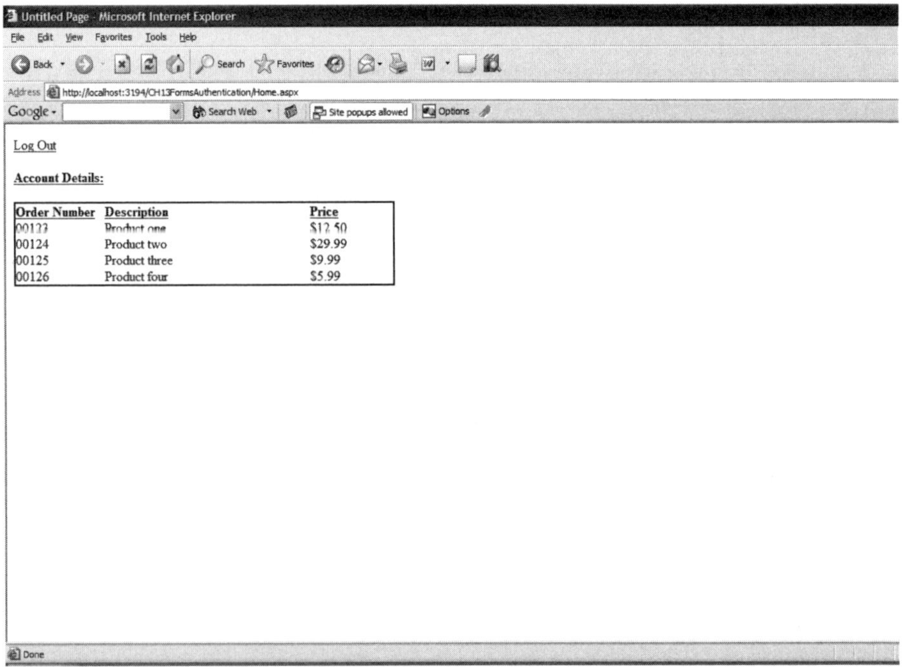

Figure 11-3. *Account details web page*

Most professional web applications have a great deal more content to which you could navigate, but for the purposes of this exercise, you can see the home page. On the home page, there is a Log Out link that will redirect you to the Logout.aspx Web Form using a Response.Redirect() method.

```
Protected Sub LinkButton1_Click(ByVal sender As Object, ByVal e As
    System.EventArgs)
    Handles LinkButton1.Click
        Response.Redirect("Logout.aspx")
End Sub
```

It then calls the following line of code within the Page_Load method of the Logout.aspx Web Form:

```
Protected Sub Page_Load(ByVal sender As Object, ByVal e As System.EventArgs)
    Handles Me.Load
        FormsAuthentication.SignOut()
End Sub
```

The `SignOut()` method from the `FormsAuthentication` class removes the cookie set from originally logging in, regardless if it is temporary or permanent.

That's all there is to it! With some configurations added to the web.config and a few web pages with FormsAuthentication code, your application is secure to only authorized users. In the exercise, we assumed the users were already created. The final section of this chapter discusses adding new users with some provided functionality and controls from the .NET Framework.

Passport Authentication

The final authentication method we discuss is the Microsoft Passport authentication. Given the scope of this book, it would be impractical to dive into great detail about this method. It is an option, however, but it requires registering your website with the Passport service from Microsoft and downloading their SDK.

For more information on using the Passport service, look at the Passport website at `http://www.passport.net`.

Membership and Roles

In addition to the authentication methods already described, there are other features that can greatly aid in the overall security of your web applications. These features come in the form of memberships and roles. Memberships and roles are classes that provide a wealth of administrative tasks, such as creating users and validating their credentials against a data store.

By using the features of memberships and roles, a great deal of work is done for you. Storing the users and their credentials is in a prebuilt accompanying package. There are programmatic methods already supplied to add, delete, search, and validate users who can access your web application. You need to know very little about how the memberships and roles are implemented and how the actual data is stored. This provides an additional security benefit in that these methods are prebuilt, tested, and use best practices within the code itself. For those of you who are new and inexperienced developers, you can use these prebuilt methods and avoid many common mistakes that otherwise could lead to potentially less secure web applications.

In this chapter, we examine the following topics:

- Learning about the `Membership` class

- Configuring the `MembershipProvider`

- Creating, searching, and deleting a user

- Verifying the user's credentials

- Managing user roles

The Membership Provider

The first priority, just as with the authentication methods, is to configure the web.config to utilize the membership functionality. We again turn to the web.config file to accomplish this setup. The prior authentication method, whether it is Windows, Forms, or Passport authentication, remains within the web.config. You will only be adding additional configuration options.

Before getting into the actual code for the configuration, note that if you do not have access to a full version or developer version of SQL Server, you can download and install SQL Server Express. For our purposes, we're assuming you selected the SQL Server Express when you originally installed Visual Web Developer 2005 Express.

Let's move on to getting everything in place. As just mentioned, you are going to keep the authentication method code and configuration in the web.config file; in this case it is Forms authentication. Add the MembershipProvider element, as outlined here, just after the authentication and authorization elements.

```
<membership>
    <providers>
      <add connectionStringName="ASPNETDB"
          applicationName="CH11Example"
          enablePasswordRetrieval="false"
          enablePasswordReset="true"
          requiresQuestionAndAnswer="false"
          requiresUniqueEmail="false"
          passwordFormat="Hashed"
          name="SqlProvider"
          type="System.Web.Security.SqlMembershipProvider" />
    </providers>
</membership>
```

Notice that the first attribute, connectionString, is set to ASPNETDB. This represents the SQL Server Express database that is going to be used along with the credentials. You will need to also add this connectionString within the <connectionStrings> element as shown next.

```
<connectionStrings>
    <add name="ASPNETDB" connectionString="Data Source=(local)
        \SQLExpress;Integrated Security=SSPI;Initial Catalog=aspnetdb;" />
</connectionStrings>
```

The entire web.config file will now resemble the following:

```
<?xml version="1.0"?>
<configuration>
  <appSettings/>
  <connectionStrings>
    <add name="ASPNETDB" connectionString="Data Source=(local)
        \SQLExpress;Integrated Security=SSPI;Initial Catalog=aspnetdb;" />
  </connectionStrings>
```

```
<system.web>
                <compilation debug="true"/>
                <authentication mode="Forms">
                <forms name=".ASPXFORMSAUTH"
                loginUrl="login.aspx"
                protection="All"
                timeout="30"
                path="/">
                </forms>
                </authentication>
                <authorization>
                                <deny users="?" />
                </authorization>
                <membership>
                                <providers>
                                <add connectionStringName="ASPNETDB"
                                        applicationName="CH11Example"
                        enablePasswordRetrieval="false"
                        enablePasswordReset="true"
                        requiresQuestionAndAnswer="false"
                        requiresUniqueEmail="false"
                        passwordFormat="Hashed"
                        name="SqlProvider"
                        type="System.Web.Security.SqlMembershipProvider" />
                                </providers>
                </membership>
        </system.web>
</configuration>
```

This might very well be your most extensive web.config configuration to this point in the examples and exercises. To avoid any confusion, let's break down each of the individual elements and their attributes just added by examining Tables 11-3 and 11-4.

Table 11-3. *ConnectionStrings*

Element or Attribute	Description
name	Provides the name of the connectionString that can be referred to later.
connectionString	The list of arguments that gives specifics about the database used and the credentials to connect. Data Source: The name of the SQL Server instance. Integrated Security: Security Support Provider Interface (SSPI). Enables the application to use various security models on the computer or network. Initial Catalog: The name of the database being used.

Table 11-4. *Membership Providers*

Element or Attribute	Description
connectionStringName	Refers to the name of the database connectionString defined in the `<connectionStrings>` element.
applicationName	The name of the web application.
enablePasswordRetrieval	A true-or-false value specifying if the provider will allow users to retrieve their password.
enablePasswordReset	A true-or-false value specifying if the provider will allow users to reset their password.
requiresQuestionandAnswer	A true-or-false value specifying if the provider will require users to supply a security question and answer.
requiresUniqueEmail	A true-or-false value specifying if the provider will only accept a unique email address.
passwordFormat	Specifies the format in which the password will be stored. Hashed, Encrypted, and Clear are the options. Note that the value chosen here will affect some of the preceding options for retrieving passwords.
name	The provider name.
type	The namespace of the provider.

One remaining item needs to be completed before you can start using the membership functionality. You need to be sure that the membership provider you just set up can connect properly to the provider. To test this connection, use the Web Site Administration Tool.

From the Website menu, select the ASP.NET Configuration option that will launch the Web Site Administration Tool. You are then presented with the home page, as shown in Figure 11-4.

Proceed to click the Provider Configuration link, which will show you the currently configured provider, which is AspNetSqlProvider (Figure 11-5).

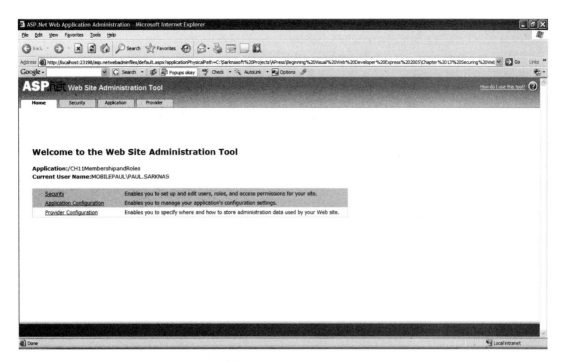

Figure 11-4. *Web Site Administration Tool home page*

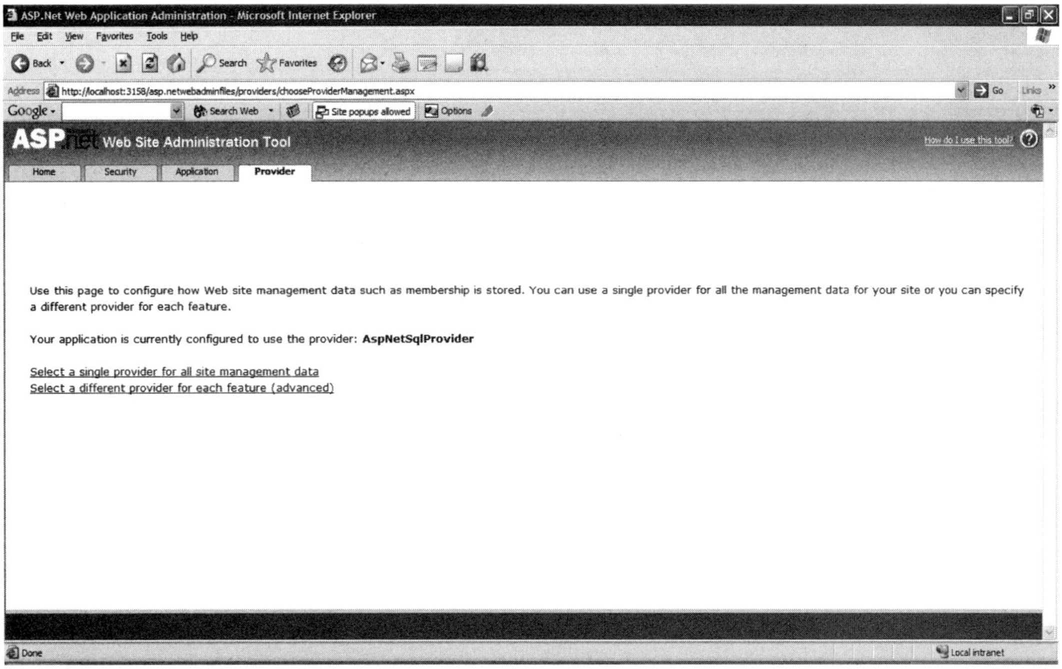

Figure 11-5. *Web Site Administration Tool: Provider tab*

From this page, you can perform two different actions. You can select and test a single provider or select a different provider that is reserved for more advanced users and applications. For our purposes here, select the first option: "Select a single provider for all site management data." This will then list the provider you just set up in the web.config file (Figure 11-6).

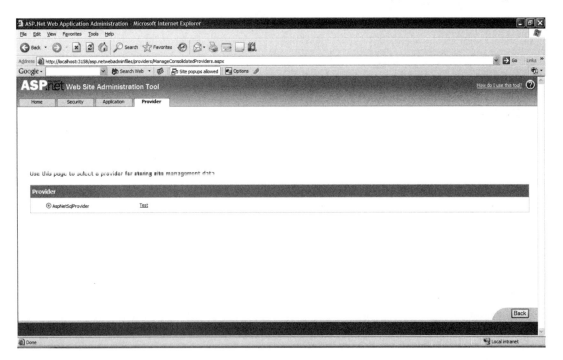

Figure 11-6. *Selecting the AspNetSqlProvider*

The AspNetSqlProvider is already selected. Click the Test link to the right to test the provider's configuration and connection to the database. If everything is successful, you should see Figure 11-7.

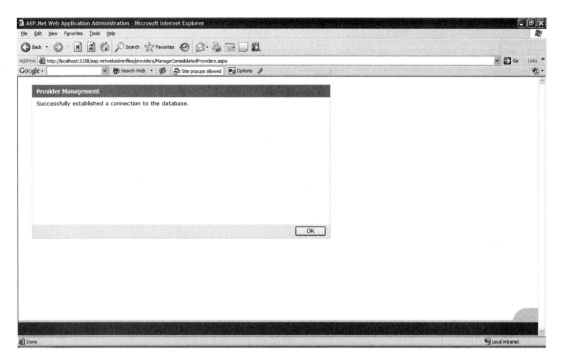

Figure 11-7. *Confirming the selection*

Click OK, and then close the Web Site Administration Tool. You are all set up to use the membership provider to enhance your web application with regard to security in adding, searching, deleting, and verifying users with little code and no database setup.

Creating a New User

The first membership sample demonstrates how to create a new user that will be stored in the database using the provider you just established. To use this feature, you will choose the `Membership.CreateUser` method, which will return a status parameter. The returned parameter will not only give you an indication as to whether the new user was successfully created, but also information on whether the username was not unique or even if the password was not in the correct format.

■**Note**   When creating users via a membership, by default the passwords need to be at least seven characters in length and must contain at least one nonalphanumeric character such as an * (asterisk) or ! (exclamation point).

Let's move on to examining the generated code from the designer. For this example, you are going to add some web controls to a Web Form named Login.aspx to capture the information needed to add a new user. The information needed to be collected is a username, password, email address, a security question, and finally the answer to the security question. All of this information will be within a panel control that is invisible by default, and when the user clicks a link button with the text "Register as a new user," it will set the visible property of the panel to true. Using a panel control in this instance is useful because it allows a section in your web page to act as a container that you define. Here is the HTML of the Login.aspx Web Form:

```
<%@ Page Language="VB" AutoEventWireup="false"
        CodeFile="Login.aspx.vb" Inherits="Login" %>

<html xmlns="http://www.w3.org/1999/xhtml" >
<head runat="server">
    <title>Untitled Page</title>
</head>
<body>
    <form id="form1" runat="server">
    <div>
        <strong><span style="font-size: 14pt">
            Please login before continuing!</span></strong>
        <br/>
        <br />
        <table border="0" cellpadding="0" cellspacing="0">
            <tr>
                <td style="width: 100px">
                    Username:</td>
                <td style="width: 100px">
                    <asp:TextBox ID="textUsername" runat="server">
                    </asp:TextBox></td>
            </tr>
            <tr>
                <td style="width: 100px">
                    Password:</td>
                <td style="width: 100px">
                    <asp:TextBox ID="textPassword"
                        runat="server" TextMode="Password">
                    </asp:TextBox></td>
            </tr>
            <tr>
                <td style="width: 100px">
                </td>
                <td style="width: 100px">
                    <asp:Button ID="Button1" runat="server" Text="Login" /></td>
            </tr>
        </table>
        <br />
```

```
<asp:LinkButton ID="LinkButton1" runat="server">
        Register as a new user.</asp:LinkButton><br />
<asp:Panel ID="panelNewUser" runat="server"
        Height="50px" Visible="False" Width="125px">
    <table border="1" style="width: 348px">
        <caption>
            Create a new user.</caption>
        <tr>
            <td style="width: 162px">
                Username:</td>
            <td style="width: 149px">
                <asp:TextBox ID="textNewUsername"
                    runat="server"></asp:TextBox></td>
        </tr>
        <tr>
            <td style="width: 162px">
                Password:</td>
            <td style="width: 149px">
                <asp:TextBox ID="textNewPassword"
                        runat="server" TextMode="Password">
                </asp:TextBox></td>
        </tr>
        <tr>
            <td style="width: 162px">
                Email:</td>
            <td style="width: 149px">
                <asp:TextBox ID="textEmail" runat="server"></asp:TextBox>
            </td>
        </tr>
        <tr>
            <td style="width: 162px">
                Security Question:</td>
            <td style="width: 149px">
                <asp:DropDownList ID="dropdownlistQuestion" runat="server">
                    <asp:ListItem>Pets Name?</asp:ListItem>
                    <asp:ListItem>Mothers Maiden Name</asp:ListItem>
                </asp:DropDownList></td>
        </tr>
        <tr>
            <td style="width: 162px; height: 21px">
                Security Question Answer:</td>
            <td style="width: 149px; height: 21px">
                <asp:TextBox ID="textAnswer" runat="server"></asp:TextBox>
            </td>
        </tr>
    </table>
```

```
                   <asp:Button ID="Button2" runat="server"
                       Text="Add User" Width="133px" /><br />
                   <br />
                   <asp:Label ID="Label1" runat="server"
                       Width="100%"></asp:Label></asp:Panel>

       </div>
       </form>
</body>
</html>
```

Let's move to the code in the Login.aspx.vb file that will actually allow you to create a new user. The first section of code is simple; it will make the panelNewUser control visible to enter the new user's information.

```
Protected Sub LinkButton1_Click(ByVal sender As Object,
       ByVal e As System.EventArgs) Handles LinkButton1.Click
               panelNewUser.Visible = True
End Sub
```

Now on to the heart of the code that will use the membership feature to create a new user with the supplied information:

```
Protected Sub Button2_Click(ByVal sender As Object,
        ByVal e As System.EventArgs) Handles Button2.Click
        Dim createresult As MembershipCreateStatus
        Membership.CreateUser(textNewUsername.Text,
            textNewPassword.Text, textEmail.Text,
            dropdownlistQuestion.SelectedItem.Value,
            textAnswer.Text, True, createresult)

        Select Case createresult
            Case MembershipCreateStatus.Success
                Label1.Text = "The user was created successfully!"
            Case MembershipCreateStatus.InvalidUserName
                Label1.Text = "The username format was invalid."
            Case MembershipCreateStatus.InvalidPassword
                Label1.Text = "The password format was invalid."
            Case MembershipCreateStatus.InvalidAnswer
                Label1.Text = "The password answer format was invalid."
            Case MembershipCreateStatus.DuplicateUserName
                Label1.Text = "The username is already in use."
            Case MembershipCreateStatus.InvalidEmail
                Label1.Text = "The email format was invalid."
            Case MembershipCreateStatus.InvalidQuestion
                Label1.Text = "The password question format was invalid."
            Case MembershipCreateStatus.DuplicateEmail
                Label1.Text = "The email address is already in use."
```

```
        Case Else
            Label1.Text = "An error occurred while creating the user."
    End Select
End Sub
```

Within this code, there certainly is a great deal of functionality happening with a minimal amount of effort. First, you declare a variable name, `createresult`, as a `MembershipCreateStatus` enumeration.

```
Dim createresult As MembershipCreateStatus
```

This variable is then passed in as a parameter with the `Membership.CreateUser` method.

```
Membership.CreateUser(textNewUsername.Text,
        textNewPassword.Text, textEmail.Text,
        dropdownlistQuestion.SelectedItem.Value,
        textAnswer.Text, True, createresult)
```

Here you can see there are several parameters passed in with the `CreateUser` method, starting with the username, `textNewUsername.Text`; the password, `textNewPassword.Text`; the email address, `textEmail.Text`; the security question, `dropdownlistQuestion.SelectedItem.Value`; the answer to the security question, `textAnswer.Text`, a Boolean value of whether the new user can access the application true, and finally, the enumerated variable of MembershipCreateStatus, `createresult`.

You are all set now to build and run the code. When doing so you will see the login page with the link to create a new user, and after clicking the link, the new user panel will appear (Figure 11-8).

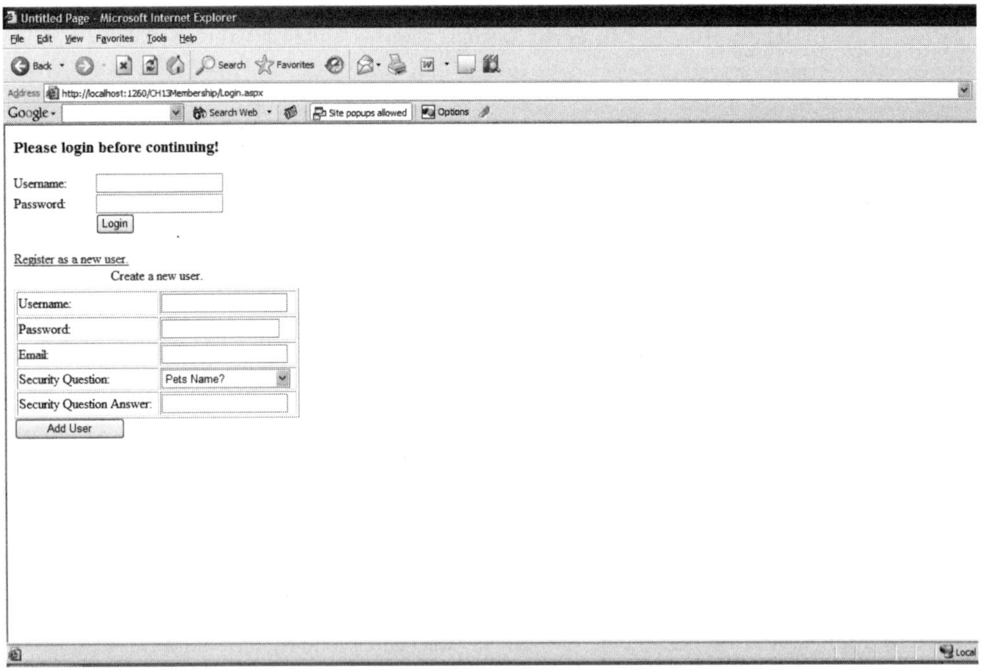

Figure 11-8. *Adding a new user*

Enter the following information for the new user to be created:

- Username: johndoe@yahoo.com

- Password: password*123

- Email: johndoe@yahoo.com

- Security question: Pet's name?

- Security question answer: Fido

When you finish entering this data, click the Add User button, and you will see the message that the user has been created successfully (Figure 11-9).

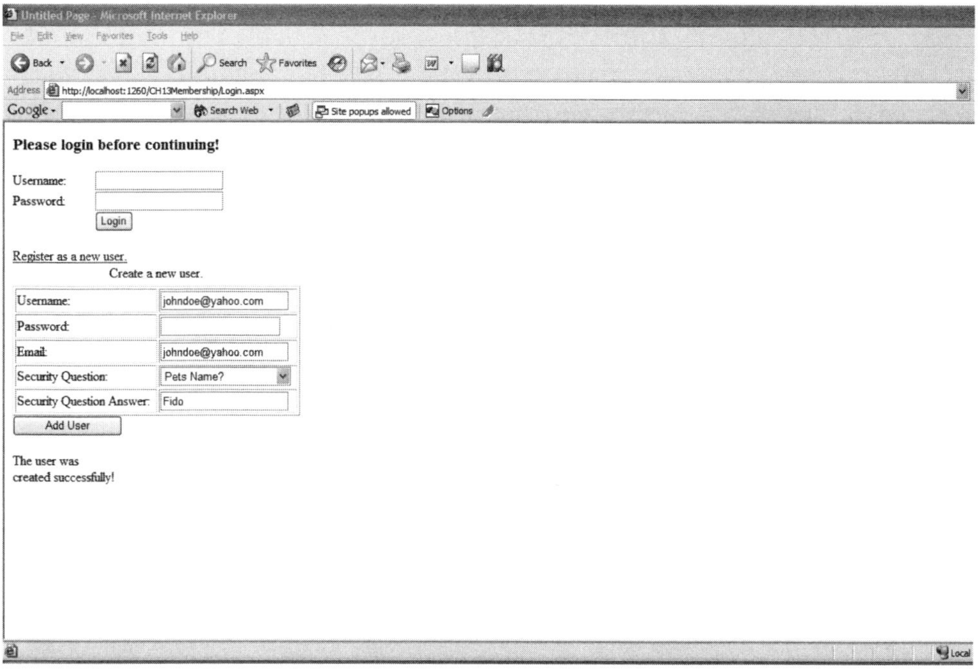

Figure 11-9. *Adding the new user information*

Congratulations! You have just created a new user by way of the membership class along with using the provider configured.

User Validation

The next step after creating a new user is of course validating his or her credentials and giving access to the content. The membership class is easily able to perform this task with the Membership.ValidateUser method. This will work in conjunction with our authentication method, Forms authentication, so that when users validate their credentials successfully, they will be redirected to the requested page to view the main content.

After successfully logging in, the Membership.GetUser method is available to retrieve the MembershipUser instance that gives the ability to access information and properties about the user who is currently logged in.

We will start off things again by going back to the Login.aspx Web Form and entering the credentials for the user you just created in the last section. When the web page is built and run, enter the following username and password:

- Username: johndoe@yahoo.com

- Password: password*123

Click the Login command button, and you will be presented with the Default.aspx page, which is the main content and home page of your application (Figure 11-10).

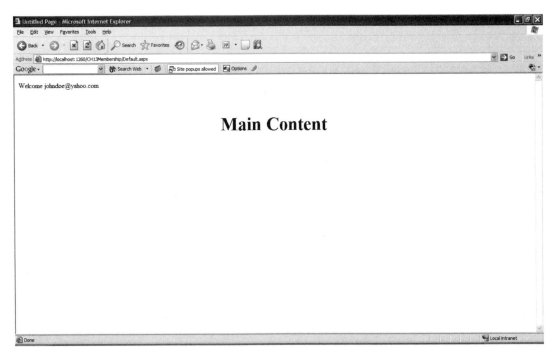

Figure 11-10. *Main Content web page demonstration*

You will also notice a welcome message displaying the user who just logged in (upper left corner). Let's examine how all this was achieved. It all begins with the login code on the Login.aspx Web Form:

```
Protected Sub Button1_Click(ByVal sender As Object,
      ByVal e As System.EventArgs) Handles Button1.Click
        If Membership.ValidateUser(textUsername.Text, textPassword.Text) Then
            FormsAuthentication.RedirectFromLoginPage(textUsername.Text, False)
        Else
            Response.Write("Invalid Login!")
        End If
End Sub
```

Here within the Click event of the Login button, you use the Membership.ValidateUser method along with passing in the username and password. This method returns a Boolean value indicating whether the user's credentials are valid or not.

After the credentials are verified, you are redirected to the Default.aspx Web Form, which is the home page of your content. The welcome message located in the upper left corner is displayed by the following code:

```
Protected Sub Page_Load(ByVal sender As Object,
      ByVal e As System.EventArgs) Handles Me.Load
              Dim currentuser As MembershipUser = Membership.GetUser()
              labelWelcome.Text = "Welcome " & currentuser.UserName
End Sub
```

A variable of the type MembershipUser is set equal to the Membership.GetUser method. From that call to the GetUser method, you can then access the current user who is logged in along with his or her information. A label's text is set to the UserName property of the MembershipUser class. Once a user is authenticated, in many instances some of the information will need to be changed and updated. Undoubtedly, you have seen in many of the more popular e-commerce applications a user profile section where users can change their password along with updating their contact information. For this demonstration, we will show you how to reset the user's password. To do so, you need to add a new Web Form named ChangePassword.aspx that supplies two textboxes in which you can supply the current password along with the new password. Let's take a look at the HTML for this:

```
<%@ Page Language="VB" AutoEventWireup="false"
     CodeFile="ChangePassword.aspx.vb"
     Inherits="ChangePassword" %>


<html xmlns="http://www.w3.org/1999/xhtml" >
<head runat="server">
    <title>Untitled Page</title>
</head>
<body>
    <form id="form1" runat="server">
    <div>
        <strong><span style="font-size: 14pt">Change Password<br />
            <br />
        </span></strong>
            <tr>        <table border="0" cellpadding="0" cellspacing="0">
                <td style="width: 126px">
                    Current Password:</td>
                <td style="width: 127px">
                    <asp:TextBox ID="textOldPassword"
                        runat="server" TextMode="Password"
                        Width="154px"></asp:TextBox></td>
            </tr>
            <tr>
                <td style="width: 126px">
                    New Password:</td>
                <td style="width: 127px">
                    <asp:TextBox ID="textNewPassword" runat="server"
                       TextMode="Password" Width="154px"></asp:TextBox>
                </td>
            </tr>
            <tr>
                <td style="width: 126px">
                </td>
```

```
            <td style="width: 127px">
                <asp:Button ID="Button1" runat="server"
                    Text="Update Password" /></td>
        </tr>
    </table>

</div>
    <br />
    <asp:Label ID="labelMessage" runat="server"></asp:Label>
</form>
</body>
</html>
```

In addition to the textboxes, you will also have a command button to execute the change of the password and a label to display a message if the task is completed. To navigate to this page, place a hyperlink on the default.aspx Web Form that links to the ChangePassword.aspx Web Form. Once users authenticate, they can click on this link and then enter their current password and click the command button named Update Password.

The code placed within the Click event of the command button will again instantiate a variable of the type MembershipUser from the Membership.GetUser method. Once instantiated, the ChangePassword method can be called, which accepts first the current password and then the new password. This method will return a Boolean value specifying if the password has been changed.

```
Protected Sub Button1_Click(ByVal sender As Object,
        ByVal e As System.EventArgs) Handles Button1.Click
            Dim currentuser As MembershipUser = Membership.GetUser()

            If currentuser.ChangePassword(textOldPassword.Text,
                textNewPassword.Text) Then
                        labelMessage.Text = "Password changed!"
            Else
                        labelMessage.Text = "An error has occurred!"
            End If
End Sub
```

Experiment with changing your password, and then try to log in again with the new password.

Deleting Users

A common task when managing users is completely deleting a user when a specific user no longer needs access to the application in question. This could be a scenario in which an employee leaves a company and hence no longer needs access. The membership class can handle this functionality by using the Membership.DeleteUser method.

Before deleting a user, you need to create an additional user for your application. You wouldn't want to attempt to delete yourself. Therefore, repeat the process to add a new user that will later be deleted. Next, add a new Web Form that will allow you to specify the username to delete. Here is the HTML:

```
<%@ Page Language="VB" AutoEventWireup="false"
        CodeFile="Manage.aspx.vb" Inherits="Manage" %>


<html xmlns="http://www.w3.org/1999/xhtml" >
<head runat="server">
    <title>Untitled Page</title>
</head>
<body>
    <form id="form1" runat="server">
    <div>
        <strong><span style="font-size: 14pt">Delete User<br /></span></strong>
            <asp:TextBox ID="textUsername" runat="server"></asp:TextBox><br />
            <asp:Button ID="Button1" runat="server" Text="Delete" />
            <br />
            <asp:Label ID="labelMessage" runat="server"></asp:Label>

    </div>
    </form>
</body>
</html>
```

As with the last demonstration, add a hyperlink to the home page that links to the new Manage.aspx Web Form. From the HTML just added, enter the following code in the command button's Click event:

```
Protected Sub Button1_Click(ByVal sender As Object,
    ByVal e As System.EventArgs) Handles Button1.Click
        If Membership.DeleteUser(textUsername.Text) Then
            labelMessage.Text = "User deleted!"
        Else
            labelMessage.Text = "An error has occurred!"
        End If
End Sub
```

Locking a User Account

The final feature to be discussed with the membership class is the ability to lock an account after a specific amount of failed attempts to log in. This provides a great security enhancement in that it prevents a user from trying to guess other users' credentials by attempting to log in numerous times with the guessed credentials. A more common prevention is that locking an account will not allow an automated process to attempt thousands or even millions of password combinations to gain access. This kind of attempt is commonly referred to as a *brute force attack* or a *dictionary attack* against the web application.

The membership feature automatically tracks the number of failed attempts to log in, and when the limit is reached, even if the correct credentials are supplied, access is denied. Access continues to be denied until the locked-out user is unlocked by another user, typically an administrator.

The code to unlock a user is slightly different than what we have seen to this point. When another user or administrator logs in, they will unlock the user with the following code:

```
Dim currentuser As MembershipUser = Membership.GetUser(textUsername.Text)
currentuser.UnlockUser()
```

The GetUser method is different here in that a specific user is passed as a parameter; the UnlockUser method can then be called from that MembershipUser object.

Roles Management

When referring to security, the first thought that comes to mind is to keep out all unauthorized users. However, there is another aspect of security: Within an application, you might only want certain users to have the authority to access certain content. For instance, a user with an administrator role might have the ability to access all content, whereas a general user is only able to view a limited amount of content.

You can also utilize roles associated with users to provide the additional point of security. Similar to memberships, roles have the ability to be stored in the same data source. With that said, you need to specify this in the web.config file:

```
<roleManager enabled="true">
    <providers>
      <add name="SqlProvider"
          type="System.Web.Security.SqlRoleProvider"
          connectionStringName="ASPNETDB"
          applicationName="CH11Example"/>
    </providers>
</roleManager>
```

Now that this is added to the web.config, all of the role information will be stored and retrieved by the same database as the membership information.

The Role class is similar to the Membership class in that the methods are self-explanatory and very easy to use. To demonstrate this functionality, let's continue on with the web project and add a hyperlink on the default.aspx Web Form to link to a new Web Form, ManageRoles.aspx. The following HTML is generated and placed in the ManageRoles.aspx Web Form:

```
<%@ Page Language="VB" AutoEventWireup="false"
    CodeFile="ManageRoles.aspx.vb" Inherits="ManageRoles" %>

<html xmlns="http://www.w3.org/1999/xhtml" >
<head runat="server">
    <title>Untitled Page</title>
</head>
<body>
    <form id="form1" runat="server">
```

```
    <div>
        <span style="font-size: 14pt"><strong>Manage User Roles<br />
        </strong><span style="font-size: 12pt">Role Name:
            <asp:TextBox ID="textRolename" runat="server"></asp:TextBox><br />
            <br />
            <asp:Button ID="Button1" runat="server" Text="Add Role" /> <br />
            <br />
        </span></span>
        <asp:ListBox ID="listboxRoles" runat="server"></asp:ListBox></div>
    </form>
</body>
</html>
```

This is quite similar to the other HTML you have added so far. It includes a textbox, a command button, and finally a ListBox that shows all roles. When a new role is added, the ListBox is automatically repopulated with the role just added. Now let's move on to the subsequent code beside:

```
Partial Class ManageRoles
    Inherits System.Web.UI.Page

    Protected Sub Page_Load(ByVal sender As Object,
        ByVal e As System.EventArgs) Handles Me.Load
            If Not IsPostBack Then
                            PopulateRoles()
            End If
    End Sub

    Protected Sub Button1_Click(ByVal sender As Object,
        ByVal e As System.EventArgs) Handles Button1.Click
            Roles.CreateRole(textRolename.Text)
            textRolename.Text = ""
            PopulateRoles()
    End Sub

    Protected Sub PopulateRoles()
            listboxRoles.DataSource = Roles.GetAllRoles()
            listboxRoles.DataBind()
    End Sub
End Class
```

Within this partial class are several pieces of functionality. First, there is a method called PopulateRoles that will populate the ListBox with all of the roles. The ListBox is populated by setting the DataSource to the GetAllRoles method, which returns a string array of all the roles. This is followed by the DataBind method of the ListBox.

The Click event of the Add Role command button used the Roles.CreateRole method, which accepts a parameter of the role name as a string. After being added, the ListBox is repopulated via the PopulateRoles method.

The role class also has many other features. Users can be added to certain roles along with verifying if they are within a role. At the same time, users can be deleted from any of the specified roles.

Security Web Controls

Now that we have thoroughly explored the different types of authentication along with memberships and roles, the last item to discuss are the included web controls that will add to the overall security of the web application. Many of these controls will look very similar to some of the web pages we created earlier in this chapter. There is a good reason for that. It is because these pieces of functionality are very common and used many times over and over again.

The controls are Login, LoginName, LoginStatus, LoginView, PasswordRecovery, and ChangePassword.

Login

Any web application that uses Forms authentication always needs a login page. Across different applications, the login page might look slightly different, but when examined closer, the content on the page is really the same.

The page consists of a textbox for each username and password, along with a link or some kind of button to execute the validation of the entered credentials. Some other items might be a checkbox that will remember your login and perhaps a link to retrieve your password if you forget it.

The login control provides all of this functionality encapsulated into a single control that can be placed on a login page by dragging and dropping. It can also easily be connected to the default membership provider. All that is left are some small property tweaks and then applying a style to give a more pleasing color scheme to the control.

To set up the Login control, drag it from the toolbox window onto the Web Form. Upon placing the control on the Web Form, you are presented with some formatting options by clicking on the Auto Format link. Let's look at the HTML:

```
<asp:Login ID="Login1" runat="server" BackColor="#EFF3FB"
      BorderColor="#B5C7DE" BorderPadding="4"
          BorderStyle="Solid" BorderWidth="1px"
          Font-Names="Verdana" Font-Size="0.8em"
          ForeColor="#333333" MembershipProvider="SqlProvider">
          <LoginButtonStyle BackColor="White" BorderColor="#507CD1"
              BorderStyle="Solid" BorderWidth="1px"
            Font-Names="Verdana" Font-Size="0.8em" ForeColor="#284E98" />
          <TextBoxStyle Font-Size="0.8em" />
          <TitleTextStyle BackColor="#507CD1" Font-Bold="True"
              Font-Size="0.9em" ForeColor="White" />
          <InstructionTextStyle Font-Italic="True" ForeColor="Black" />
</asp:Login>
```

There are other properties that can be enabled, such as displaying a checkbox to remember the login and the option to create a new user.

LoginName

The LoginName control is quite simple yet very useful. It is similar to a label control in that it displays the user's name on the web page where it is placed. There is only one property we are concerned about here: the FormatString property.

```
<asp:LoginName ID="LoginName1" runat="server" FormatString="Welcome {0}" />
```

The FormatString property accepts a text value where the user's name will be displayed. Enter any other text that you want to display in the message with the user's name.

LoginStatus

The LoginStatus control is also similar to a label control in that it is used for display. It indicates the state of the authentication for the current user and often works in conjunction with the LoginName control. Unlike a label, the LoginStatus control has a link button to either log in or log out, depending on what the current user login or authentication state is.

```
<asp:LoginStatus ID="LoginStatus1" runat="server" />
```

Utilizing this control facilitates the task of having a login link on certain web pages and having a logout link on another. All that needs to be done is set the property for the LogoutPageUrl.

LoginView

The LoginView control serves as a dashboard for the user when logged in. It will take a combination of both the LoginStatus and LoginName controls. This control determines and separates what unauthenticated users see compared to those who have been authenticated.

PasswordRecovery

The PasswordRecovery control is a useful control that encapsulates functionality and delivers an out-of-the-box component to the user. This control allows users to retrieve or reset their password, which will then be delivered in an email message. The HTML resembles the following:

```
<asp:PasswordRecovery ID="PasswordRecovery1" runat="server"
    BackColor="#EFF3FB" BorderColor="#B5C7DE"
        BorderPadding="4" BorderStyle="Solid" BorderWidth="1px"
      Font-Names="Verdana"
        Font-Size="0.8em">
        <InstructionTextStyle Font-Italic="True" ForeColor="Black" />
        <SuccessTextStyle Font-Bold="True" ForeColor="#507CD1" />
        <TextBoxStyle Font-Size="0.8em" />
```

```
        <TitleTextStyle BackColor="#507CD1" Font-Bold="True"
            Font-Size="0.9em" ForeColor="White" />
        <SubmitButtonStyle BackColor="White" BorderColor="#507CD1"
            BorderStyle="Solid" BorderWidth="1px"
            Font-Names="Verdana" Font-Size="0.8em" ForeColor="#284E98" />
</asp:PasswordRecovery>
```

This control too will easily use the default membership provider from which the password will be extracted.

ChangePassword

The ChangePassword control is a very simple control as well that requires practically no code to allow users to change their current password. If this type of functionality sounds familiar, it certainly is, because the underlying code for this control uses the membership class to change the password that we discussed in the earlier section. Here is the HTML rendered when the control is placed on the web page and formatted:

```
<asp:ChangePassword ID="ChangePassword1" runat="server"
        BackColor="#EFF3FB" BorderColor="#B5C7DE"
            BorderPadding="4" BorderStyle="Solid" BorderWidth="1px"
            Font-Names="Verdana"
            Font-Size="0.8em">
        <CancelButtonStyle BackColor="White" BorderColor="#507CD1"
        BorderStyle="Solid" BorderWidth="1px"
            Font-Names="Verdana" Font-Size="0.8em" ForeColor="#284E98" />
        <ChangePasswordButtonStyle BackColor="White" BorderColor="#507CD1"
            BorderStyle="Solid"
            BorderWidth="1px" Font-Names="Verdana" Font-Size="0.8em"
            ForeColor="#284E98" />
        <ContinueButtonStyle BackColor="White" BorderColor="#507CD1"
            BorderStyle="Solid"
            BorderWidth="1px" Font-Names="Verdana" Font-Size="0.8em"
            ForeColor="#284E98" />
        <TextBoxStyle Font-Size="0.8em" />
        <TitleTextStyle BackColor="#507CD1" Font-Bold="True" Font-Size="0.9em"
            ForeColor="White" />
        <PasswordHintStyle Font-Italic="True" ForeColor="#507CD1" />
        <InstructionTextStyle Font-Italic="True" ForeColor="Black" />
</asp:ChangePassword>
```

Again, the beauty with this control, like the others, is that no additional code needs to be added on the server side to actually call the method to change the password. All of this code is included with the control.

Summary

We certainly covered a great deal of material within this chapter. It is extremely important to become familiar with the techniques discussed to give your web application the best security possible. As mentioned earlier, it is inevitable that someone may try to gain access to your sensitive data. Luckily, the .NET Framework 2.0 provides many options and methods that you can implement to stop these unauthorized attempts. You can never achieve or guarantee total security 100% of the time; however, implementing the methods we discussed in this chapter will give you the safeguards necessary to gain the greatest security possible.

CHAPTER 12

■ ■ ■

Debugging Your Website

When developing websites and any software application, regardless of your experience level or how many applications you have developed, undoubtedly you will find the need for debugging. *Debugging* is examining the actual source code step by step within the application to determine where an error or unexpected result is occurring. The error could be a severe error that prevents the application from running or a logical error where perhaps a calculation is not quite yielding the result desired. Regardless of the error, you need to take a step back and consider what might be the possible cause. Typically, this will mean you must examine the source code line by line to narrow down the cause. Oftentimes this process can be long and tedious, but after reading this chapter, you will be better prepared for the challenge.

Enabling Debugging

When creating a new web project within Visual Web Developer Express 2005, support for the debugging is not automatically enabled. You will notice when a new web project is created that no web.config file is included in the project. From reading the previous chapters, you might have guessed that the ability to debug stems from the configuration to do so within the web.config file.

However, with that said, when a new web project is built and run, if there is no web.config file, Visual Web Developer Express 2005 will prompt you to select the option to enable debugging. The message appears as shown in Figure 12-1.

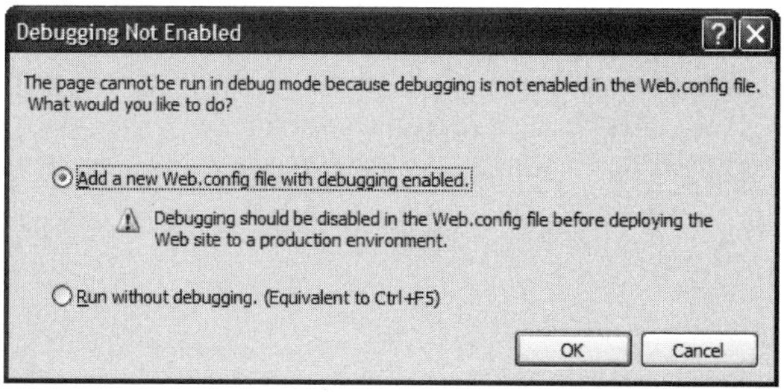

Figure 12-1. *Enabling debugging*

The message will default to the option of adding a new web.config file to your web project. After you click OK, the web project will run and debugging will be enabled. This message will not appear again when running the application. Now that you have a web.config file added to the web project, let's take a look at the web.config.

Note As an alternative to hand-editing this file, you can use the Web Admin tool to configure settings for your application. Use the Website ➤ ASP.NET Configuration option in Visual Studio.

```xml
<?xml version="1.0"?>
<!--
/* A full list of settings and comments can be found in
machine.config.comments usually located in
\Windows\Microsoft.Net\Framework\v2.x\Config */
-->
<configuration xmlns="http://schemas.microsoft.com/.NetConfiguration/v2.0">
<appSettings/>
<connectionStrings/>
<system.web>
        <!--
/* Set compilation debug="true" to insert debugging symbols
into the compiled page. Because this affects performance,
set this value to true only during development. */
        -->
        <compilation debug="true"/>
        <!--
/*The <authentication> section enables configuration of the
security authentication mode used by ASP.NET to identify
an incoming user. */
        -->
        <authentication mode="Windows"/>
        <!--
/ *The <customErrors> section enables configuration of what to
do if/when an unhandled error occurs during the execution of a
request. Specifically, it enables developers to configure html error
pages to be displayed in place of a error stack trace. */
```

```
        <customErrors mode="RemoteOnly" defaultRedirect="GenericErrorPage.htm">
            <error statusCode="403" redirect="NoAccess.htm"/>
            <error statusCode="404" redirect="FileNotFound.htm"/>
        </customErrors>
        -->
</system.web>
</configuration>
```

You can see that the added web.config file has some comments with helpful tips, but the element you are concerned with is the compilation with its attribute debug set to true.

```
<compilation debug="true"/>
```

A best practice to follow during development is to enable the debugging, which essentially loads debugging symbols. However, when the web application is ready for deployment or a production type of environment, it is best to disable or set the debugging to false, which will not load the debugging symbols. This will aid in the overall performance because the debugging symbols can add extra overhead.

Breakpoints

When debugging your web application, one of the first items to deal with is breakpoints. A *breakpoint* is a marker or flag that instructs the application to suspend the execution. When this occurs, the application is in break mode but it doesn't end or terminate the overall execution of the web application. During break mode, you can resume the execution at any time by clicking the Run button. However, the biggest advantage of using breakpoints while debugging is that all of the current variables, objects, and functions are still contained in memory. This can be compared to your favorite sporting event when a time-out is taken. During a time-out, the players remain on the field but their actions come to a stop. When a breakpoint is encountered, all objects and variables are still active but they too have come to a stop.

Inserting a Breakpoint

Now that you know what a breakpoint is and how it is used, let's move on to actually adding or inserting a breakpoint into your code. The code you are going to use is quite simple. It will declare a variable with a string value and write that value to the browser.

```
Dim stringvariable As String = "Breakpoint Example"
Response.Write(stringvariable)
```

You can add a breakpoint by simply right-clicking on the line of code and choosing Insert Breakpoint from the submenu as shown in Figure 12-2.

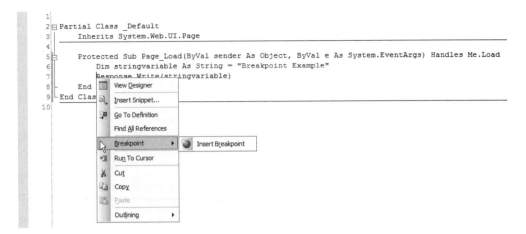

Figure 12-2. *Inserting a breakpoint*

After selecting this item, you can see that a breakpoint is added to the line of code by a red circle placed in the leftmost margin and the line of code selected highlighted in red. Figure 12-3 demonstrates this.

Figure 12-3. *A breakpoint*

You can add a breakpoint just as easily by clicking in the margin to the left where the red circle appears. You have just added a breakpoint to your code, and even though the code used in the example is very simple, you are nonetheless ready to debug and explore the web application in break mode.

Note in this example, however, that there is no bug or flaw within the code, and we are just examining some simple lines of code to demonstrate how to set breakpoints and debug. Run the web application, and you will see that within the Page_Load method of this particular Web Form, the execution will come to a stop and resemble Figure 12-4.

The application stops executing at the breakpoint and highlights the line of code in bright yellow. As mentioned, this code sample is very basic, and when you debug in a real-world application, there will be a great deal of additional code. However, this example will suffice in that you can see firsthand that within break mode, all the information within the code is still in memory.

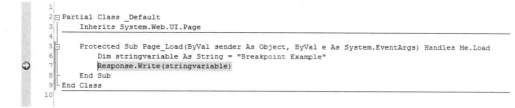

Figure 12-4. *A breakpoint during runtime*

Let's take a look at this. While the web application is still in break mode from stopping at the breakpoint, hover the cursor over the variable `stringvariable` within the `Response.Write` method. You can see that the variable is currently still in memory because a tool tip appears near the variable that displays the string value. In this case, the string value is "Breakpoint Example," which was declared in the previous line of code (Figure 12-5).

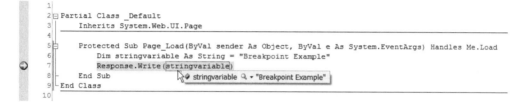

Figure 12-5. *Viewing a variable during break mode*

You will learn more about this very helpful tool tip window later in the chapter. However, with these few steps, you can see how easy it is to add breakpoints to your code and how beneficial it will be to examine the code in break mode to ultimately fix the error or bug in your application. To resume the execution of the code, click on the Run command again, and the application will resume.

What if you needed to examine more that just one or a few lines of code? In the next section, you will learn how to handle such a situation.

Now that you know how to insert, turn off, or delete a breakpoint, you can click on the red circle in the left margin and the breakpoint will delete.

Navigation During Break Mode

As we mentioned before, most applications have a greater amount of code than just a line or two. When this is the case, oftentimes to debug the application thoroughly, you will need to continue to examine the code while in break mode. To achieve this task, there are three different methods you can use to navigate throughout the code while still being in break mode: Step Into, Step Over, and Step Out. Each of these methods executes the code one line at a time, but depending on the situation, one method might be more advantageous than the others. Table 12-1 provides details of each method.

Table 12-1. *Navigation Methods*

Method	Description
Step Into	Executes the next line of code. Will enter into a method or function call, regardless if the method is contained within the same file or in a separate class.
Step Over	Executes the next line of code. Will *not* enter into a method or function call but instead executes the method or function and returns the value.
Step Out	Executes the next line of code. Returns the execution out of a method or function to the level above the current code execution.

Step Into

The Step Into method executes the very next line of code. This proves helpful when the code is broken out into different methods and functions. By using the Step Into method, you can force the execution of the code to navigate down inside any of the methods or functions. To step into a method or function, click on the icon to the left of the three navigation methods on the Debug toolbar. If you are not sure which icon is correct, hover over each of them to view the tool tip as shown in Figure 12-6.

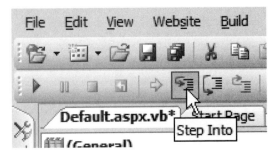

Figure 12-6. *Step Into*

To demonstrate this kind of navigation, we will use the code from earlier in the chapter, but we will change the functionality slightly to use a method to write to the browser. Let's look at the changed code:

```
Protected Sub Page_Load(ByVal sender As Object, ByVal e As System.EventArgs)
Handles Me.Load
        Dim stringvariable As String = "Breakpoint Example"
        WriteToBrowser(stringvariable)
End Sub

Protected Sub WriteToBrowser(ByVal whattowrite As String)
        Response.Write(whattowrite)
End Sub
```

The only difference with the altered code is that instead of having the `Response.Write` method within the `Page_Load` method, we added a separate method named `WriteToBrowser` to demonstrate the act of stepping into a method.

```
Protected Sub WriteToBrowser(ByVal whattowrite As String)
        Response.Write(whattowrite)
End Sub
```

This method simply uses the same `Response.Write` method to write to the browser. It will use the string parameter value `whattowrite` that is passed in when the method is called. Let's use the step into a method by placing a breakpoint on the `WriteToBrowser` method in the `Page_Load` (Figure 12-7). When running the application and the execution stopping at the breakpoint, click on the Step Into method on the Debug toolbar. The debugger will move to the `WriteToBrowser` method and in turn to the `Response.Write` method.

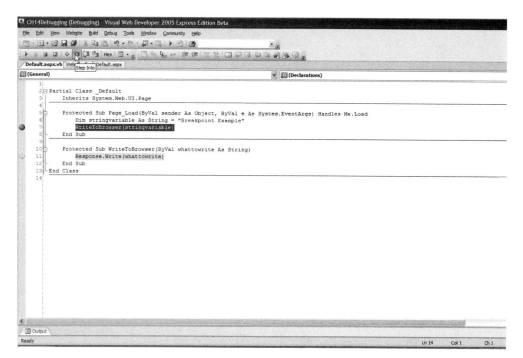

Figure 12-7. *Stepping into a method*

From this point, you can run the application to achieve the end result of writing the text to the browser.

Within this demonstration of inserting a breakpoint and halting the execution of the code, you can see that as your web applications grow in size and numbers of lines of code, using breakpoints will come in quite handy to examine code closer and find where unexpected results are occurring or where the system is breaking.

Step Over

The Step Over method executes the next line of source code; however, the main difference is that it will not navigate down into a separate method or function. The method or function will be executed and the value will be returned. Using this kind of debugging navigation can speed up the debugging process because it does not take you through a possible set of methods and functions. This is helpful when you determine that the error or exception is not occurring within one of these methods or functions.

To demonstrate, we will use the same code. However, instead of actually running the debugger into the WriteToBrowser method, we will use Step Over and you will see that the same result will be achieved. Keep the breakpoint that was set in the last section and run the project. When you encounter the breakpoint, click on the middle arrow icon within the Debug toolbar as shown in Figure 12-8.

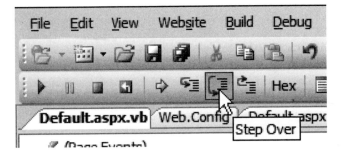

Figure 12-8. *Step Over*

As opposed to the debugger stepping into the WriteToBrowser method, by clicking on the Step Over method, the same result will occur.

Step Out

The Step Out method is typically used after using the Step Into method. To be more precise, oftentimes when you are debugging code and stepping into a method or function, there will be an instance when you want to return to the section of code where the method or function was called. The reason for this is that when looking for a bug and stepping into a method, there will be occasions where the bug is not found in the method and you need to continue from where the method was called. This can easily be performed by clicking the Step Out navigation method. As you might have guessed by now, the icon is located at the right of the three debugging navigation icons, as shown in Figure 12-9.

Again, you will use the Step Out method after using the Step Into navigational method. When the execution of the code hits the breakpoint and steps into the method, you continue to step into the code; however, at the end of the method, you can click the Step Out method to return to the code that called the method or function.

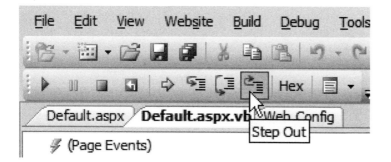

Figure 12-9. *Step Out*

Debugging Windows

Now that we have examined adding or inserting breakpoints within the code along with navigating throughout during break mode, there are some other tools available that will really help your debugging efforts. These tools come in the form of different windows in which you can analyze the data, objects, and variables within the code. These different windows are the Quick Watch window, Watch window, Locals window, Immediate window, and Call Stack window.

Quick Watch Window

The Quick Watch window is slightly different than its counterparts in that it really doesn't resemble a window but works more like a tool tip instead. However, it does provide a great deal of information. The Quick Watch window looks at a single object or variable to examine its details further. You have actually already used this tool earlier in the breakpoints section. To use the tool again, while in break mode, simply hover the cursor over a variable or object. Let's try this with our example code as shown in Figure 12-10.

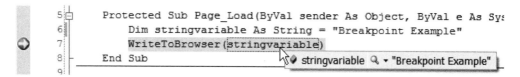

Figure 12-10. *Quick Watch window*

You can immediately see the evaluated variable. At this point, it is clear that this tool will prove to be very useful. However, there is another aspect you can use to examine the value of the variable or object in further detail. Within the tool tip, notice the magnifying glass and the small arrow. Click on the small arrow and notice the additional choices (Figure 12-11).

The additional choices given are Text Visualizer, XML Visualizer, and HTML Visualizer. These options are ways to view the data or information being examined in different formats.

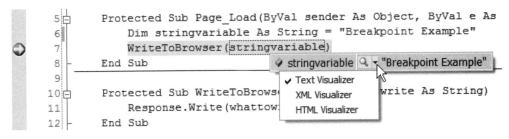

Figure 12-11. *Quick Watch formats*

Watch Window

The Watch window is used to evaluate variables and expressions within the code, and it also has the ability to maintain the results. When viewing the Watch window, three different columns present information: Name, Value, and Type, which you can see in Figure 12-12. In the Name column, any valid expression can be typed in to gain more information. The Value column displays the evaluation of the expression or variable corresponding to that in the Name column. Last, the Type column exhibits what kind of data type the variable or expression is.

After running the code and encountering a breakpoint, to open the Watch window, click on the Debug menu item, choose Windows, and select the Watch menu item. You will continue to use the same code and keep the breakpoint inserted at the same line of code. Figure 12-12 shows you what the Watch window will look like.

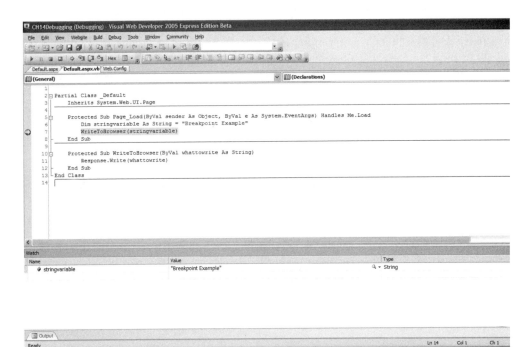

Figure 12-12. *Watch window*

You can see the three columns in the Watch window, and in this scenario you see the string variable with a value of "Breakpoint Example," which has a type of string. Practice and explore adding more variables to your code and then typing the names into the Watch window to see how they are evaluated.

Locals Window

The Locals window displays all of the variables that are local to the current context while in break mode. When referring to the current context, it is referring to the current method in which the code is being executed. This window also has three different columns of information: Name, Value, and Type. The Name column lists all of the variables in the current context scope. The variables displayed are not only ones that you have defined yourself in the code, but also any structure or array variables. For instance, you will be able to evaluate the Page object.

To open the Locals window, click on the Debug menu item, choose Windows, and select the Locals menu item. Figure 12-13 resembles what you will see.

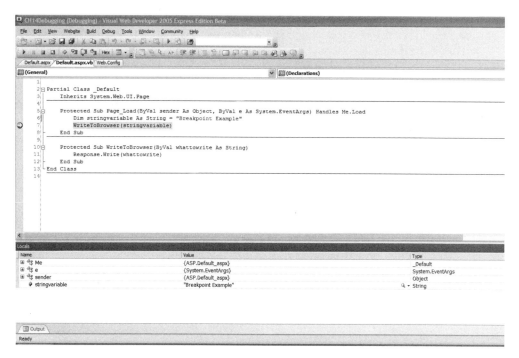

Figure 12-13. *Locals window*

In Figure 12-13 you can see the code in break mode and the Locals window open at the bottom of the Integrated Development Environment (IDE). Not only the variable that you declared in the code is evaluated but also the Me object and the two parameters that are passed into the Page_Load method: e and sender. Let's take a closer look at the Locals window by itself in Figure 12-14.

Locals		
Name	Value	Type
⊞ ◦ Me	{ASP.Default_aspx}	_Default
⊞ ◦ e	{System.EventArgs}	System.EventArgs
⊞ ◦ sender	{ASP.Default_aspx}	Object
◦ stringvariable	"Breakpoint Example"	String

Figure 12-14. *Close-up view of the Locals window*

Notice that the Me, e, and sender objects are part of a tree and can be uncollapsed to explore the objects in greater detail.

Oftentimes when you are debugging, you need to examine the value of the variables or objects and when they change. Using the different windows just described will greatly aid in this process.

Immediate Window

The Immediate window is a debugging window that allows you to evaluate expressions or issue commands within the IDE during break mode. Any of the variables can have their values changed, functions can be executed, along with statements as well.

To launch the Immediate window, click on the Debug window during runtime, choose Windows, and then select the Immediate option. When launched, it will resemble Figure 12-15.

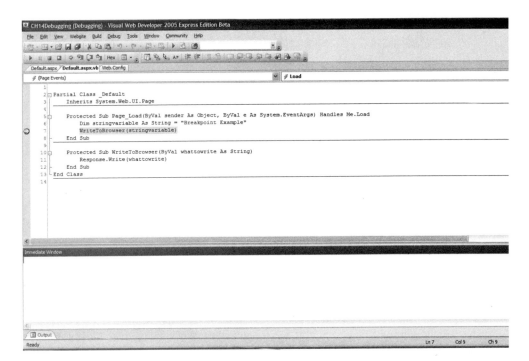

Figure 12-15. *Immediate window*

You can see that the Immediate window is launched and docked at the bottom of the IDE, similar to the other debugging windows. From here, if you are debugging, you can find many very useful techniques that will aid you during the process. Within the Immediate window, before evaluating any expression, be sure to type a question mark followed by the expression. For instance, let's first start out with a simple calculation. Type the following into the Immediate window and then press Enter: **? 10+10**.

The Immediate window will evaluate the mathematical expression to 20 (Figure 12-16).

```
Immediate Window
? 10+10
20
```

Figure 12-16. *Close-up view of the Immediate window*

Granted, this is a very simple example of calculating two different numbers, but the important concept to remember is that oftentimes there will be many variables in your application that represent numbers. Then these variables will be used in expressions to be calculated in some manner. To take this idea further, let's add some variables to your code base. The following variables should be added to the Page_Load method coming right after the stringvariable variable.

```
Dim i As Integer = 100
Dim a As Integer = 5
```

After adding these two variables to the code, run the application, and when the breakpoint is encountered, practice entering some expressions into the Immediate window for it to evaluate. We entered some simple division and multiplication in Figure 12-17.

```
Immediate Window
? i/a
20.0
? a/i
0.05
? i*a
500
```

Figure 12-17. *Using the Immediate window*

You can see that the Immediate window allows you to evaluate different variables and expressions during break mode that will aid in the overall debugging process.

> ■**Tip**   To delete or clear all the expressions in the Immediate window, at any time you can right-click in the Immediate window and choose the Clear All menu option.

Call Stack Window

The Call Stack window gives you the ability to view the current execution of the function or procedural calls that are currently on the stack. The term *stack* refers to a data structure in which objects or variables are kept in memory. It is called a stack because once an object is placed in memory, the next encountered object will be placed on top of the previous, hence the term.

To launch the Call Stack window while in break mode, click on the Debug menu, choose Windows, and select Call Stack Window. When launched, it will resemble Figure 12-18.

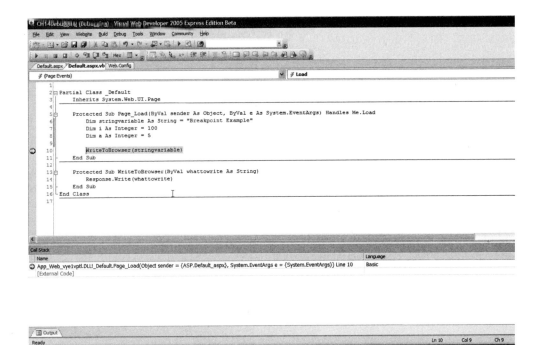

Figure 12-18. *Call Stack window*

The Call Stack window is docked in the lower section of the IDE. Let's take a closer look in Figure 12-19 at what the Call Stack window shows.

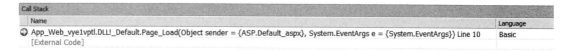

Figure 12-19. *Close-up view of the Call Stack window*

You can see that the Call Stack window shows the current Dynamic Link Library (DLL) from which the code is executing, along with the method or event that is being executed from the class. This type of examination is important when a web application is larger and has many different DLLs that are being executed and referenced. When this is the case, looking at the stack trace will help you determine where the current execution is originating from.

Tracing

The last item with regard to debugging an application is called *tracing*, which within the .NET Framework is like taking a look at the big picture within a web page. When you used break-points and the debugging windows, your objective was to dig into the details during break mode, which would allow you to do so within the code. Tracing displays information and messages about the actions occurring when the web page is processing and can also include any information that you want included. For instance, you may want to have a value at a given time included in the tracing output, such as the string variable from our previous example. Tracing will also give information on the data that is exchanged from the client or browser and then back to the server. This also includes any web controls, server variables, or cookies. Lastly, tracing can be enabled at the individual page level or at the application level.

Tracing at the Page Level

When a single web page is needed to display tracing information, this functionality can be enabled by configuring the page directive, which is found at the top of the web page within the Source view. Again, only perform this during development and not within the production environment because you do not want the end user to view this output. The page directive is quite simple; all that needs to be added is the following:

```
<%@ Page language="VB"      Trace="true" %>
```

When you build and run this page, any controls or other items placed on the web page will show at the top of the page. Below the controls the tracing information is displayed. This information is quite thorough and includes the sequence of the page events that occurred during the page running; any of the types, names, and size of any web controls used; cookies and their contents; and finally, any server variables, which are the collection of the information that was sent to the client or browser and back to the server. After adding the page directive, let's run the application with your prior code base and examine the tracing output information (Figures 12-20 through 12-24).

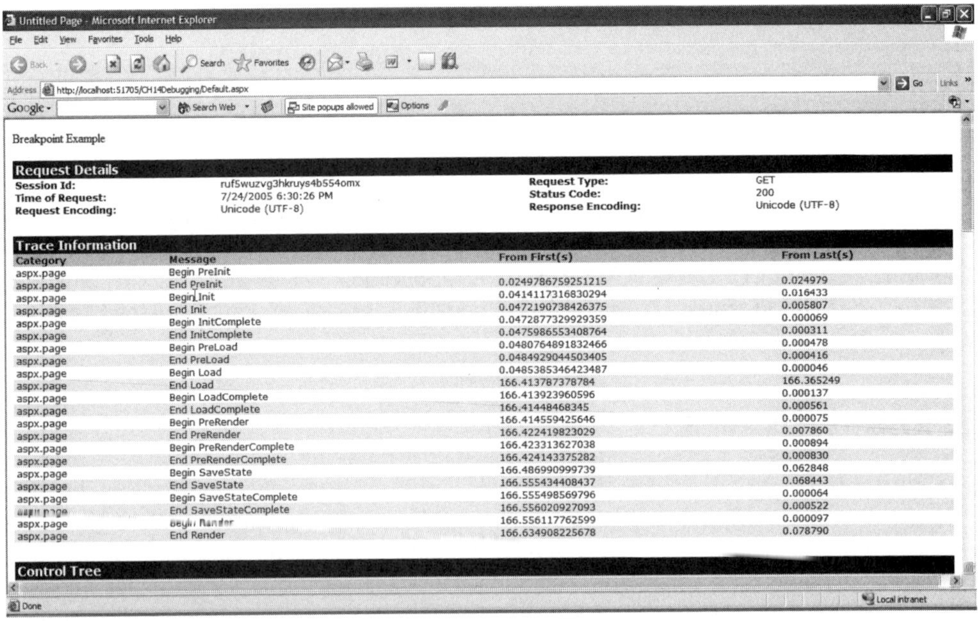
Untitled Page - Microsoft Internet Explorer
http://localhost:51705/CH14Debugging/Default.aspx
Breakpoint Example
Request Details
Session Id: ruf5wuzvg3hkruys4b554omx
Time of Request: 7/24/2005 6:30:26 PM
Request Encoding: Unicode (UTF-8)
Request Type: GET
Status Code: 200
Response Encoding: Unicode (UTF-8)
Trace Information
Category Message From First(s) From Last(s)
aspx.page Begin PreInit
aspx.page End PreInit 0.0249786759251215 0.024979
aspx.page Begin Init 0.0414117316830294 0.016433
aspx.page End Init 0.0472190738426375 0.005807
aspx.page Begin InitComplete 0.0472877329929359 0.000069
aspx.page End InitComplete 0.0475986553408764 0.000311
aspx.page Begin PreLoad 0.0480764891832466 0.000478
aspx.page End PreLoad 0.0484929044503405 0.000416
aspx.page Begin Load 0.0485385346423487 0.000046
aspx.page End Load 166.413787378784 166.365249
aspx.page Begin LoadComplete 166.413923960596 0.000137
aspx.page End LoadComplete 166.41448468345 0.000561
aspx.page Begin PreRender 166.414559425646 0.000075
aspx.page End PreRender 166.422419823029 0.007860
aspx.page Begin PreRenderComplete 166.423313627038 0.000894
aspx.page End PreRenderComplete 166.424143375282 0.000830
aspx.page Begin SaveState 166.486990999739 0.062848
aspx.page End SaveState 166.555434408437 0.068443
aspx.page Begin SaveStateComplete 166.555498569796 0.000064
aspx.page End SaveStateComplete 166.556020927093 0.000522
aspx.page Begin Render 166.556117762599 0.000097
aspx.page End Render 166.634908225678 0.078790
Control Tree
Done
Local intranet

Figure 12-20. *Stack trace output, view 1*

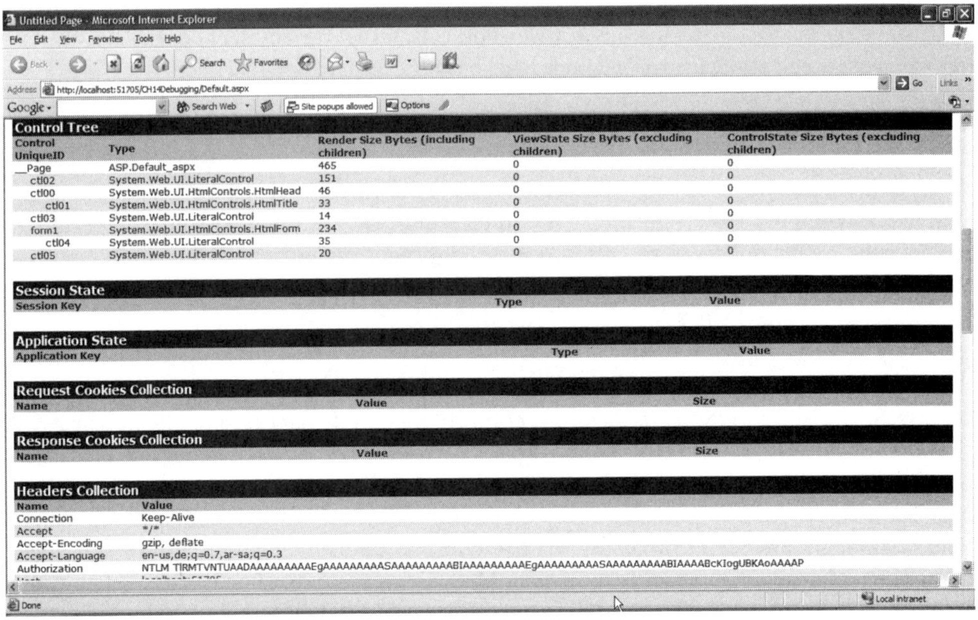
Untitled Page - Microsoft Internet Explorer
http://localhost:51705/CH14Debugging/Default.aspx
Control Tree
Control UniqueID Type Render Size Bytes (including children) ViewState Size Bytes (excluding children) ControlState Size Bytes (excluding children)
__Page ASP.Default_aspx 465 0 0
ctl02 System.Web.UI.LiteralControl 151 0 0
ctl00 System.Web.UI.HtmlControls.HtmlHead 46 0 0
ctl01 System.Web.UI.HtmlControls.HtmlTitle 33 0 0
ctl03 System.Web.UI.LiteralControl 14 0 0
form1 System.Web.UI.HtmlControls.HtmlForm 234 0 0
ctl04 System.Web.UI.LiteralControl 35 0 0
ctl05 System.Web.UI.LiteralControl 20 0 0
Session State
Session Key Type Value
Application State
Application Key Type Value
Request Cookies Collection
Name Value Size
Response Cookies Collection
Name Value Size
Headers Collection
Name Value
Connection Keep-Alive
Accept */*
Accept-Encoding gzip, deflate
Accept-Language en-us,de;q=0.7,ar-sa;q=0.3
Done
Local intranet

Figure 12-21. *Stack trace output, view 2*

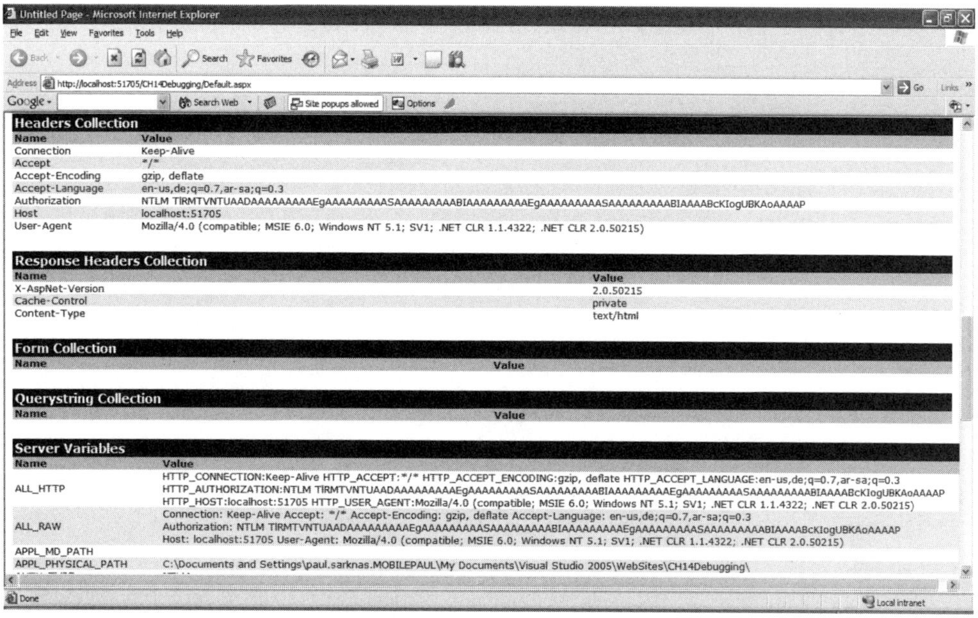

Figure 12-22. *Stack trace output, view 3*

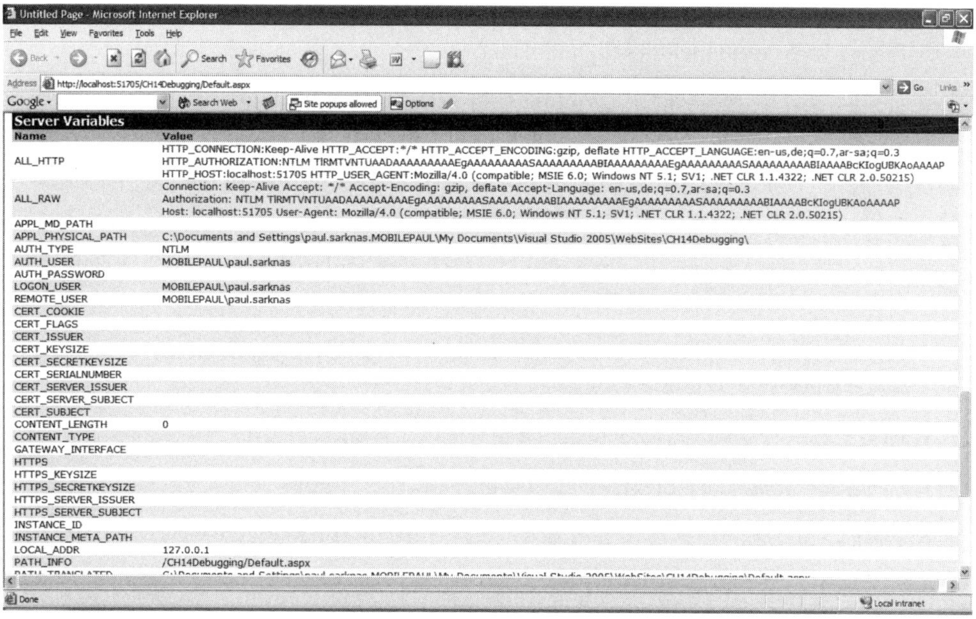

Figure 12-23. *Stack trace output, view 4*

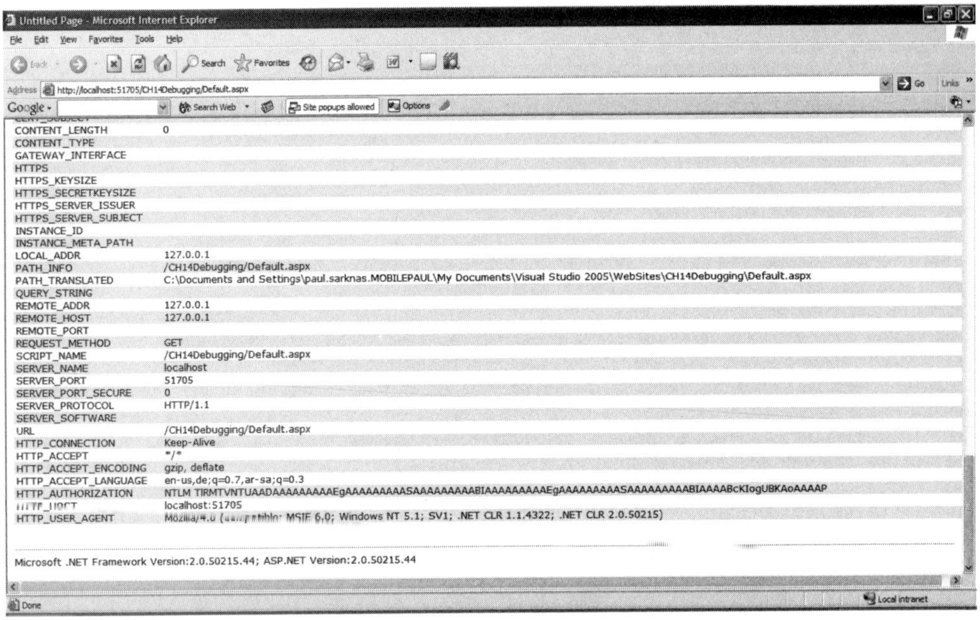

Figure 12-24. *Stack trace output, view 5*

You can see that tracing provides a wealth of information. To expand on the information given, the tracing output includes the following:

- *Request details*: Basic information including the Session ID Request time, Request encoding, Request type, Request status, and Response encoding.

- *Trace information*: Page-level trace messages that were written to the tracing output by using the `Trace.Write` and `Trace.Warn` methods.

- *Controls*: A list of controls within the ASP.NET page and their hierarchy. For each control, this section details the ID type, render size, and view-state size.

- *Cookies collection*: A list of all cookies with their values and size. These are all the cookies that clients send to the server.

- *Headers collection*: All HTTP headers.

- *Server variables*: A list of all server variables and their values.

Having all of this output information will give you a thorough macro view of what is happening on the individual web page.

Tracing at the Application Level

We have just examined how to enable tracing for an individual page; however, there may be times when you want to have every web page within the application to display the tracing information. It is true that you could add page directives to all the web pages within your application, but there is a far easier way to accomplish the same result. You will start off by using the Web Site Administration Tool.

To refresh your memory, click on the Web Site menu and chose the ASP.NET configuration menu item. When the home page is displayed, click on the Application Configuration link. Then click on the Configure Debugging and Tracing link under the Debugging and Tracing section. Here there are several options you can enable. The main item you will want to address is to check the option for Capture Tracing Information. The setting will automatically save the option, and then you can close the Web Site Administration Tool. Notice the newly added element to the web.config file:

```
<system.web>
        <trace enabled="true" localOnly="false" />
</system.web>
```

An element is added; trace which attribute is set to true. From this point, you can build and run the application as normal. There is something different here that you will notice right away. If you run the web page we have been dealing with, notice that no trace of information is displayed. You might be thinking that the settings didn't work. Actually, they did work, but when the tracing information is set at the application level, to view the web pages with the trace information you need to take an additional step. To perform this step, you must run the application and specify a certain web page that has been created for you. This page's name is trace.axd, which can be appended to the URL in the browser. For instance, within our web project configuration, we appended the URL as follows:

```
http://localhost:51705/CH14Debugging/trace.axd
```

When navigating to this web page in the browser, you will see the application trace as shown in Figure 12-25.

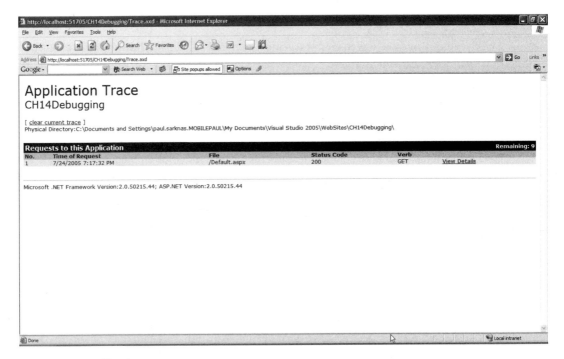

Figure 12-25. *Application trace*

Here you see all of the web pages within your application that you can navigate to by clicking on the View Details link for the respective web pages. Configuring tracing at the application level provides some advantages, in that it provides a single entry to enable or disable tracing along with, of course, saving a great deal of time compared to adding a page directive for all of the web pages in the web project.

When finished, remember to set the tracing back to false, which will turn off the feature so that end users do not see this output.

Custom Trace Output

The default trace information displayed oftentimes is adequate for web applications. However, there will be times when you want to include some of your own content that is displayed along with the default trace information. To display your own custom trace information, you can utilize two methods from the trace class within the code: Trace.Write and Trace.Warn. The biggest difference between the two is that Trace.Warn displays its contents in red, which can greatly help in distinguishing your own trace information from the rest. This functionality is handled by the two different methods of the Trace class: the Write and Warn methods. Let's take our existing code base and add the following code:

```
Protected Sub WriteToBrowser(ByVal whattowrite As String)
        Response.Write(whattowrite)
        Trace.Write(whattowrite)
        Trace.Warn(whattowrite)
End Sub
```

You will simply add two tracing statements to the `WriteToBrowser` method, one using `Trace.Write` and one using `Trace.Warn`. This will distinguish between the two different methods within all of the tracing information. Run the application and let's examine the output (Figure 12-26).

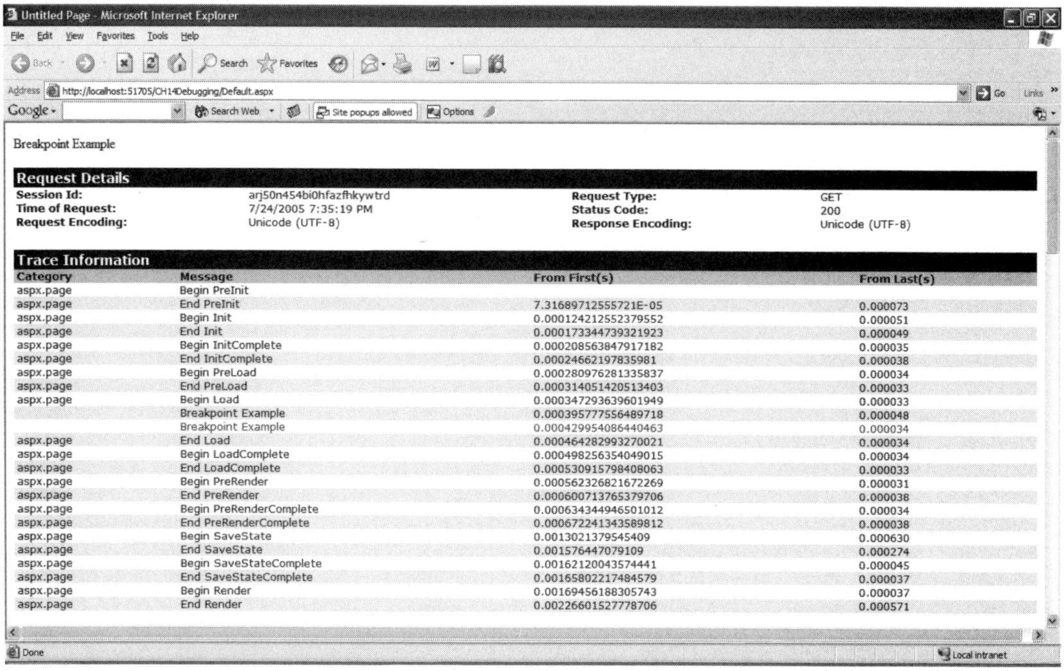

Figure 12-26. *The Trace.Write output*

You can clearly see the two different customized trace output statements. The only difference is that the `Trace.Warn` method is easily contrasted from the rest of the tracing information. Using the `Trace.Warn` method is helpful to use within the code when your code needs to demonstrate an exception or display a possible outcome that is not desired.

Summary

In this chapter we explored many different techniques you can use to explore and examine your application to find exceptions and errors, a process otherwise known as debugging. Regardless of the size of the application or your experience level, there will undoubtedly come a time when your application will need to be debugged. By using a combination of all the items described in this chapter, including breakpoints, the debugging windows, and tracing, you will have some of the best tools available to exterminate any bugs or exceptions and finalize your applications so they have the most stability possible.

CHAPTER 13

■■■

Deployment

Agreat deal of time and effort is spent designing web applications. At the conclusion of the design, development, and testing phase, one last step is needed: deploying the application. *Deployment* occurs when an application is designed and coded to a point where it has been run through a battery of tests. Upon passing these tests, the application is ready to be used. The application typically is deployed to a production server or maybe even a test environment.

In addition to deployment, we are also going to discuss some techniques to prepare your code and the advantages and disadvantages of the different methods you can use to compile the code prior to the actual deployment. We show you how to make a decision that will best fit your scenario.

In this chapter, we cover the following topics:

- XCOPY deployment

- How to transfer files with File Transfer Protocol (FTP)

- How to create a batch file for XCOPY

- How to use the Copy Web Site tool

- In-place compilation

- Precompilation

Deployment Methods

The bottom line with deployment is that the tested code taken from development needs to be copied to the production platform or server. Next we discuss two main methods you can use: XCOPY and the Copy Web Site tool.

XCOPY

The term *XCOPY* (meaning *external copy*) originated from the MS-DOS operating system. Within MS-DOS, XCOPY was a command that could copy multiple files from one directory to another on the file system. This method of deploying applications provides some additional flexibility that the Web Copy Tool cannot provide.

When using the XCOPY method, there is no automation provided as there is with a utility or predesigned tool. Instead, it is up to you, the developer, to understand and know what to copy.

If you need additional flexibility, you can create your own deployment utilities. Oftentimes these small utilities are called batch files, which essentially consist of several XCOPY command statements.

Let's take a look at a few different options and scenarios in which you can use the XCOPY method to deploy your web applications. We will walk through two different exercises that demonstrate the capabilities of dragging and dropping, and also the use of a batch file. In the examples, we explore different options in which to use the XCOPY or drag-and-drop methods.

Drag and Drop

The term *drag and drop* refers to a Windows function in which the user can click on a file or a grouping of files with the mouse and drag, or move them, to the target location. When this action occurs, the Windows operation system is essentially performing an XCOPY method; however, users can accomplish this through the graphical interface. To demonstrate, try Exercise 13-1.

Exercise 13-1. Drag-and-Drop Deployment

In this exercise, you will deploy to a production server by using File Transfer Protocol (FTP).

1. Our first priority is to ensure that your Internet settings allow you to view an FTP folder. To do so, click on the Internet Properties from the Control Panel. When the Internet Properties window opens, proceed to the Advanced tab. In the Browsing category, look for the "Enable folder view for FTP sites" option and make sure it is checked (Figure 13-1).

2. You can now log in to an FTP site. Most hosting companies will give you an FTP URL along with a user-name and password in which to log in to (Figure 13-2). You can type this URL directly into Internet Explorer. When the browser connects to the FTP site, you will be prompted to enter your credentials.

3. After entering your credentials, click Log On, and if the credentials are correctly authenticated, the window will open and look the same as a window from your local Windows Explorer. However, the content will be on a hosted server and not your local machine. While the FTP window is open, proceed to open the window you used earlier that contains the precompiled code for deployment.

4. Align the FTP window and your local window with the precompiled code so it is easy to see the contents for both windows. Click on the first file in the local window, and then hold down the Shift key while you click on the remaining files. This action will highlight and select all the files.

5. When all files are highlighted, click on the grouping of files, hold down the left mouse button, and drag the group of files to the FTP window as shown in Figure 13-3.

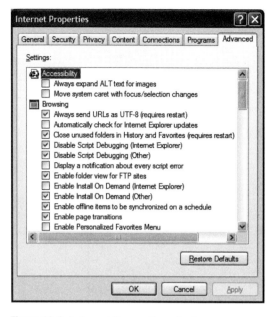

Figure 13-1. *Internet Properties window*

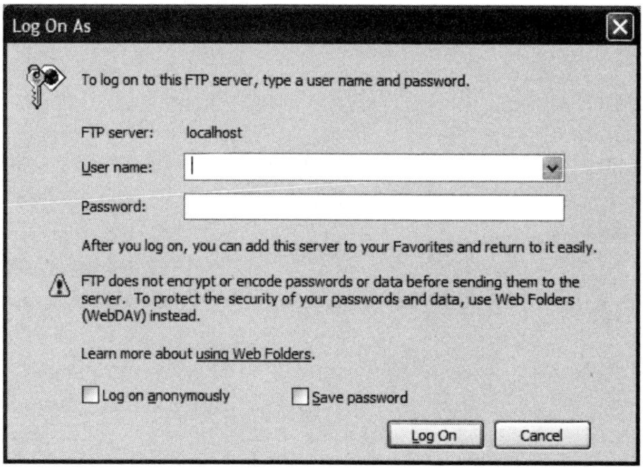

Figure 13-2. *FTP Log On As dialog*

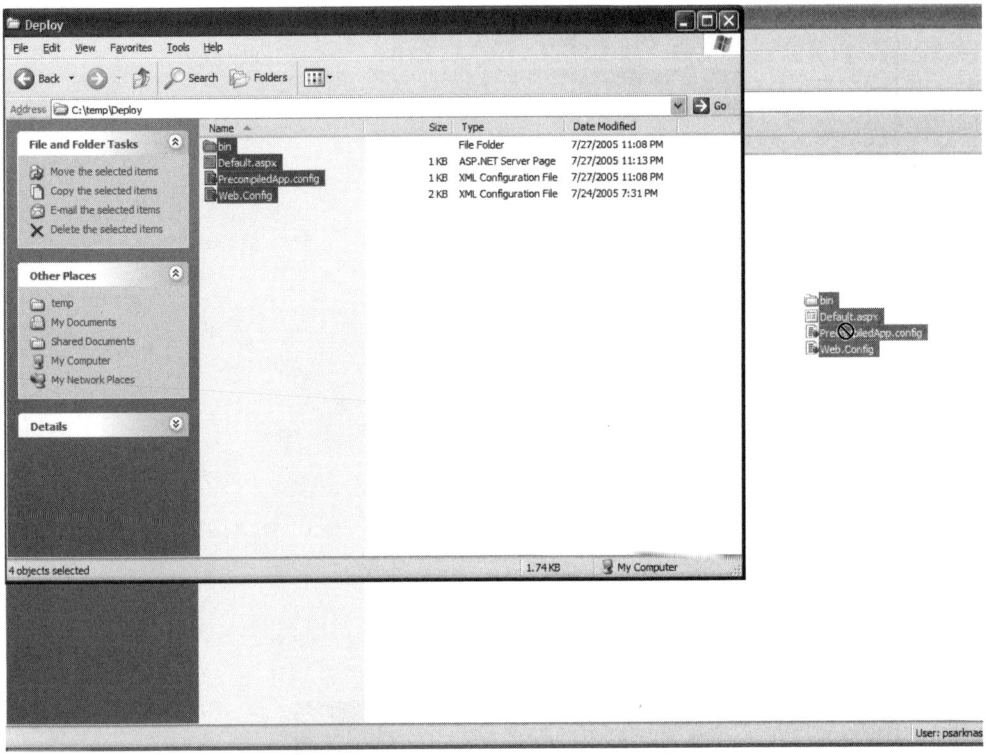

Figure 13-3. *Dragging and dropping*

6. When the group of files is within the FTP window, release the mouse button (i.e., "drop" the files), and the grouping of files will be uploaded to the target location.

Congratulations! You have just uploaded and deployed your application to the target server.

Using the drag-and-drop functionality in Windows provides a very simple way to copy files to and from the local computer and a target server. It gives additional flexibility in that it is up to the individual or developer to choose what files to be deployed. It is a manual process, and in the next section we discuss how to write a simple batch file to provide some simple XCOPY automation.

Batch File

The second method we discuss that you can use to deploy your application is writing a simple batch file with XCOPY commands. A *batch file* is a simple text file with specific commands that is saved to the file system with a .bat extension. You can click on this file and the command window will be displayed while the commands execute. Upon completing the commands, the command window will close. Try Exercise 13-2 for a thorough demonstration.

Exercise 13-2. Using a Batch File for Deployment

For this batch file exercise, you are going to create a simple batch file to XCOPY your application to another location on your local machine.

1. To create a batch file, open the Notepad application. Add the following commands to the file:

   ```
   XCOPY C:\temp\Deploy\web.config C:\Deploy
   ```

   ```
   XCOPY C:\temp\Deploy\Default.aspx C:\Deploy
   ```

   ```
   XCOPY C:\temp\Deploy\PreCompiledApp.config C:\Deploy
   ```

   ```
   md C:\Deploy\bin
   ```

   ```
   XCOPY C:\temp\Deploy\bin\*.dll C:\Deploy\bin
   ```

   ```
   XCOPY C:\temp\Deploy\bin\*.compiled C:\Deploy\bin
   ```

   Each of these commands consists of the XCOPY command followed by the source directory and file name, followed by the target directory. You will notice that the other command, md C:\Deploy\bin, creates the bin directory at the target location.

■**Tip** When specifying different files and directories in the source and target locations, you can specify either all the files of a certain type by using the wildcard character * and the file extension or all the files in a certain location by using the wildcard character twice: *.*.

---

2. When finished, save the file to your desktop or to any location on your local computer with the name **Deploy.bat**. Be sure to include the batch file extension .bat. Proceed to the directory in which you saved the file. The icon of the file is shown in Figure 13-4.

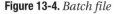

Figure 13-4. *Batch file*

3. When you are ready to deploy the application, double-click on the Deploy.bat file to execute the commands. You will see the Command window launch and execute the commands you added. The size of all the files will impact the time it takes to copy to the target. The Command window may only appear for a brief amount of time.

> ■**Caution** Make sure you have write privileges enabled on the target directory; otherwise, access will be denied.

    4. After the Command window closes, proceed to the target location, and if all the commands executed successfully, you will see the contents copied as shown in Figure 13-5.

Figure 13-5. *Target directory*

Congratulations again! You have deployed the application by using a simple batch file.

    By creating a batch file, you can save a great deal of time when deploying the application. Throughout the development phase, there will most certainly be several times when you have to deploy the application to the target location. If you take the time to create a batch file, deploying the application will be faster, especially for applications that have many files and directories.

Copy Web Site Tool

The Copy Web Site tool is a deployment tool included within the Visual Web Developer 2005 Express edition. This tool, easily used from within the IDE, is very similar to a third-party FTP utility. You can open the directory on the target server and then upload the source code. It is also possible to download code from the target server to your local computer. The Copy Web Site tool also has a synchronization feature that examines files on both the client and target server and automatically ensures that both targets have the most up-to-date versions of the source code. With this said, it is important to point out some advantages and disadvantages of using the Copy Web Site tool. Let's take a closer look.

Here are the advantages of using the Copy Web Site tool:

- Simple deployment by copying files from the local computer to the target server.

- Variety of protocols can be used. Files can be copied by FTP or across a local area network.

- Ability to copy files from the target server to the local computer, thus having the tool work in two directions.

- Ability to synchronize the files.

Here are the disadvantages of using the Copy Web Site tool:

- Source code files copied as is.

- Inability to precompile the source code.

After reading the previous section regarding the precompiling of the source code and the benefits associated, clearly the greatest downfall of the Copy Web Site tool is that the code cannot be precompiled first. With that said, it still can come in handy in certain scenarios, such as for projects that are very small or simple where precompilation will not provide greater performance. Let's walk through using the tool itself.

As we mentioned before, this tool can be used directly from within the IDE. To launch the Copy Web Site tool, open the Solution Explorer window and click on the Copy Web Site icon as shown in Figure 13-6.

Figure 13-6. *Copy Web Site icon*

This will open a new window that contains the Copy Web Site tool and has the current web project as the source website (Figure 13-7).

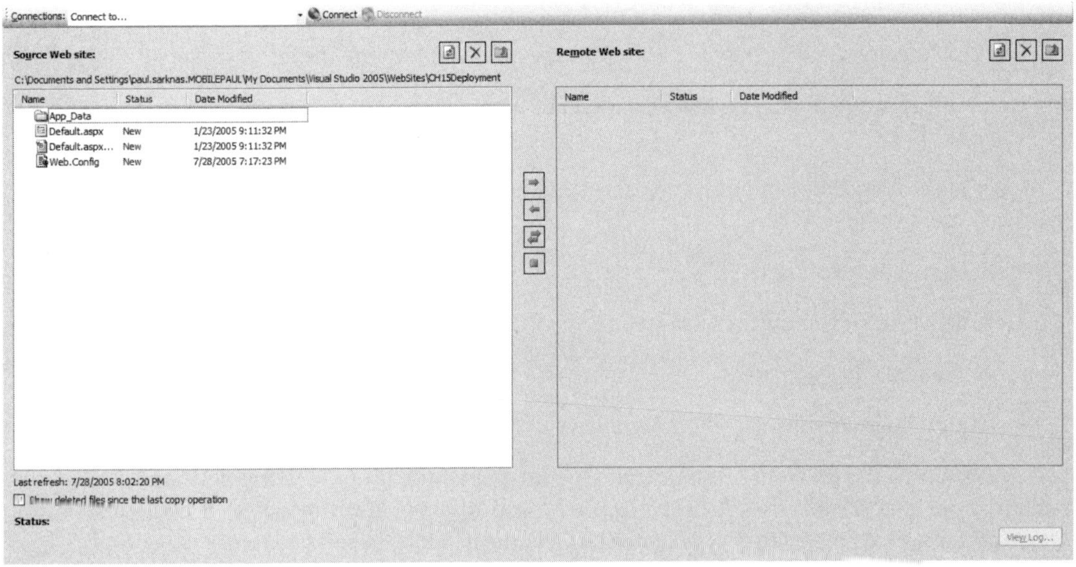

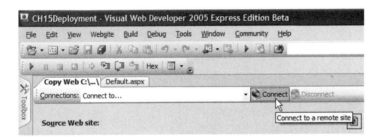

Figure 13-7. *Copy Web Site tool*

When the new window opens in the IDE, the section on the right, Remote Web site, is not enabled. You must first connect to a remote or target website before continuing. To connect to a target site, click on the Connect button located in the upper-left section of the window.

Figure 13-8. *Connecting with the Copy Web Site tool*

After you click on the Connect button, a dialog window will open with several options regarding the target to connect. Figure 13-9 represents what you will see.

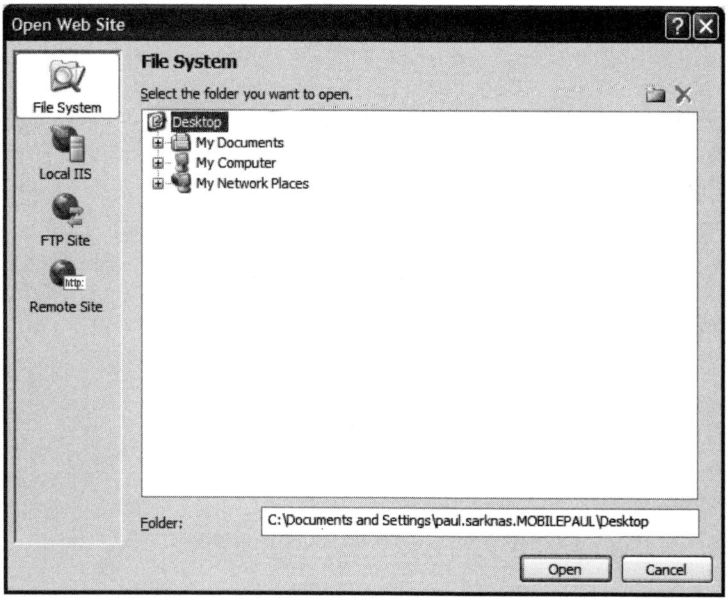

Figure 13-9. *Copy Web Site tool destination*

In the column on the left, you can see the four different choices of how to make the connection. The File System will browse through the different directories located on the local computer. The Local IIS (Internet Information Server) will browse throughout the IIS default directory. The FTP Site option will allow you to specify an FTP URL along with the ability to supply a username and password to connect. Last, the Remote Site option will need a URL to connect. Select one of the options and click Open. If you connect to the chosen option successfully, you will be returned to the Copy Web Site tool main window. At this point, you can use the tool to copy the files to or from the client or server. Additionally, the files can be synchronized by using the synchronization option. All of these actions can be performed by either right-clicking the files in either section of the window or selecting the Command buttons located in the center of the window.

Compilation

The term *compilation*, or *compiling*, refers to building and checking the source code for errors, which results in some sort of an executable program. The .NET Framework 2.0 provides you with some great features.

Compilation is important to discuss when dealing with deployment in that when deploying an application, you need every advantage available with regard to performance. By taking advantage of the precompilation methods available within the .NET Framework 2.0, you can meet some of the performance enhancements and fine-tune the source code prior to the actual deployment.

In-Place Compilation

In-place compilation is the default method used with ASP.NET 2.0. When creating a web project and adding either Web Forms or class files, the code-beside files have a .vb extension. These files are directly related to the .aspx and .ascx pages that contain the HTML code. When deployed, the ASP.NET 2.0 runtime will compile each of the pages as they are requested. This type of model is ideal during the development phase of the project; however, you might want to think twice before deploying your application under this compilation. Table 13-1 lists some of the advantages and disadvantages of this compilation model.

Table 13-1. *In-Place Compilation Comparison*

Advantage/ Disadvantage	Description
Pros	Easy to use and implement. Changes code and runs without recompiling. Ideal during development efforts.
Cons	Source code is present when deployed to production environment. Presents a security risk. More prone for errors to be bypassed because compiled at runtime. .aspx and code-beside files need to be in sync.

You can see that although this model is easy to use, there are drawbacks to other aspects. The most important aspect is that the source code in a clear text version must be placed on the deployment platform. Luckily, the .NET Framework 2.0 provides some additional options and techniques to use so the disadvantages are minimized. We will start off the discussion in the next section with precompilation.

Precompilation

The direct opposite of in-place compilation is the model called *precompilation*. It is the opposite of in-place compilation because the source code along with all pages in the project are compiled prior to any deployment. However, the .NET Framework 2.0 actually will first compile the code into MSIL, or Microsoft Intermediate Language, which is what allows you to use different languages within the source code. After this occurs, the requested class or web page is translated or compiled into actual machine code.

There are two different types of precompilation: *in-place precompilation* and *precompilation for deployment*. Both of these methods are made available by using the command-line utility ASPNET_COMPILER. This tool is included when the .NET Framework 2.0 is installed and you can find it in the following directory:

```
%WINDIR%\Microsoft.NET\Framework\v2.x.xxxx
```

Before continuing with more detail on the precompilation methods, let's examine the ASPNET_COMPILER tool so you have a better understanding of it. To use the ASPNET_COMPILER utility, open a command window by clicking the Start button and then choosing the Run menu item.

■**Note** The reason the command line is being used as opposed to the IDE is to take advantage of some included tools within the .NET Framework that are utilized by the command line.

When the Run window opens, type in **cmd** as shown in Figure 13-10.

Figure 13-10. *The command line*

Click the OK button and a command prompt window will launch. When the command prompt window launches, you will need to change the directory in which the prompt is located. You can do this easily by typing the change directory DOS command to the path of where the ASPNET_COMPILER utility is located. At the prompt, type the following:

```
cd %WINDIR%\Microsoft.NET\Framework\v2.x.xxxx
```

Notice that the version of the .NET Framework 2.0 being used at the time of this writing is v2.0.50215. Be sure to check the version of the Framework used on your computer and replace the version in the command with the version you are using. Press Enter and the command prompt will now look similar to Figure 13-11.

```
C:\WINDOWS\system32\cmd.exe

Microsoft Windows XP [Version 5.1.2600]
(C) Copyright 1985-2001 Microsoft Corp.

C:\Documents and Settings\paul.sarknas.MOBILEPAUL>cd %WINDIR%\Microsoft.NET\Fram
ework\v2.0.50215

C:\WINDOWS\Microsoft.NET\Framework\v2.0.50215>
```

Figure 13-11. *The command-line window*

From this point, you can get a quick glimpse of the different switches available with the ASPNET_COMPILER utility by typing the following at the prompt:

```
aspnet_compiler -?
```

Press Enter once again, and with this switch, the utility will print the help text associated (Figure 13-12).

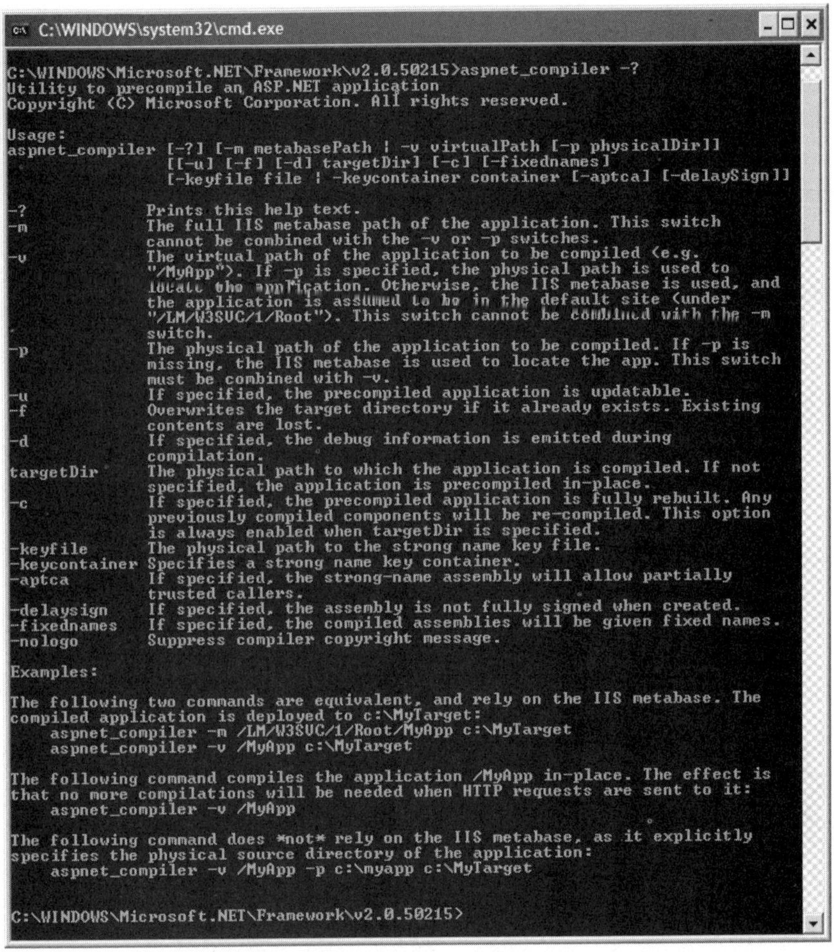

Figure 13-12. *ASPNET_COMPILER utility help text*

You can see that the Help files are displayed, listing the different options you can use with the utility.

Now that you have some exposure to the ASPNET_COMPILER utility, let's look at how it is going to perform the precompilation for your code.

In-Place Precompilation

As mentioned earlier, the first method of precompilation is called in-place precompilation. When performing this type of precompilation, the code will end up inside the temporary ASP.NET file directory. This is the identical location in which the ASP.NET runtime compiles files for the browser requests. To perform this action, return to the command prompt as demonstrated in the last section and enter the following for the ASPNET_COMPILER utility:

```
aspnet_compiler -v /ch15deployment
```

To review, the switch used with the utility, -v, represents an IIS virtual directory followed by the name of the virtual directory. After pressing Enter, if the utility completes without any errors, you will be presented with a new command prompt. Let's see what exactly was precompiled from the utility. To do so, navigate to the temporary ASP.NET file directory, and look in the directory with the same name as the virtual directory that you specified.

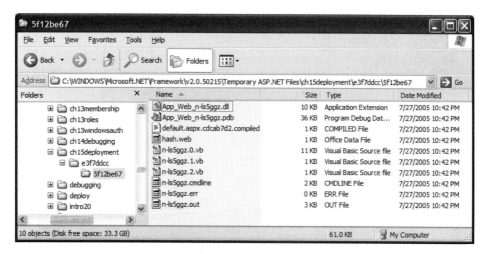

Figure 13-13. *In-place precompilation*

You can see the compiled files in the temporary directory. With this output, the web application will have a better performance at the startup, but the main benefit to using in-place precompilation is to verify that the web application is free from errors. If the application happens to have errors that were caused from a modification to a class or Web Form, the utility will fail and display the error or warnings.

Precompilation for Deployment

Precompilation for deployment is a more extensive type of precompilation in that it creates an executable version of the web application. This executable does not contain any of the source code in a clear text version that can be read by the naked eye. The difference when using the ASPNET_COMPILER utility is that two different paths or parameters are used. The first path is the location of the source code of the web application, and the second is the target directory that will contain the compiled results. Let's take the same sample web application used with the in-place method and perform the precompilation for deployment method to it. Enter the following at the command prompt:

```
aspnet_compiler -v /ch15Deployment c:\temp\deploy
```

Again, the name of the virtual directory is specified with the -v switch command followed by the target directory, c:\temp\deploy. If the utility completes without error, navigate to the target directory to examine the precompiled output (Figure 13-14).

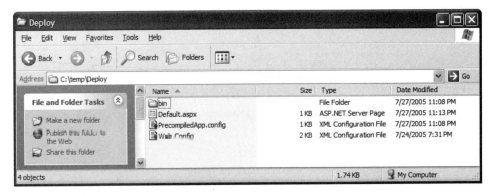

Figure 13-14. *The target directory*

Within the root directory of the target, you can see the Web Form Default.aspx, the web.config file, a PrecompiledApp.config file, and a bin directory. Navigate to the bin directory (Figure 13-15).

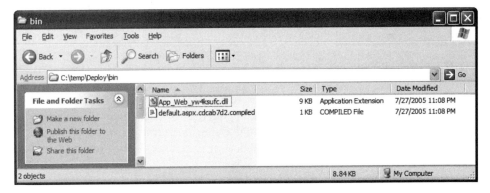

Figure 13-15. *Target bin directory*

Here within the bin directory is the .dll along with an accompanying compiled file. At this point, this content could be uploaded to a production or deployment server. Not only will the start-up have better performance, but the main advantage is that no source code will have to be included.

Summary

In this chapter, we examined the different precompilation methods and their advantages and disadvantages, along with the different methods used to deploy the application content. After developing your application, the work is not finished, however. A great deal of attention needs to be dedicated to considering the different precompilation options that will best fit your individual scenario.

CHAPTER 14

■■■

Post Development

We have come to the end of the book and the end of your project. You should feel a great sense of satisfaction and accomplishment. Not only have you developed a web application using the different functionality provided with the .NET 2.0 Framework, you have also deployed the application to a production platform where your end users are able to use the end product. At this point, there are just a few more issues to keep in mind.

Monitoring the application and how it performs over time and addressing any poor performance issues that arise is the subject of this final chapter, which addresses these issues in detail by showing ways the application can be monitored, optimized, and have the highest degree of scalability possible. The following topics are highlighted:

- Performance

- Caching techniques and methods

Performance

One of the most important tasks to address after a web application is deployed to a production environment is monitoring the overall performance. This type of maintenance is important because there is no true test on how the application will perform until it is placed in and deployed to the production environment and the users begin to use it.

One such tool is a performance monitor, which can give you real-time statistics with regard to an ASP.NET application running on a server. These statistics come in the form of the amount of central processing unit (CPU) cycles being used, the number of threads, and the amount of memory being consumed. To use this tool, click on the Windows Start button and then the Run command. Type the command **perfmon** in the Run command window. The abbreviation perfmon represents a command for a performance monitor. When you execute this command, the performance monitor window will launch (Figure 14-1).

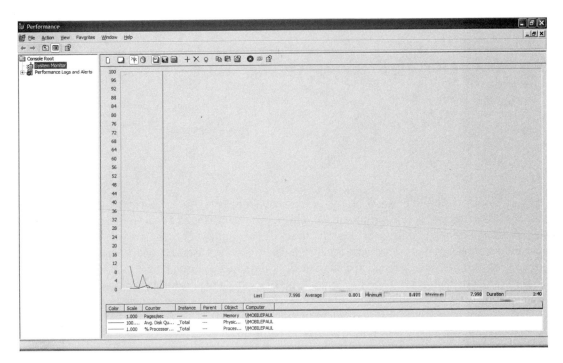

Figure 14-1. *Performance monitor*

When the performance monitor window is displayed, there are three default counters that you can examine: pages/sec, average queue disk length, and % processor time. Because we are more concerned with ASP.NET counters, add ASP.NET-specific counters by right-clicking on the main window and choosing the menu item Add Counters. When you choose this menu item, the Add Counters window will launch, as shown in Figure 14-2.

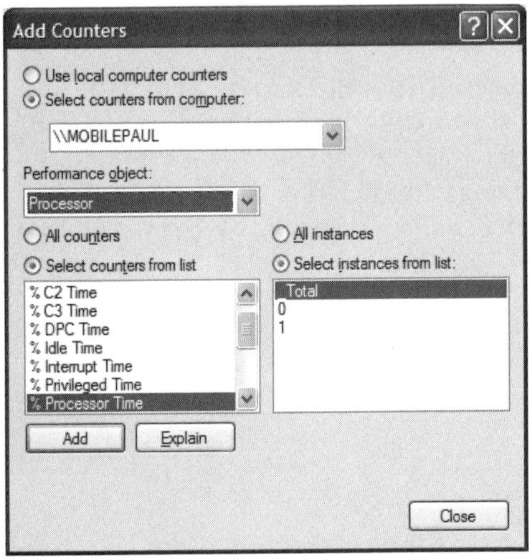

Figure 14-2. *Adding performance monitors*

When the Add Counters window is displayed, you will see a drop-down list of many different performance objects. Again, let's focus on the ASP.NET objects in particular. Choose the ASP.NET object and select All Counters. This will add performance counters to the monitor, all pertaining to the ASP.NET applications running on the specified machine. At the top menu, click on the various different choices of views. Finally, run your web application and view the different counters to monitor your web application.

Caching

When discussing performance and optimization with regard to web applications, the most effective tool is *caching*, a function within ASP.NET 2.0 where specified data or information can be saved into memory and later accessed from memory instead of accessing the information by making a round-trip to the server. There are different types of caching, and certain types are better in different scenarios. In this section we discuss two types of output caching: SQL Server caching and output caching.

You must take extreme care when your website's content is completely dynamic because there is a danger of incorrect information being displayed. In situations such as these, SQL Server caching is the preferred technique.

SQL Server Caching

SQL Server caching is a form of output caching that depends on the data stored within a SQL Server database. This technique is basically centered on caching data within a web page until the information records within a specified database change. This can prove to be very helpful when an application has a database that does not change or is not updated very frequently. For example, perhaps your application contains a product catalog in which a certain number of products are added and then new products are very seldom added. This content could be considered static in the sense that the number of products remains the same for a long period of time. To enable this kind of optimization, specific configurations need to be added to the web.config file along with utilizing the ASPNET_REGSQL utility to configure the database. Exercise 14-1 will walk you through an example of how to configure and execute this functionality.

Exercise 14-1. Implementing SQL Server Caching

In this exercise you will use the Northwind sample database that is included when installing SQL Server.

1. The first order of business is to configure the web.config file for SQL Server caching. To do so, you need to add a connection string for the database along with enabling SQL caching as demonstrated here:

```
<?xml version="1.0"?>
<configuration>
    <appSettings/>
        <connectionStrings>
```

```
            <add name="SQLCON"
                    connectionString="Server=localhost;Integrated
    Security=True;Database=Northwind;
    Persist Security Info=True" />
                </connectionStrings>
        <system.web>
                        <compilation debug="true"/>
                        <authentication mode="Windows"/>
                        <caching>
                                    <sqlCacheDependency enabled="true">
                                    <databases>
                                    <add name="Northwind"
                                     connectionStringName="SQLCON" />
                                    </databases>
                                    </sqlCacheDependency>
                        </caching>
                </system.web>
        </configuration>
```

Within the web.config, the database connection string named SQLCON is set to use the local database and the Northwind database. SqlCacheDependency is enabled to true and also references SQLCON as the connection string to use.

2. Now that the web.config is taken care of, you need to configure the actual database and table to achieve SQL caching. As mentioned, this is accomplished by using the ASPNET_REGSQL utility, which is included when the .NET 2.0 Framework is installed and placed in the following directory:

```
%windir%\Microsoft.NET\Framework\FrameworkVersion
```

Be sure that %windir% represents the Windows default directory in which the .NET Framework 2.0 is installed along with the version. At the time of this writing, v2.0.50215 of the .NET Framework 2.0 is being used, so the full file path would look like this:

```
C:\WINDOWS\Microsoft.NET\Framework\v2.0.50215
```

This path will be needed in the Command window in the next step.

3. In step 2 you determined where the ASPNET_REGSQL utility is located. Now you can use the utility by opening a Command window. Click on the Start button and then click Run. In the Run window, type **cmd** and click OK. A Command window will launch. Change the directory to the path in which the utility is located by using the following command:

```
cd C:\WINDOWS\Microsoft.NET\Framework\v2.0.50215
```

The command prompt will be set in the Command window and look like Figure 14-3.

Figure 14-3. *The Command window*

From this point, you can focus on the utility itself. The ASPNET_REGSQL utility needs specific information passed as parameters, including the server name, username, password, database name, and database table name. Enter the following command:

```
aspnet_regsql -S <Server> -U <Username>
     -P <Password> -ed -d Northwind -et -t Orders
```

As we mentioned previously, the ASPNET_REGSQL utility requires a certain number of parameters. There are also two other switches that need to be specified. As shown earlier, the server name, username, and password are specified. However, after the password, a switch, -ed, is specified, meaning to enable a database for SQL cache dependency. Following the switch is the database name, Northwind, and then the final switch: -et. The -et switch simply instructs the utility to enable a database table for SQL cache dependency. Finally, the command is ended using the name of the table: Orders.

4. After entering in the complete utility command with the specified parameters, press Enter, and if the utility executes without error, a message will be displayed indicating that the command has finished (Figure 14-4).

■Note Administrative access will need to be granted to the database being specified with the ASPNET_REGSQL utility.

Figure 14-4. *Finishing the ASPNET_REGSQL utility*

5. One last piece of configuration remains, which will bo within the actual Web Form where the SQL caching will take place. Let's proceed to the Default.aspx Web Form in your project and click on the Source
tab. Add the following page directive:

```
<%@ Page Language="VB" AutoEventWireup="false"
        CodeFile="Default.aspx.vb" Inherits="_Default" %>
<%@ OutputCache Duration="3600"
        SqlDependency="Northwind:Orders"
        VaryByParam="none" %>
```

These page directives specify the SqlDependency using the Northwind database and the Orders table.
When this is placed in a Web Form, any data being displayed from the Orders table from the Northwind
database will be cached until a change or update is made to the Orders table.

6. Switch back to the design view of the Default.aspx Web Form. Open the Database Explorer window by
clicking on the View menu and choosing the Database Explorer menu item. The Database Explorer window will launch near the Solution Explorer window. Click on the Connect to Database icon as shown in
Figure 14-5.

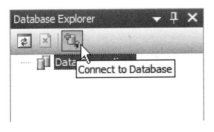

Figure 14-5. *Connecting to the database*

The Add Connection dialog window will launch, as shown in Figure 14-6.

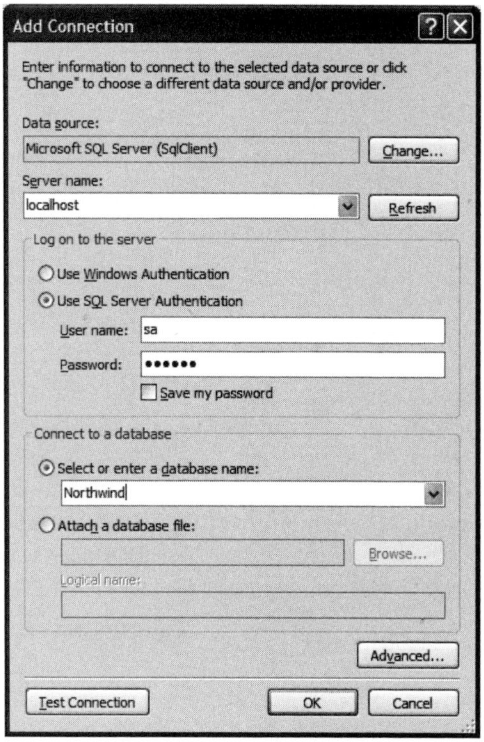

Figure 14-6. *Adding a connection*

Set the data source to use the localhost with the specified authentication credentials as used in the ASPNET_REGSQL utility. Click on the Test Connection if you wish to test the current settings, and when finished, click OK. Proceed back to the Database Explorer window, and you will notice that a new connection is listed. Expand the connection as well as the tables (Figure 14-7).

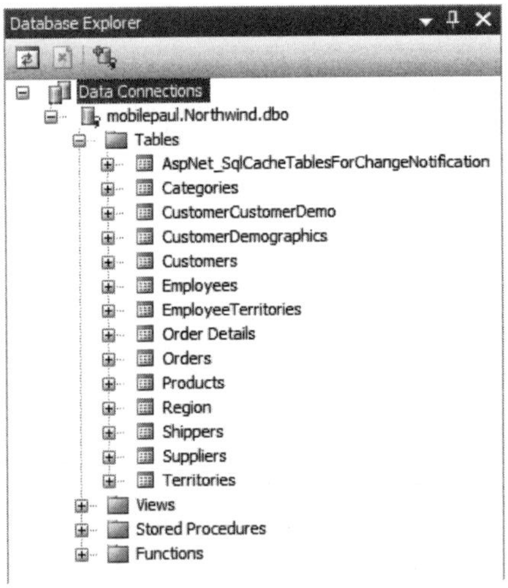

Figure 14-7. *Exploring the database tables*

7. Select the Orders table and drag the table over to the Default.aspx Web Form. This will automatically create a GridView control on the Web Form that uses the database connection to the Orders table. You can also experiment with the auto formatting to give the grid a more pleasing appearance.

8. In the final step, add a Label control above the GridView control on the Default.aspx Web Form as shown in Figure 14-8.

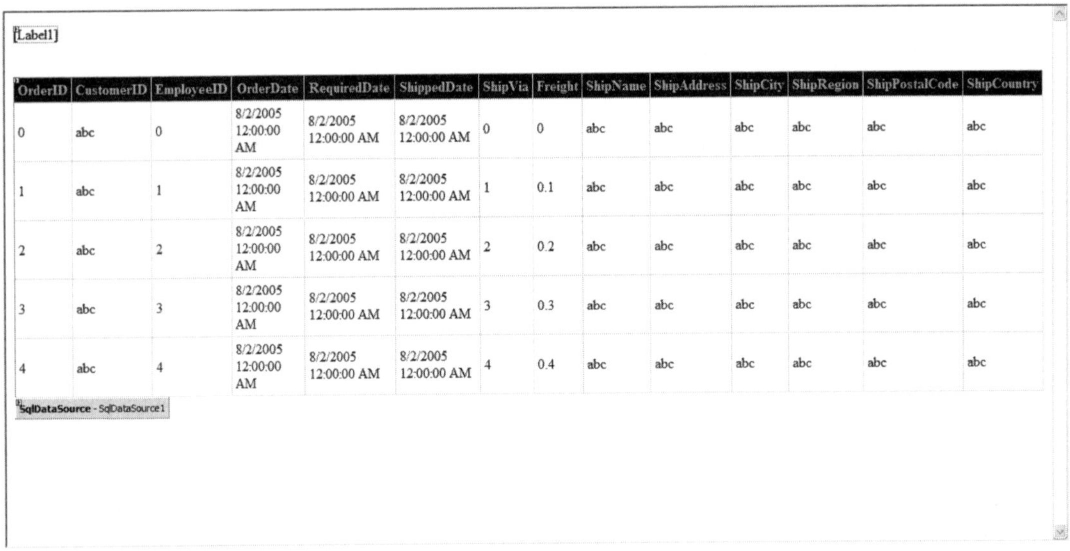

[Label1]

OrderID	CustomerID	EmployeeID	OrderDate	RequiredDate	ShippedDate	ShipVia	Freight	ShipName	ShipAddress	ShipCity	ShipRegion	ShipPostalCode	ShipCountry
0	abc	0	8/2/2005 12:00:00 AM	8/2/2005 12:00:00 AM	8/2/2005 12:00:00 AM	0	0	abc	abc	abc	abc	abc	abc
1	abc	1	8/2/2005 12:00:00 AM	8/2/2005 12:00:00 AM	8/2/2005 12:00:00 AM	1	0.1	abc	abc	abc	abc	abc	abc
2	abc	2	8/2/2005 12:00:00 AM	8/2/2005 12:00:00 AM	8/2/2005 12:00:00 AM	2	0.2	abc	abc	abc	abc	abc	abc
3	abc	3	8/2/2005 12:00:00 AM	8/2/2005 12:00:00 AM	8/2/2005 12:00:00 AM	3	0.3	abc	abc	abc	abc	abc	abc
4	abc	4	8/2/2005 12:00:00 AM	8/2/2005 12:00:00 AM	8/2/2005 12:00:00 AM	4	0.4	abc	abc	abc	abc	abc	abc

SqlDataSource - SqlDataSource1

Figure 14-8. *The GridView at design time*

9. Double-click on the Web Form to view the code-beside file. Add the following code for the label in the Page_Load event:

```
Protected Sub Page_Load(ByVal sender As Object,
    ByVal e As System.EventArgs) Handles Me.Load
    Label1.Text = DateTime.Now.ToShortDateString & " " &
DateTime.Now.ToLongTimeString
    End Sub
```

This code will display the current date and time with the seconds when the Web Form loads.

10. Build and run the web project, and the Orders table from the Northwind database will be displayed along with the current date and time (Figure 14-9).

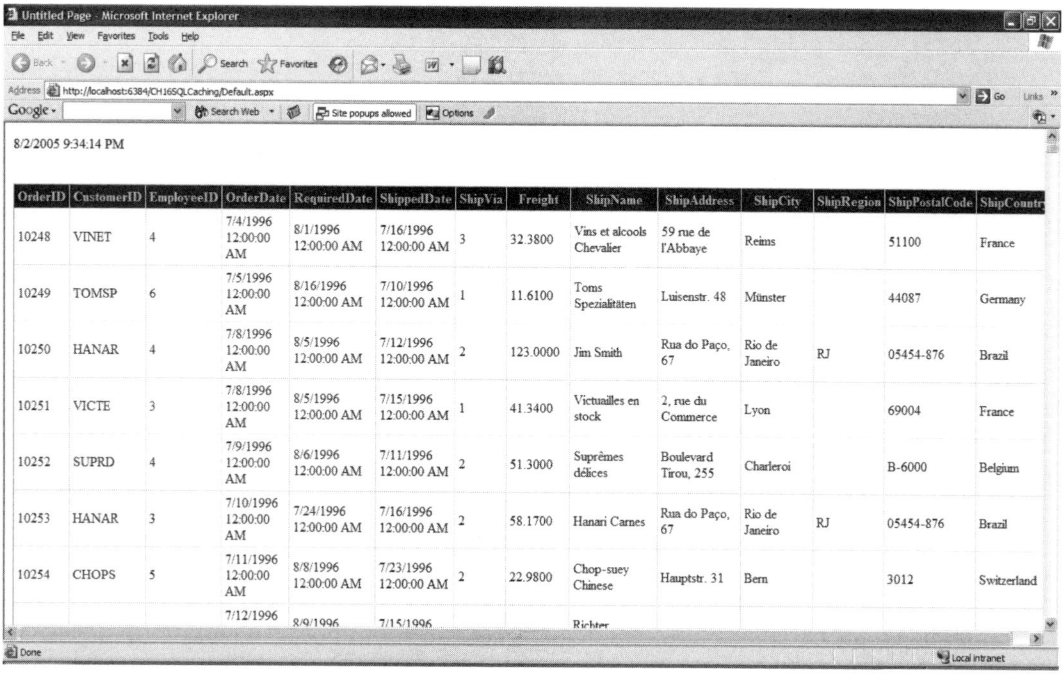

Figure 14-9. *The GridView at runtime*

11. Notice the date and especially the time with the seconds. Click the Refresh button in the browser, and note that the time will not change. Keep refreshing the browser three or four times. The date and time will remain the same because the page has been loaded into the cache and is going to be retrieved from the cache when requested until the Orders table changes.

12. Let's test the cache by making a change to the Orders table. To do so, proceed back to the Database Explorer window while the web application is still running. Right-click on the Orders table, and choose the Show Table Data menu item (Figure 14-10).

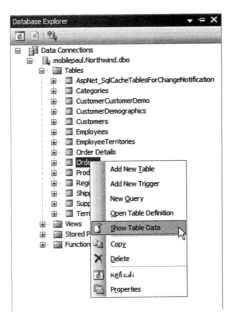

Figure 14-10. *Showing the table data from the Database Explorer*

This will then show the actual records from the Orders table of the Northwind database (Figure 14-11).

OrderID	CustomerID	EmployeeID	OrderDate	RequiredDate	ShippedDate	ShipVia	Freight	ShipName	ShipAddress	ShipCity	ShipRegion
10248	VINET	4	7/4/1996 12:00:...	8/1/1996 12:00:...	7/16/1996 12:00...	3	32.3800	Vins et alcools C...	59 rue de l'Abbaye	Reims	NULL
10249	TOMSP	6	7/5/1996 12:00:...	8/16/1996 12:00:...	7/10/1996 12:00...	1	11.6100	Toms Spezialitäten	Luisenstr. 48	Münster	NULL
10250	HANAR	4	7/8/1996 12:00:...	8/5/1996 12:00:...	7/12/1996 12:00...	2	123.0000	Jim Smith	Rua do Paço, 67	Rio de Janeiro	RJ
10251	VICTE	3	7/8/1996 12:00:...	8/5/1996 12:00:...	7/15/1996 12:00...	1	41.3400	Victuailles en stock	2, rue du Comm...	Lyon	NULL
10252	SUPRD	4	7/9/1996 12:00:...	8/6/1996 12:00:...	7/11/1996 12:00...	2	51.3000	Suprêmes délices	Boulevard Tirou,...	Charleroi	NULL
10253	HANAR	3	7/10/1996 12:00...	7/24/1996 12:00...	7/16/1996 12:00...	2	58.1700	Hanari Carnes	Rua do Paço, 67	Rio de Janeiro	RJ
10254	CHOPS	5	7/11/1996 12:00...	8/8/1996 12:00...	7/23/1996 12:00...	2	22.9800	Chop-suey Chinese	Hauptstr. 31	Bern	NULL
10255	RICSU	9	7/12/1996 12:00...	8/9/1996 12:00...	7/15/1996 12:00...	3	148.3300	Richter Supermarkt	Starenweg 5	Genève	NULL
10256	WELLI	3	7/15/1996 12:00...	8/12/1996 12:00...	7/17/1996 12:00...	2	13.9700	Wellington Impor...	Rua do Mercado...	Resende	SP
10257	HILAA	4	7/16/1996 12:00...	8/13/1996 12:00...	7/22/1996 12:00...	3	81.9100	HILARION-Abastos	Carrera 22 con ...	San Cristóbal	Táchira
10258	ERNSH	1	7/17/1996 12:00...	8/14/1996 12:00...	7/23/1996 12:00...	1	140.5100	Ernst Handel	Kirchgasse 6	Graz	NULL
10259	CENTC	4	7/18/1996 12:00...	8/15/1996 12:00...	7/25/1996 12:00...	3	3.2500	Centro comercial...	Sierras de Grana...	México D.F.	NULL
10260	OTTIK	4	7/19/1996 12:00...	8/16/1996 12:00...	7/29/1996 12:00...	1	55.0900	Ottilies Käseladen	Mehrheimerstr. ...	Köln	NULL
10261	QUEDE	4	7/19/1996 12:00...	8/16/1996 12:00...	7/30/1996 12:00...	2	3.0500	Que Delicia	Rua da Panificad...	Rio de Janeiro	RJ
10262	RATTC	8	7/22/1996 12:00...	8/19/1996 12:00...	7/25/1996 12:00...	3	48.2900	Rattlesnake Can...	2817 Milton Dr.	Albuquerque	NM
10263	ERNSH	9	7/23/1996 12:00...	8/20/1996 12:00...	7/31/1996 12:00...	3	146.0600	Ernst Handel	Kirchgasse 6	Graz	NULL
10264	FOLKO	6	7/24/1996 12:00...	8/21/1996 12:00...	8/23/1996 12:00...	3	3.6700	Folk och fä HB	Åkergatan 24	Bräcke	NULL
10265	BLONP	2	7/25/1996 12:00...	8/22/1996 12:00...	8/12/1996 12:00...	1	55.2800	Blondel père et fils	24, place Kléber	Strasbourg	NULL
10266	WARTH	3	7/26/1996 12:00...	9/6/1996 12:00:...	7/31/1996 12:00...	3	25.7300	Wartian Herkku	Torikatu 38	Oulu	NULL
10267	FRANK	4	7/29/1996 12:00...	8/26/1996 12:00...	8/6/1996 12:00:...	1	208.5800	Frankenversand	Berliner Platz 43	München	NULL
10268	GROSR	8	7/30/1996 12:00...	8/27/1996 12:00...	8/2/1996 12:00:...	3	66.2900	GROSELLA-Rest...	5ª Ave. Los Palo...	Caracas	DF
10269	WHITC	5	7/31/1996 12:00...	8/14/1996 12:00...	8/9/1996 12:00:...	1	4.5600	White Clover Ma...	1029 - 12th Ave...	Seattle	WA
10270	WARTH	1	8/1/1996 12:00:...	8/29/1996 12:00...	8/2/1996 12:00:...	1	136.5400	Wartian Herkku	Torikatu 38	Oulu	NULL
10271	SPLIR	6	8/1/1996 12:00:...	8/29/1996 12:00...	8/30/1996 12:00...	2	4.5400	Split Rail Beer & Ale	P.O. Box 555	Lander	WY
10272	RATTC	6	8/2/1996 12:00:...	8/30/1996 12:00...	8/6/1996 12:00:...	2	98.0300	Rattlesnake Can...	2817 Milton Dr.	Albuquerque	NM
10273	QUICK	3	8/5/1996 12:00:...	9/2/1996 12:00:...	8/12/1996 12:00...	3	76.0700	QUICK-Stop	Taucherstraße 10	Cunewalde	NULL

Figure 14-11. *Viewing the table data*

To continue with our example, let's update a record to test the SQL Cache. Change the first record under the ShipName column to read John Doe. Right-click on the newly added text, and choose Execute SQL to update the entry (Figure 14-11).

Figure 14-12. *Executing the database table update*

13. Return back to the running Default.aspx Web Form, and click the browser Refresh button. Notice that the time has changed on the page along with the newly added entry (Figure 14-13).

OrderID	CustomerID	EmployeeID	OrderDate	RequiredDate	ShippedDate	ShipVia	Freight	ShipName	ShipAddress	ShipCity	ShipRegion	ShipPostalCode	ShipCountry
10248	VINET	4	7/4/1996 12:00:00 AM	8/1/1996 12:00:00 AM	7/16/1996 12:00:00 AM	3	32.3800	John Doe	59 rue de l'Abbaye	Reims		51100	France
10249	TOMSP	6	7/5/1996 12:00:00 AM	8/16/1996 12:00:00 AM	7/10/1996 12:00:00 AM	1	11.6100	Toms Spezialitäten	Luisenstr. 48	Münster		44087	Germany
10250	HANAR	4	7/8/1996 12:00:00 AM	8/5/1996 12:00:00 AM	7/12/1996 12:00:00 AM	2	123.0000	Jim Smith	Rua do Paço, 67	Rio de Janeiro	RJ	05454-876	Brazil
10251	VICTE	3	7/8/1996 12:00:00 AM	8/5/1996 12:00:00 AM	7/15/1996 12:00:00 AM	1	41.3400	Victuailles en stock	2, rue du Commerce	Lyon		69004	France
10252	SUPRD	4	7/9/1996 12:00:00 AM	8/6/1996 12:00:00 AM	7/11/1996 12:00:00 AM	2	51.3000	Suprêmes délices	Boulevard Tirou, 255	Charleroi		B-6000	Belgium
10253	HANAR	3	7/10/1996 12:00:00 AM	7/24/1996 12:00:00 AM	7/16/1996 12:00:00 AM	2	58.1700	Hanari Carnes	Rua do Paço, 67	Rio de Janeiro	RJ	05454-876	Brazil
10254	CHOPS	5	7/11/1996 12:00:00 AM	8/8/1996 12:00:00 AM	7/23/1996 12:00:00 AM	2	22.9800	Chop-suey Chinese	Hauptstr. 31	Bern		3012	Switzerland
			7/12/1996	8/9/1996	7/15/1996			Richter					

8/2/2005 9:51:14 PM

Figure 14-13. *Viewing the changes*

As a result of the SQL caching, the Web Form stayed within the cache and was served from it until a change was made to the database table. This technique can provide great optimization for web applications.

Output Caching

Output caching is different from SQL Server caching in that the former will cache the data or information for a specified amount of time regardless of any database changes or updates. Using this type of caching is best in scenarios in which a web application will have a great deal of traffic and the content is mostly static. Perhaps the content within the application is not critical if it changes. For instance, maybe the application displays some historical data that once added to the site will likely not change. Therefore, adding output caching can aid in the overall optimization and performance. Exercise 14-2 demonstrates output caching.

Exercise 14-2. Implementing Output Caching

1. As mentioned earlier, implementing output caching is less involved than its counterpart SQL Server caching. The first step is to add the page directives to the Web Form in which to cache:

```
<%@ Page Language="VB" AutoEventWireup="false"
    CodeFile="Default.aspx.vb" Inherits=" Default" %>
<%@ OutputCache Duration="10" VaryByParam="none" %>
```

Here you can see that there are only two page directives: the OutPutCache Duration and the VaryByParam. The Duration indicates the number of seconds the data or information will remain in the cache. The VaryByParam directive indicates if the page will still cache regardless of any parameters that are included. For our example, we simply specify none.

2. Proceed to the code beside of the Default.aspx Web Form. Add the following code to the `Page_Load` event, which will write the date and time to the browser:

```
Protected Sub Page_Load(ByVal sender As Object,
  ByVal e As System.EventArgs) Handles Me.Load
    Response.Write(DateTime.Now.ToShortDateString & " " &
    DateTime.Now.ToLongTimeString)
  End Sub
```

3. Build and run the web project. When the Default.aspx Web Form is loaded, it will resemble Figure 14-14.

4. When the page is loaded, continue to click the Refresh button in the browser. Notice that the date and timestamp does not change each time you click the Refresh button. However, after a ten-second interval, the page will display the updated date and timestamp because the cache duration has expired.

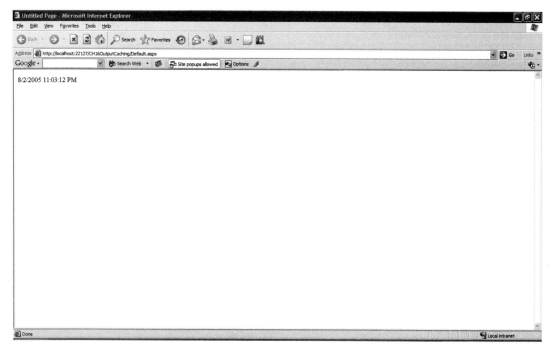

Figure 14-14. *Viewing the cached date timestamp*

By implementing this kind of caching, a great deal of processing can be saved on the web server, hence aiding in overall performance. Depending on the content and its propensity for change, be cautious of the duration specified.

Summary

In this chapter, we examined some techniques that can monitor the overall health and performance of your web application. We also looked at adding different types of caching to web applications that will add performance enhancements. Undoubtedly, the maintenance and monitoring of web applications will continue to be a task after you develop the application. The length of this task will vary depending on the size and complexity of the overall application.

INDEX